CW00821648

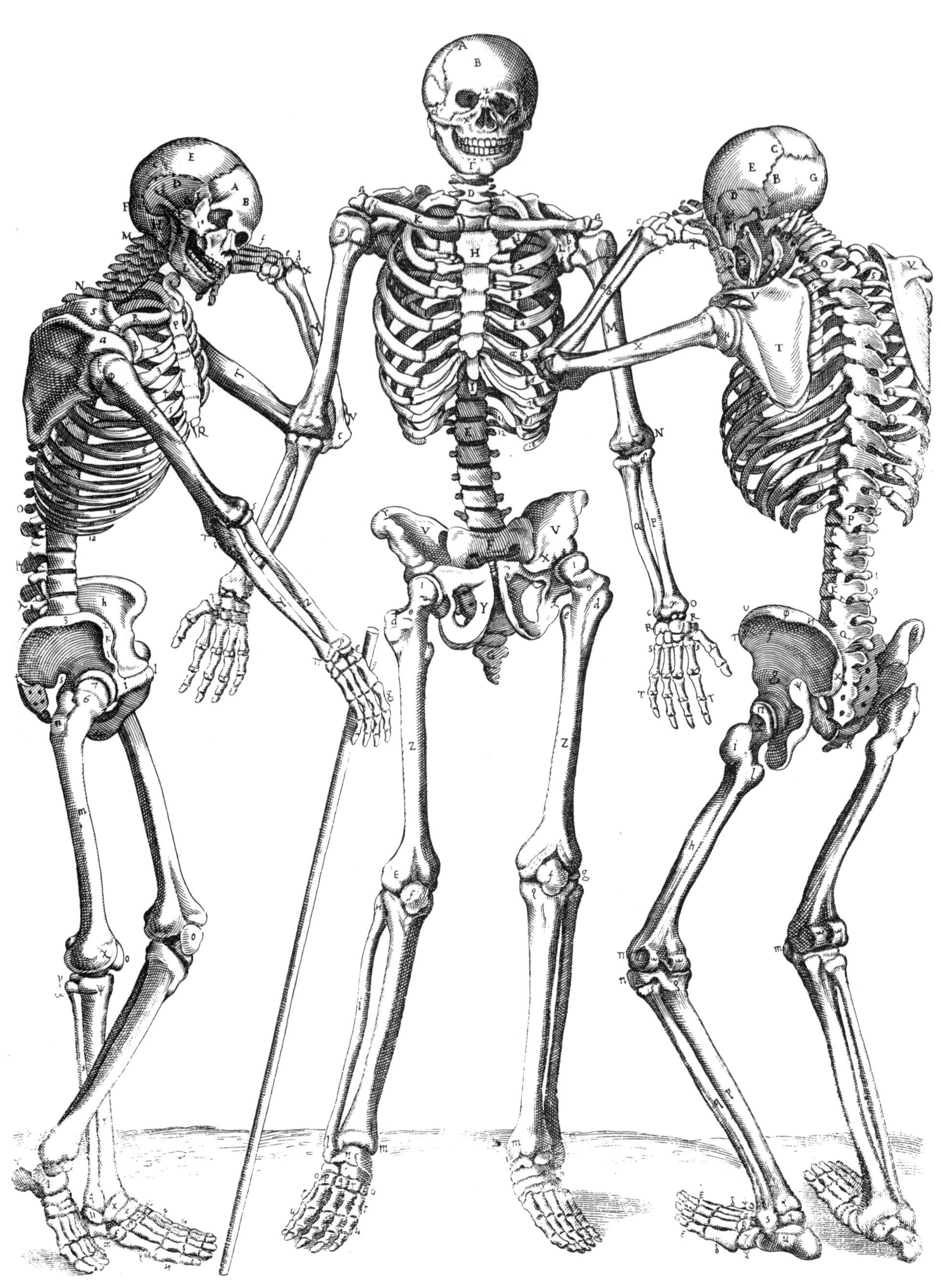

Da Cortona. Three Views of the Skeleton

Classic Anatomical Illustrations

Vesalius, Albinus, Leonardo and Others

DOVER PUBLICATIONS, INC.
Mineola, New York

Contents

ANDREAS VESALIUS (1514–1564) *1*
BERNARD SIEGFRIED ALBINUS (1697–1770) *20*
LEONARDO DA VINCI (1452–1519) *38*
PIETRO DA CORTONA (1596–1669) *58*
BARTOLOMMEO EUSTACHIUS (1520?–1574) *72*

Copyright

Bibliographical Note

Classic Anatomical Illustrations is a new work, first published by Dover Publications, Inc., in 2008.

DOVER *Pictorial Archive* SERIES

Library of Congress Cataloging-in-Publication Data

Classic anatomical illustrations : Vesalius, Albinus, Leonardo, and others.
p. cm. — (Dover pictorial archive series)
"A new selection of ninety plates reprinted from standard sources"—T.p. verso.
ISBN-13: 978-0-486-46162-5
ISBN-10: 0-486-46162-9
1. Anatomy, Artistic—Pictorial works.

NC760.C48 2008
743.4'9—dc22

2007046758

Manufactured in the United States of America
Dover Publications, Inc., 31 East 2nd Street, Mineola, N.Y. 11501

Publisher's Note

THE SHEER BEAUTY OF THE HUMAN BODY has long fascinated artists in every medium of art. As a requisite subject in the study of art, anatomy was skillfully mastered in order to convey fluidity of movement. An artistic representation of the human body necessitated a comprehensive knowledge of anatomy and a full appreciation for the efficiency of the body's processes. The chief components of this intricate flesh-and-blood machine are clearly revealed in these meticulously accurate and precise engravings.

This treasury of detailed anatomical illustrations presents the work of a distinguished group of artists who were drawn to the exploration of bodily proportions and the amazing inner workings of the human form. During the time these artists flourished—the fifteenth through the eighteenth centuries—any exploration into the inner processes of the human body was severely limited. From a historical context, doctors and anatomists at that time obviously lacked the technological advances of today, and would use these drawings for reference since contemporary diagnostic tools such as MRIs and CAT scans had yet to be invented.

A work of great scientific merit as well as a remarkable collection of art, this compilation of ninety plates includes realistic drawings by five magnificent anatomists. Drawings include studies of the skeleton and spinal column, cardiovascular and nervous systems, as well as a glimpse at internal organs, muscle structure, and other subjects. Executed with vitality, originality, and anatomical accuracy, these illustrations by artists such as Vesalius and Albinus enabled art students to study the body from varying perspectives and positions. Historians in the fields of medicine and art owe an enormous debt of gratitude for the unique contributions of such innovative and talented artists. An enthralling combination of beauty and symmetry, the anatomical images in this book illuminate the incredibly complex and highly specialized workings of the human body.

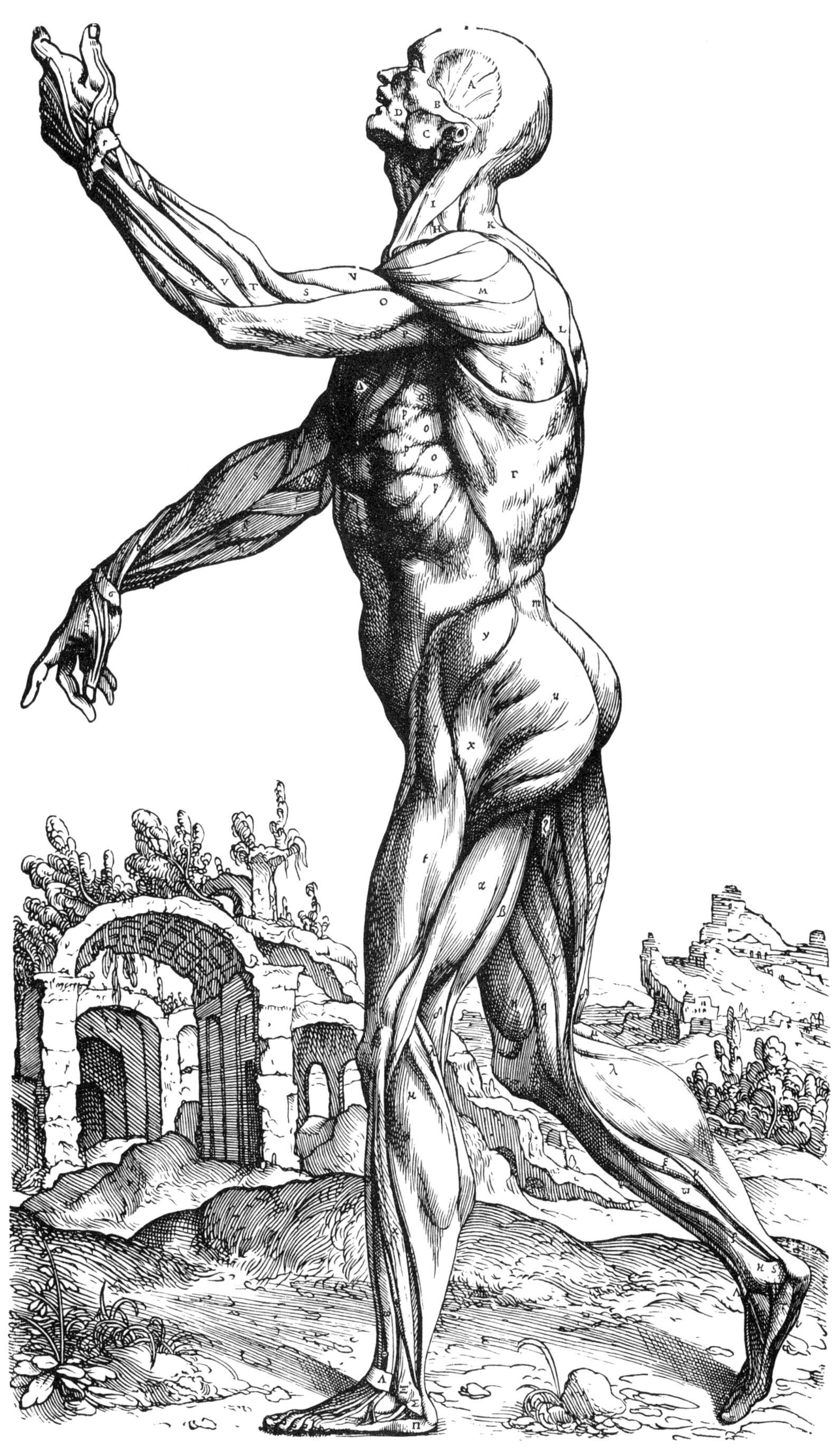

The Muscles

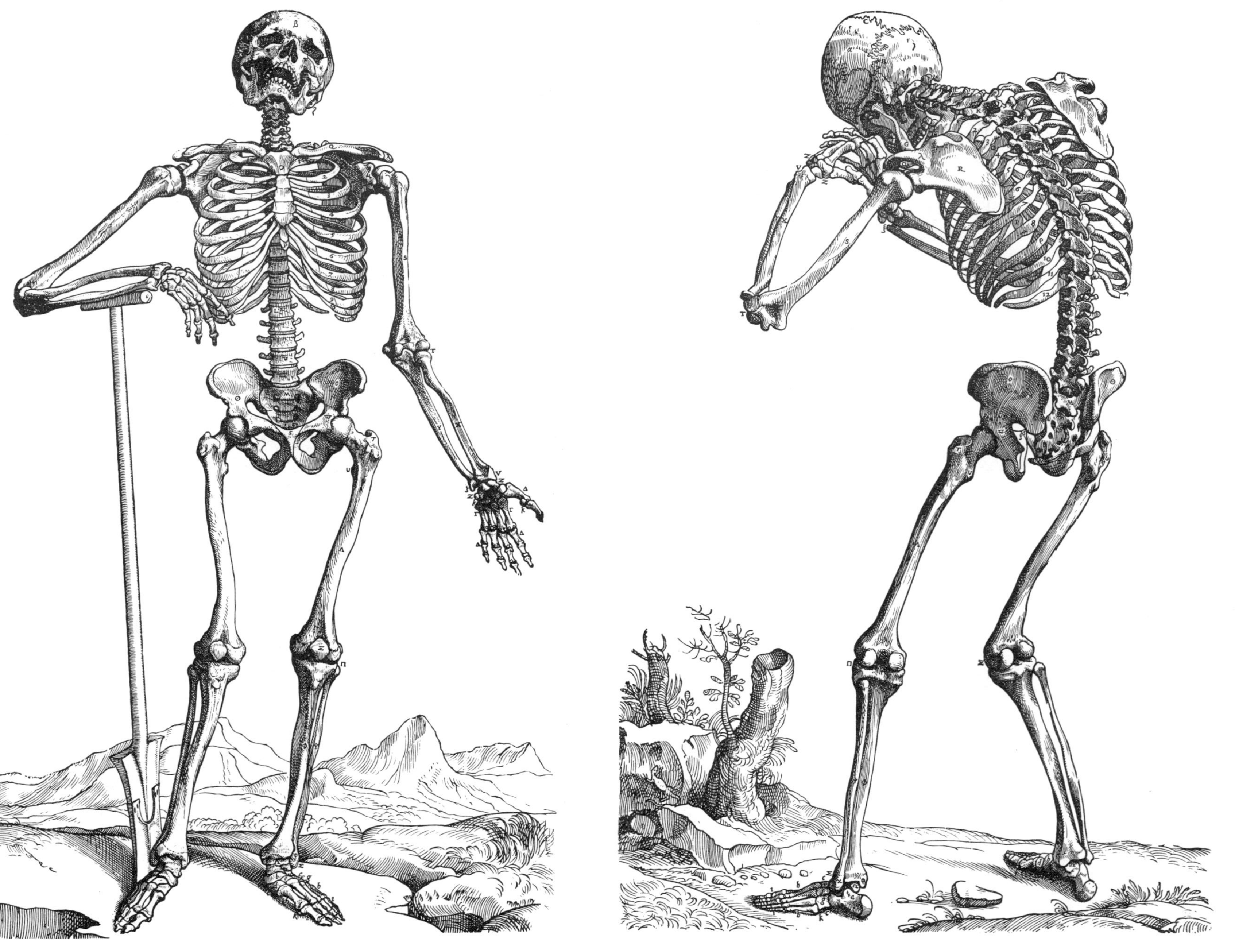

Left: The Skeleton, front view. *Right:* The Skeleton, back view.

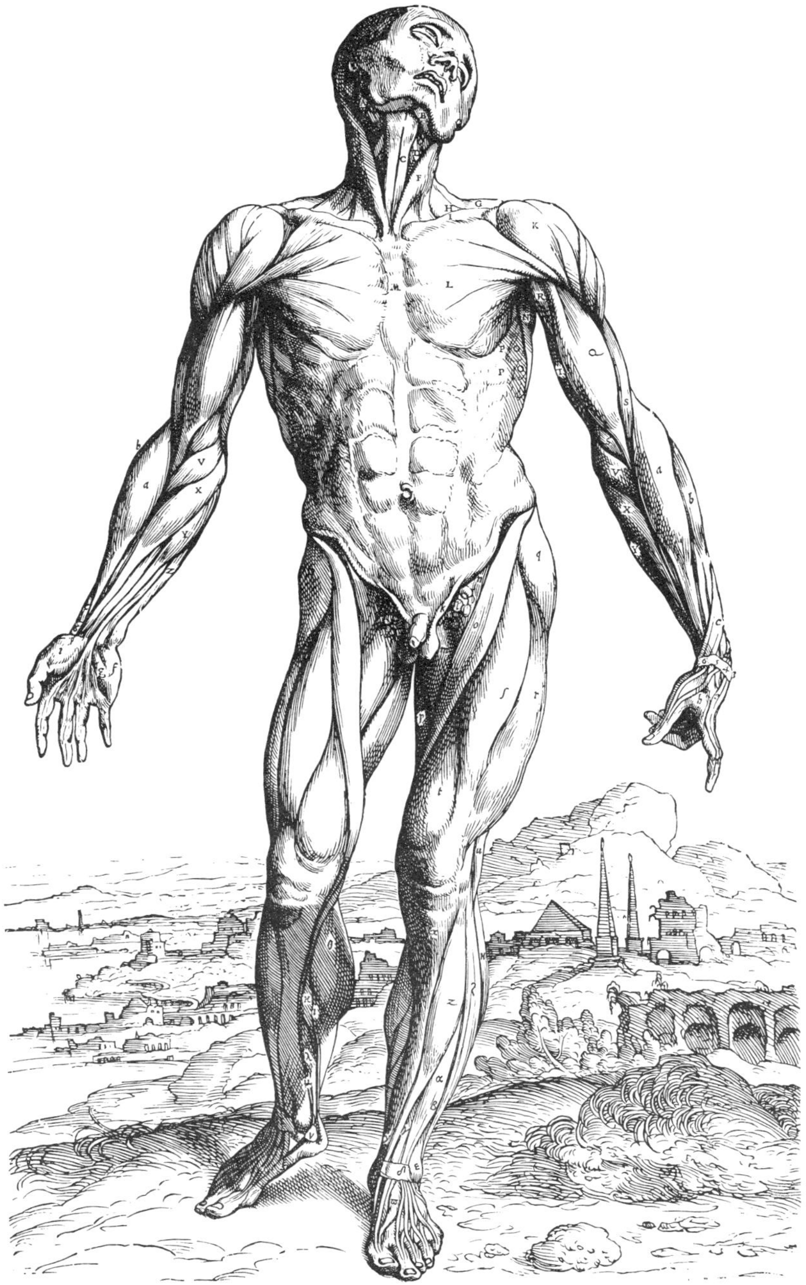

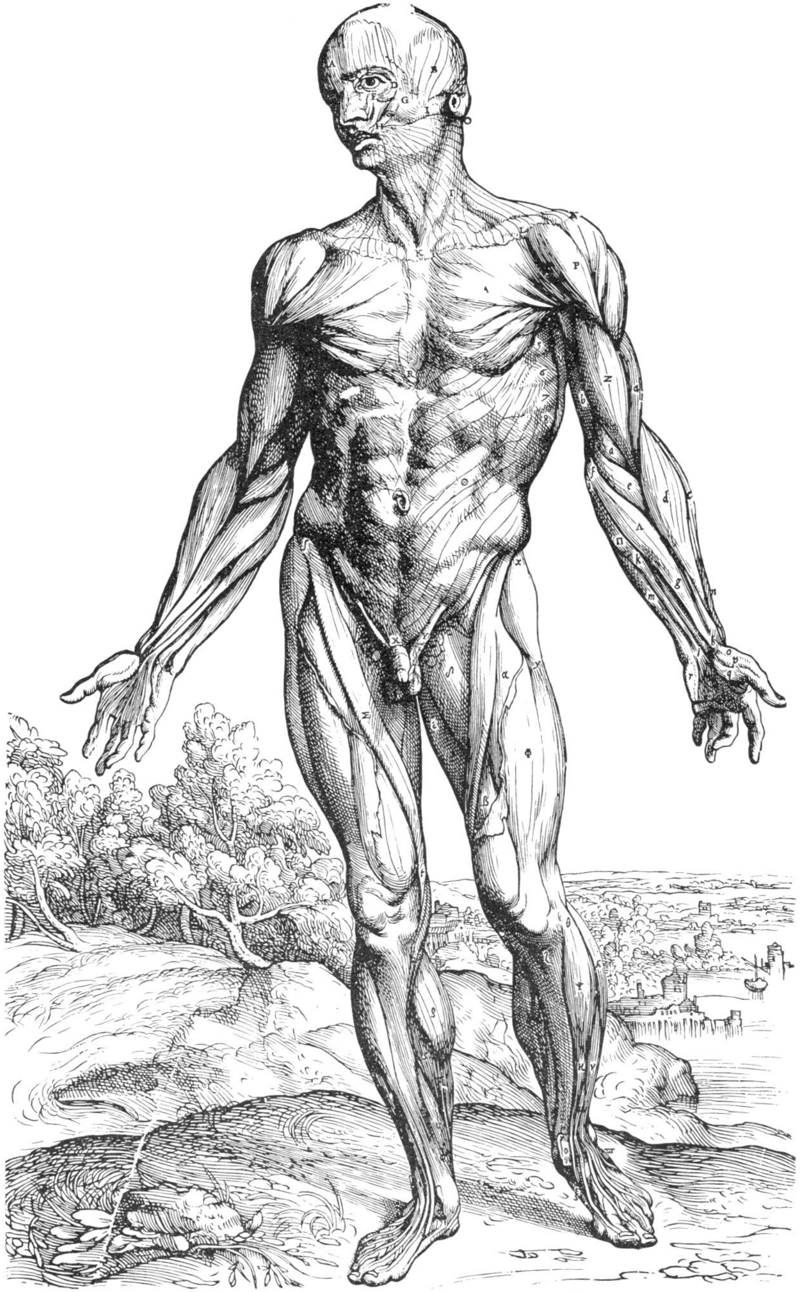

Left: The Muscles, front view. *Right:* The Muscles, front view.

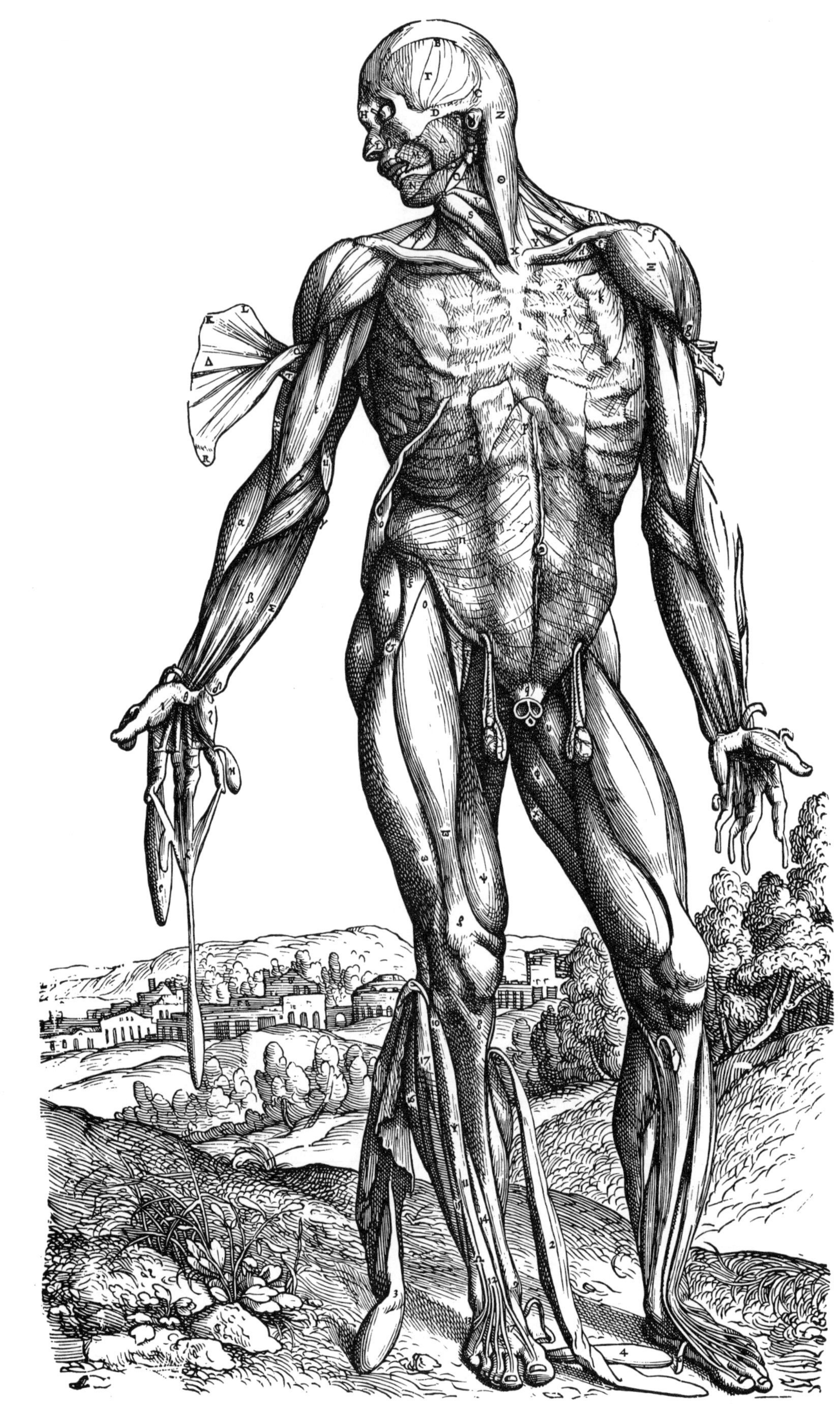

The Muscles

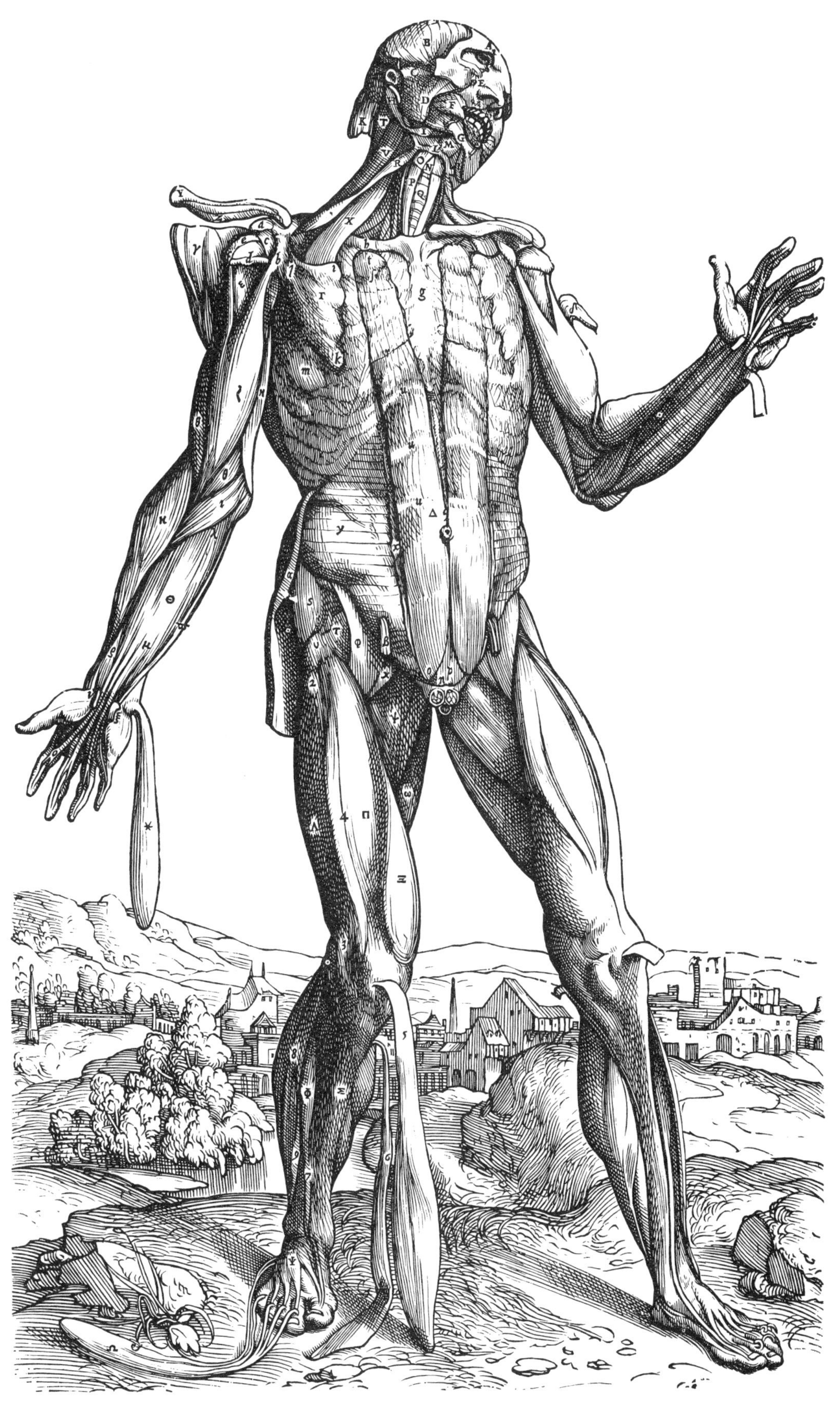

The Muscles

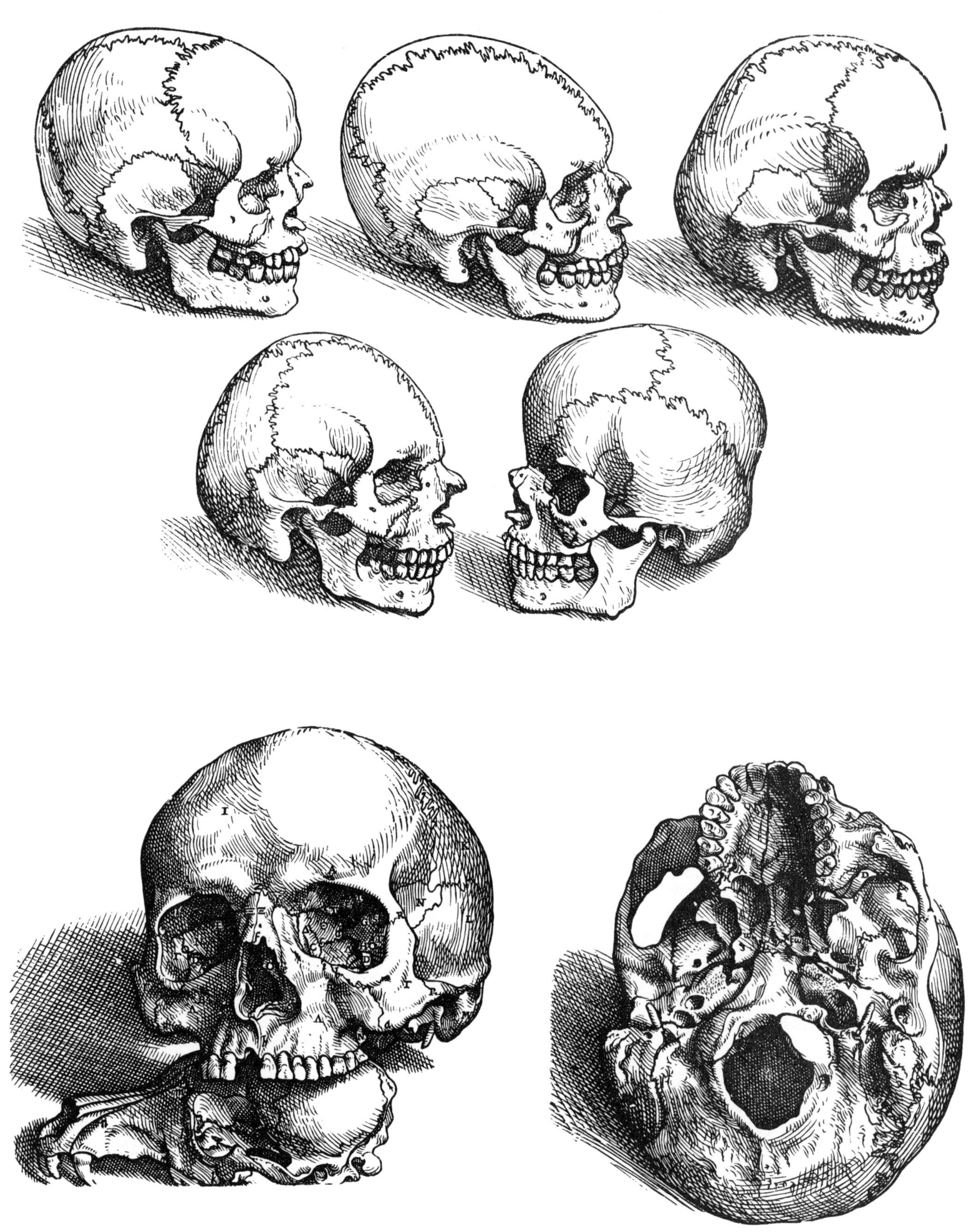

Top: Variants of Skull Shape. *Bottom:* Two Views of the Skull.

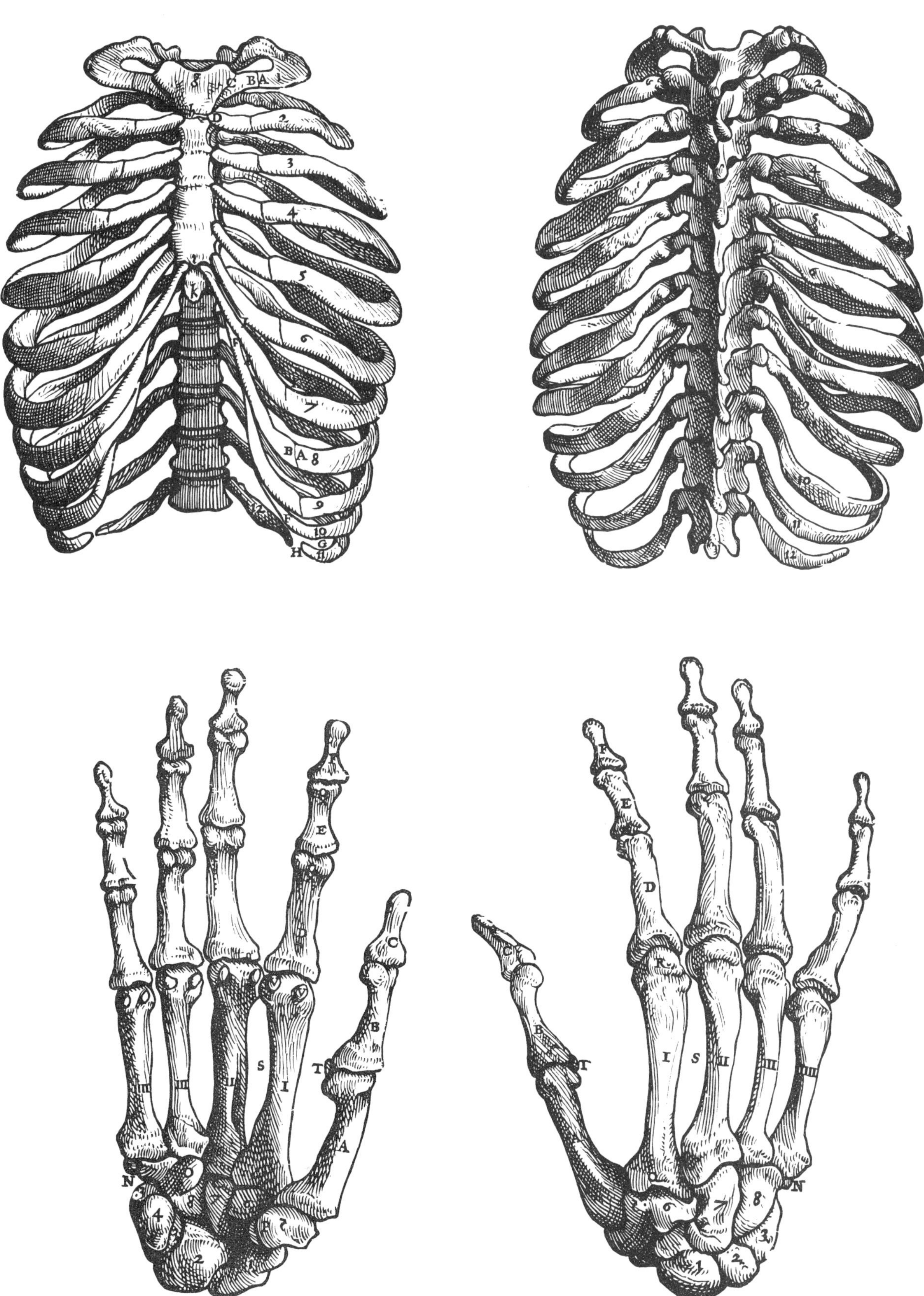

Top: Bones of the Thorax. *Bottom:* Bones of the Hand.

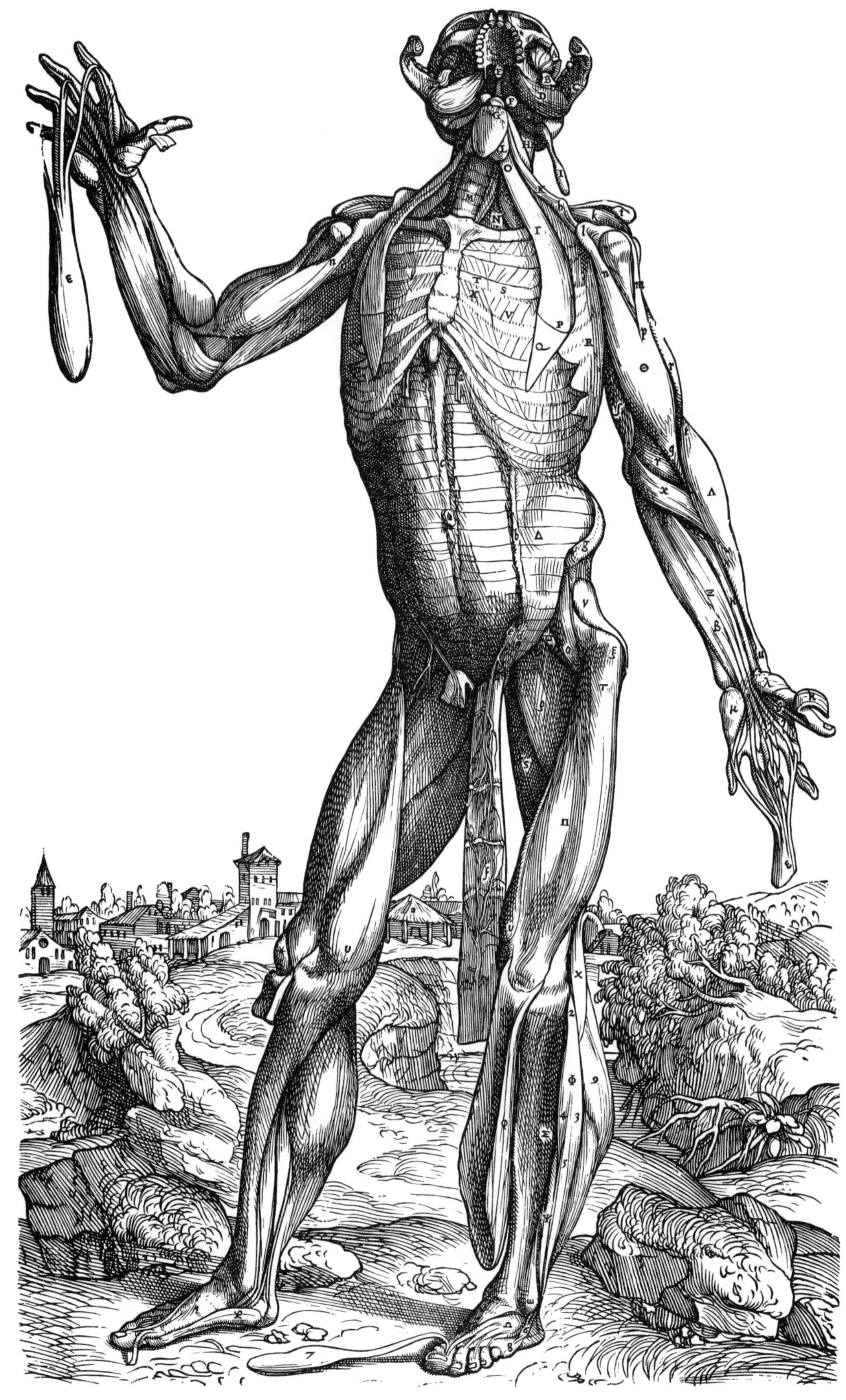

The Muscles

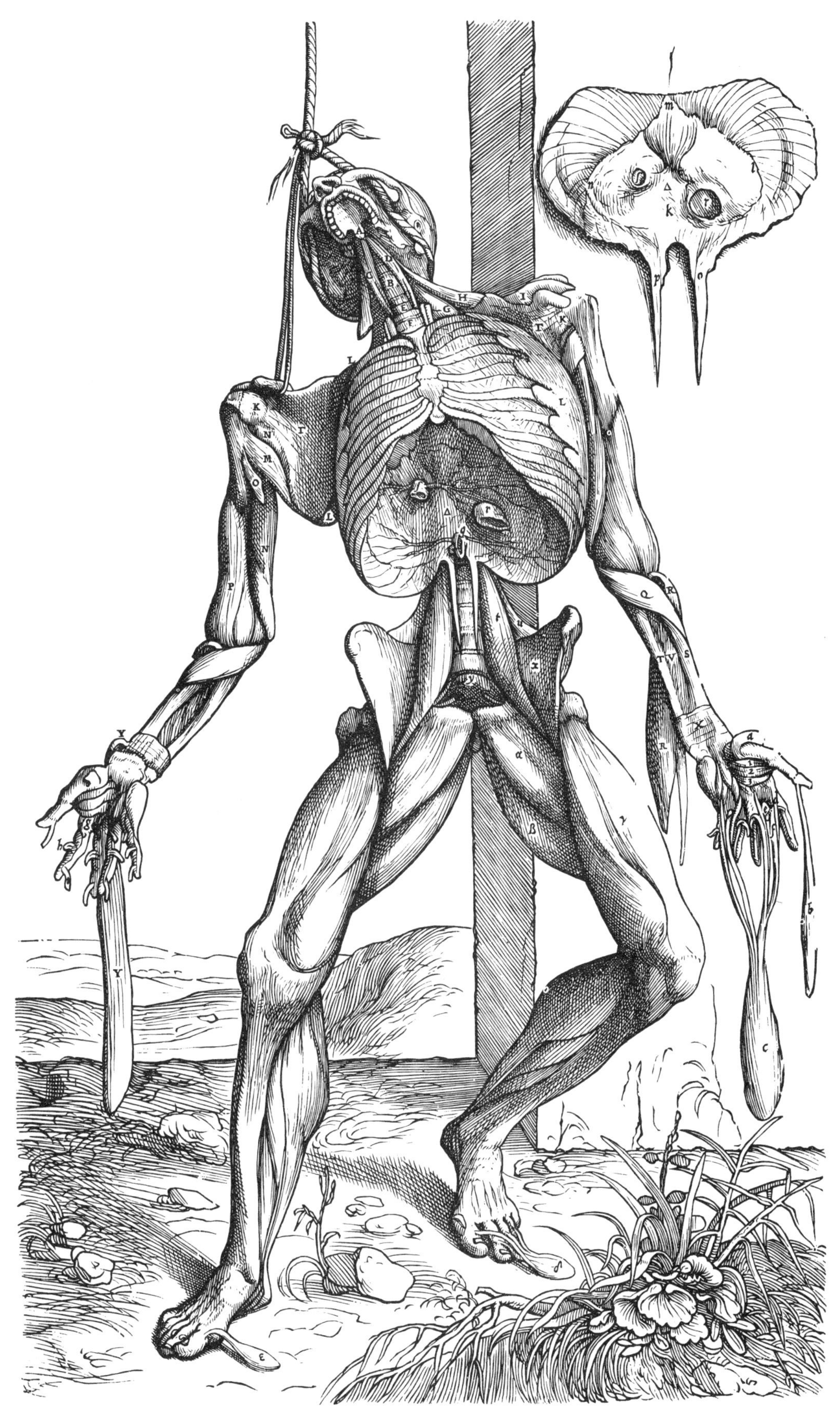

The Muscles

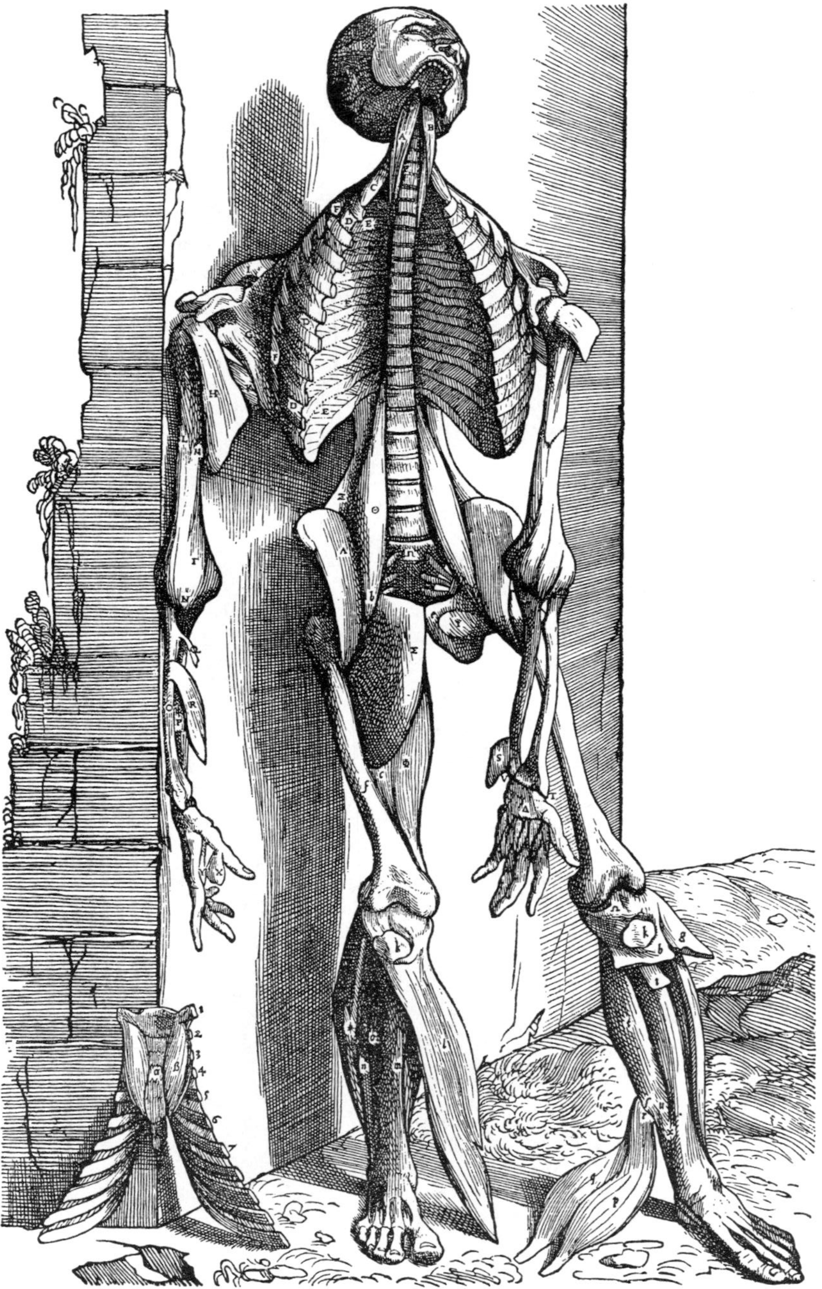

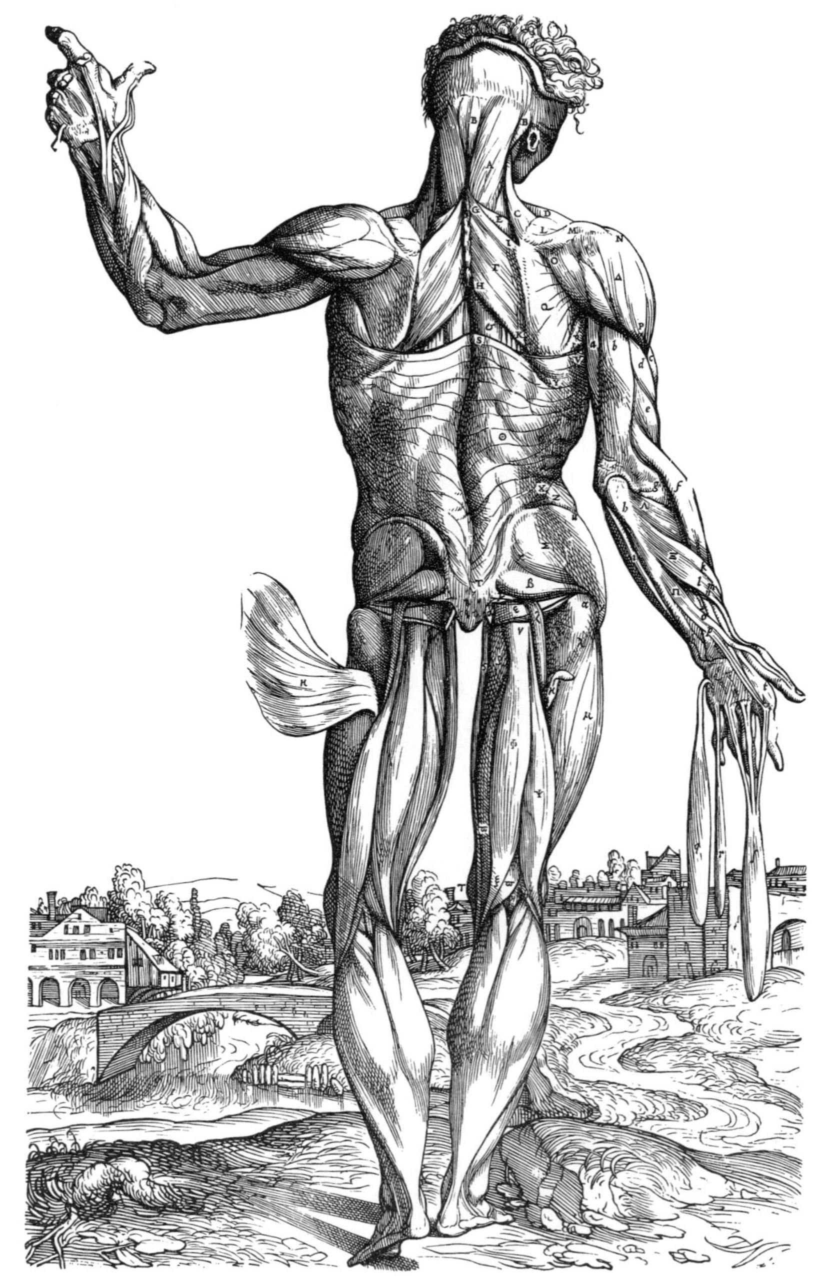

The Muscles

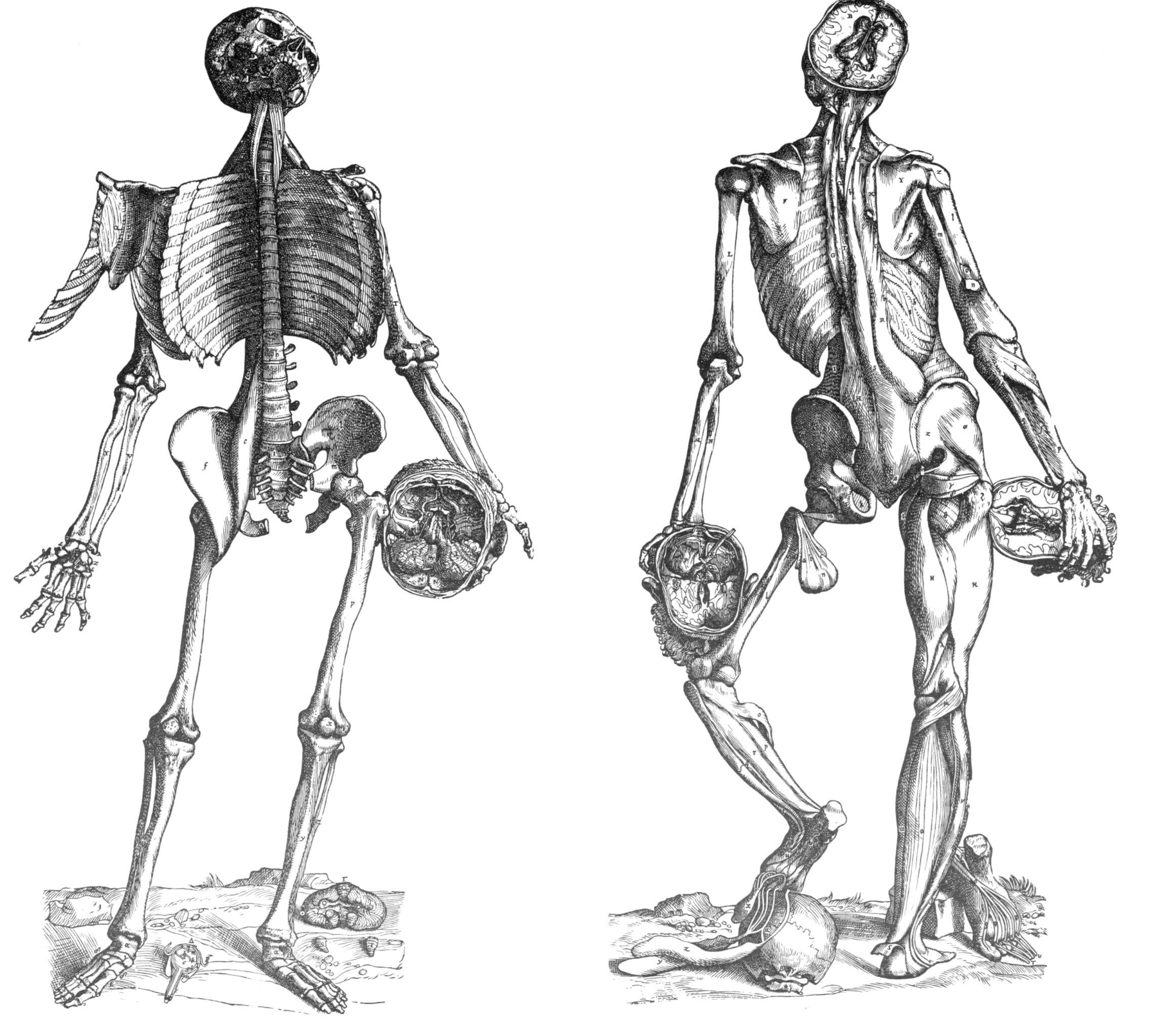

The Skeleton, front and back views

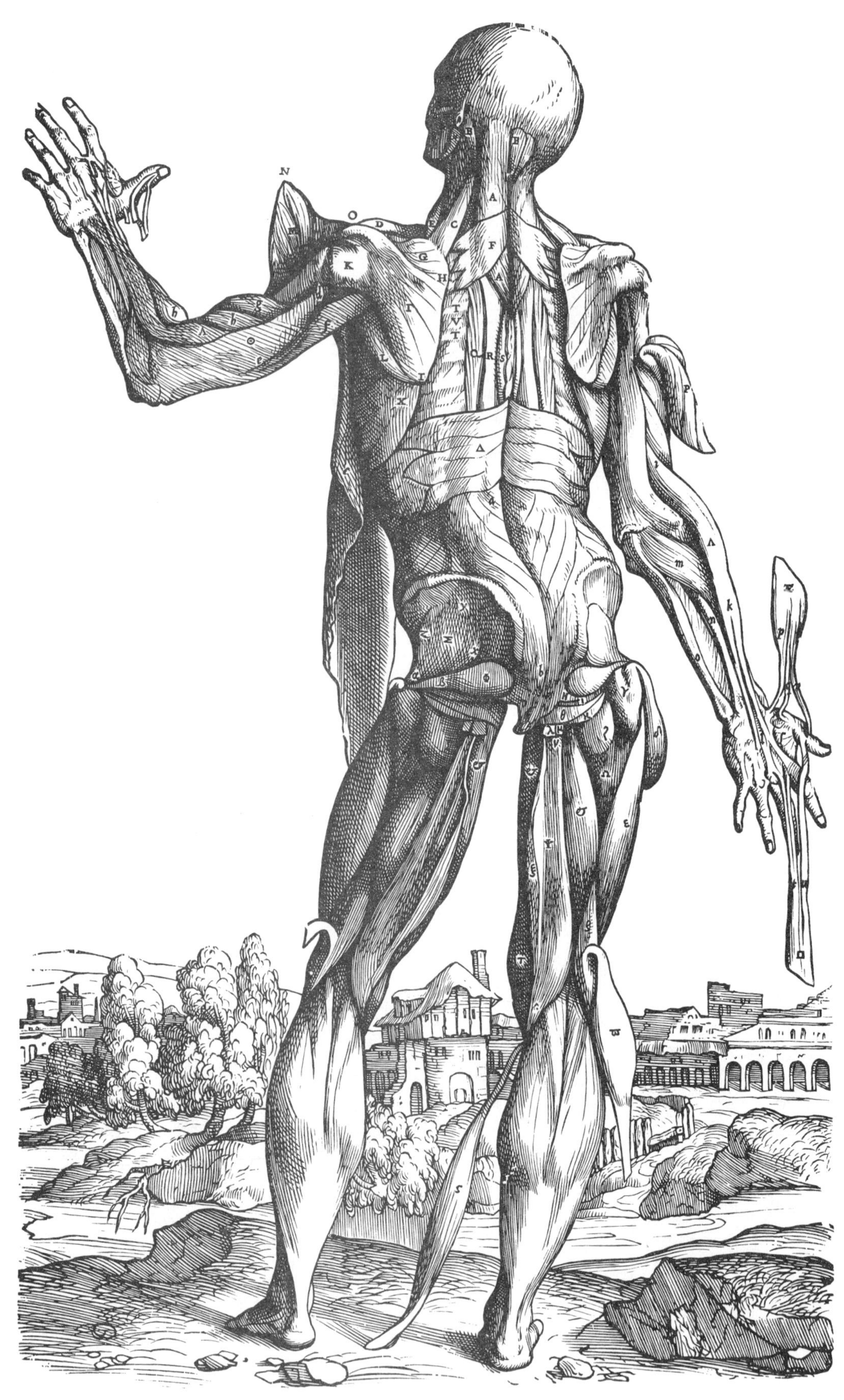

The Muscles, back view

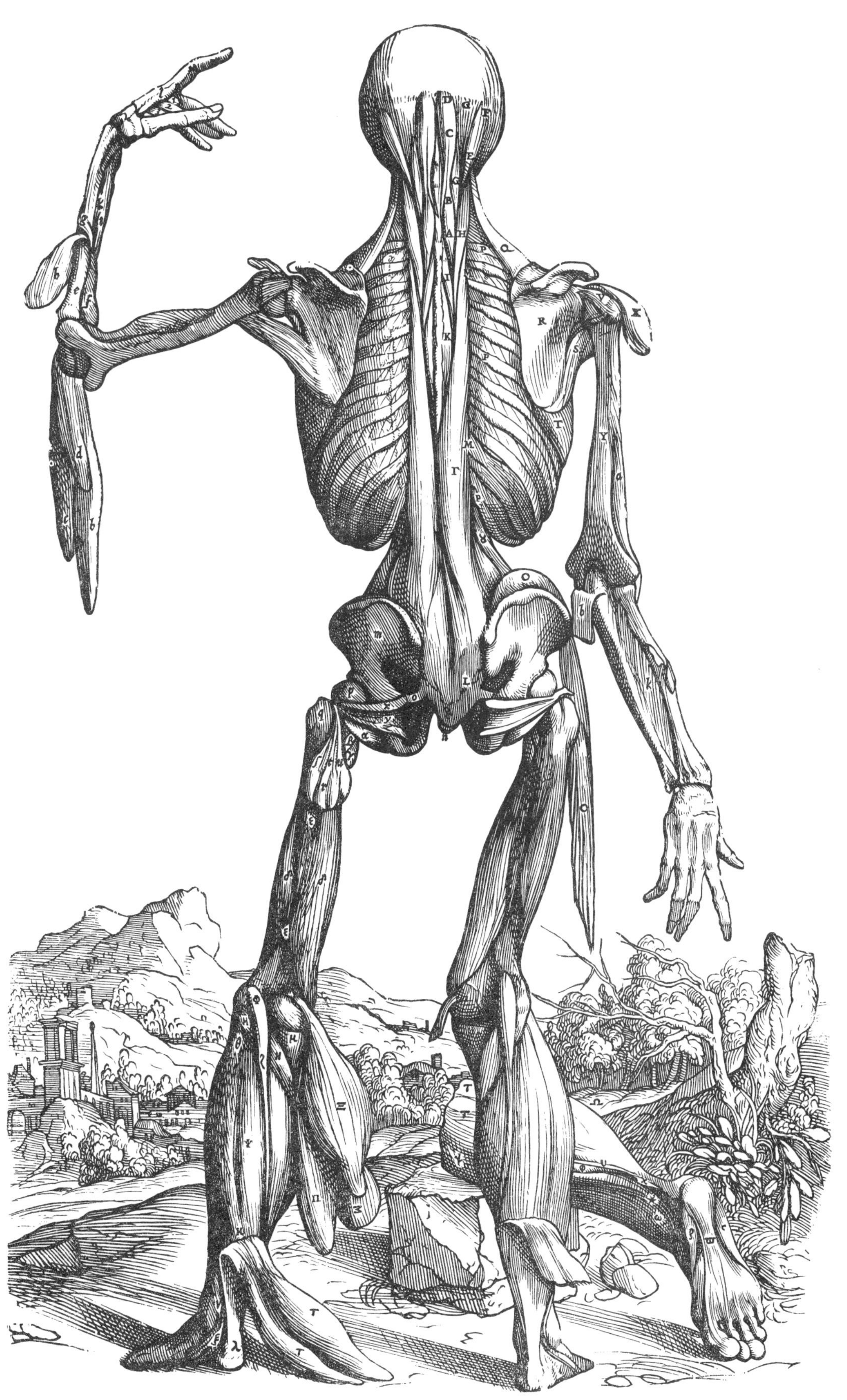

The Muscles, back view

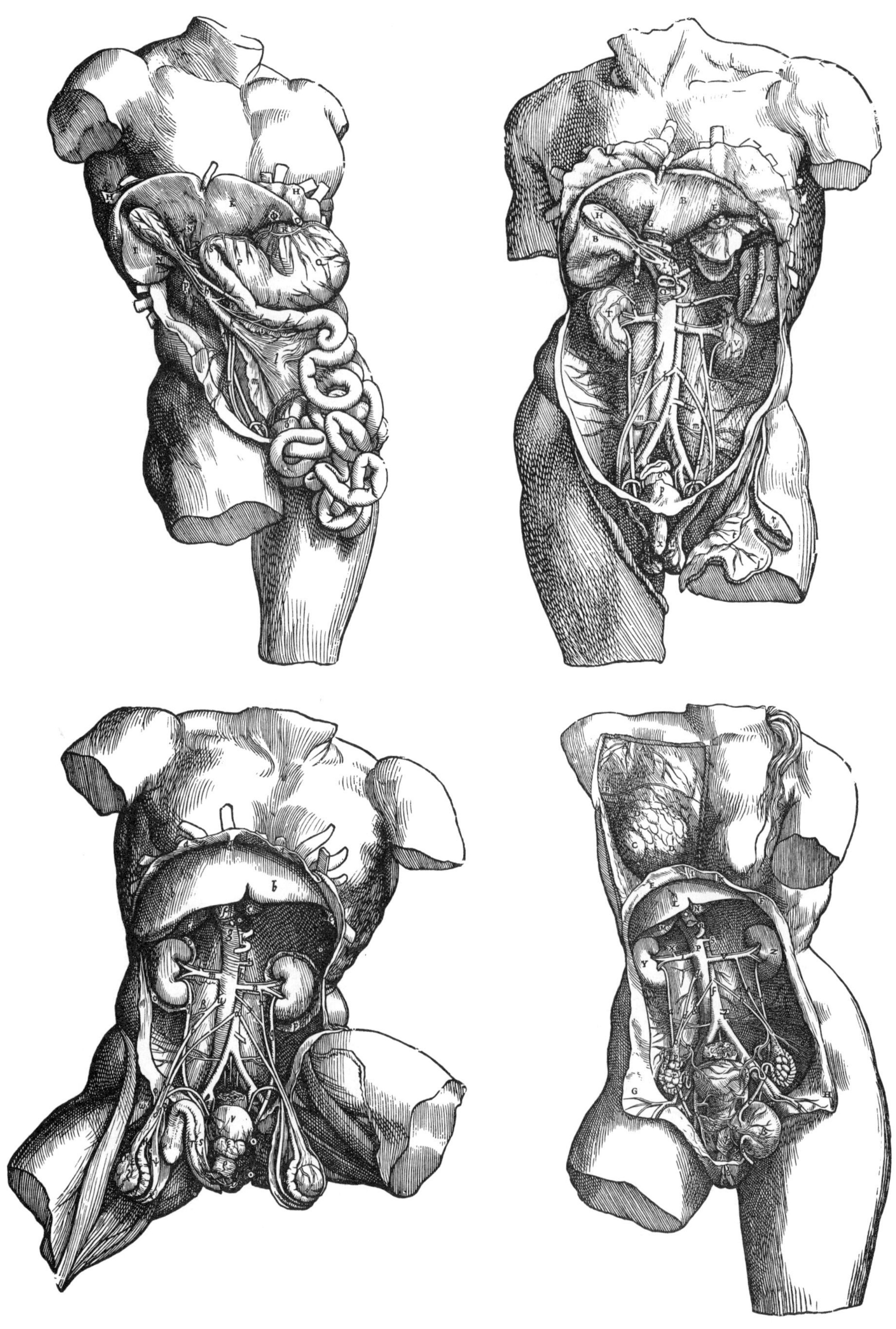

Internal Organs of the Trunk. *Top, left:* Stomach and esophagus. *Top, right:* Abdominal cavity, liver, spleen, and kidneys. *Bottom, left:* Male Genito-Urinary Tract. *Bottom, right:* Female Reproductive Organs.

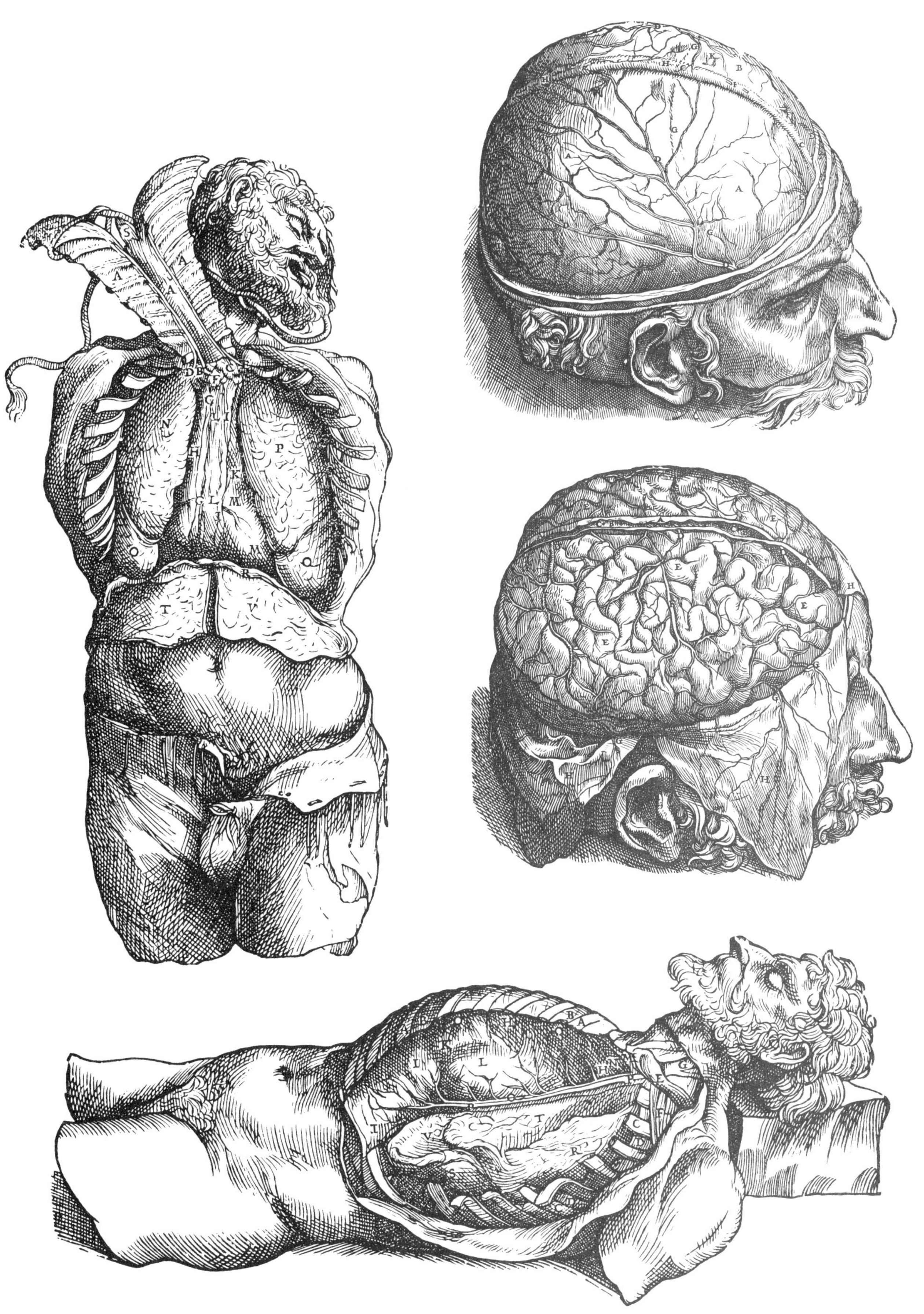

Thoracic Cavity and the Brain

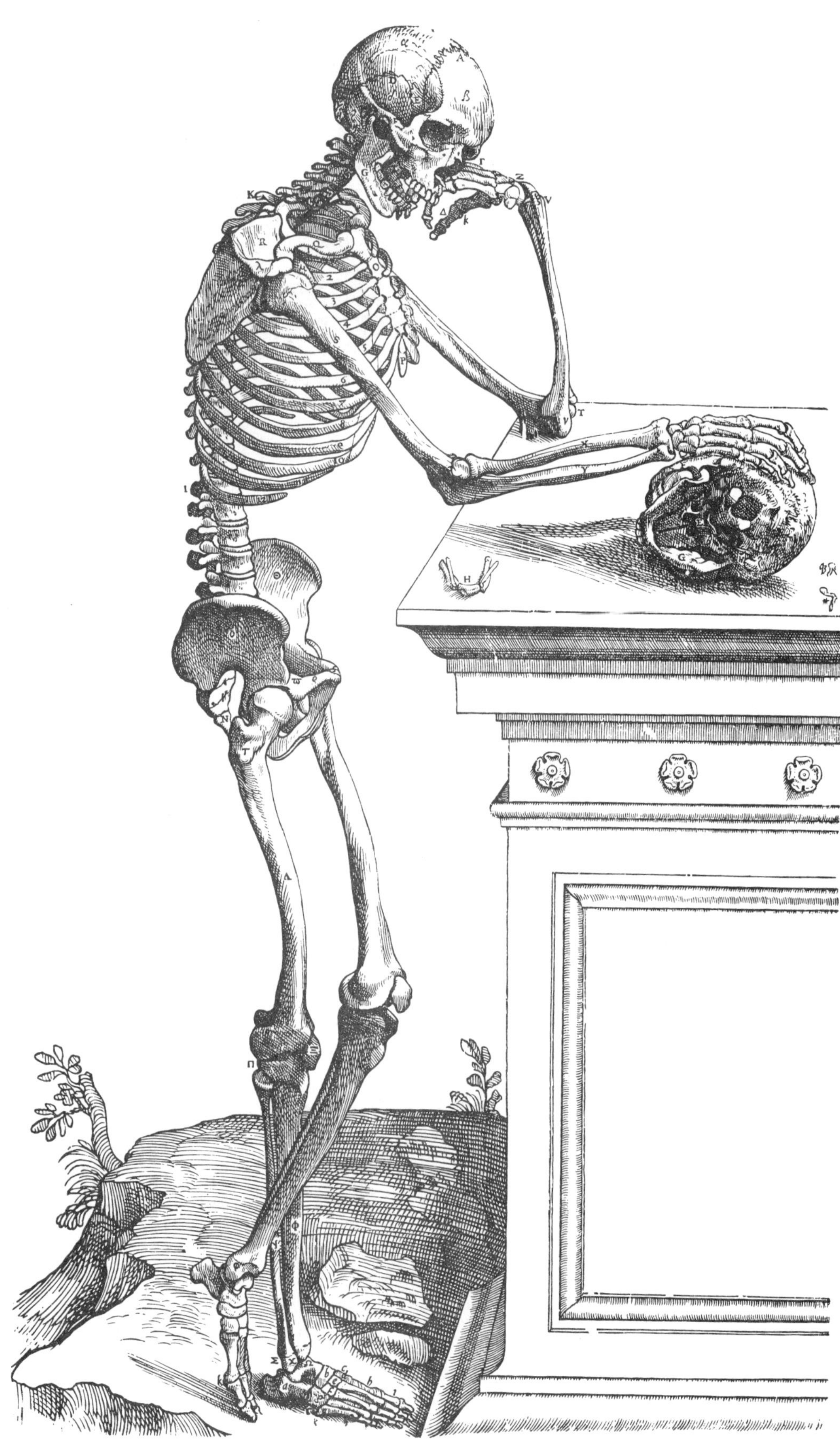

The Skeleton

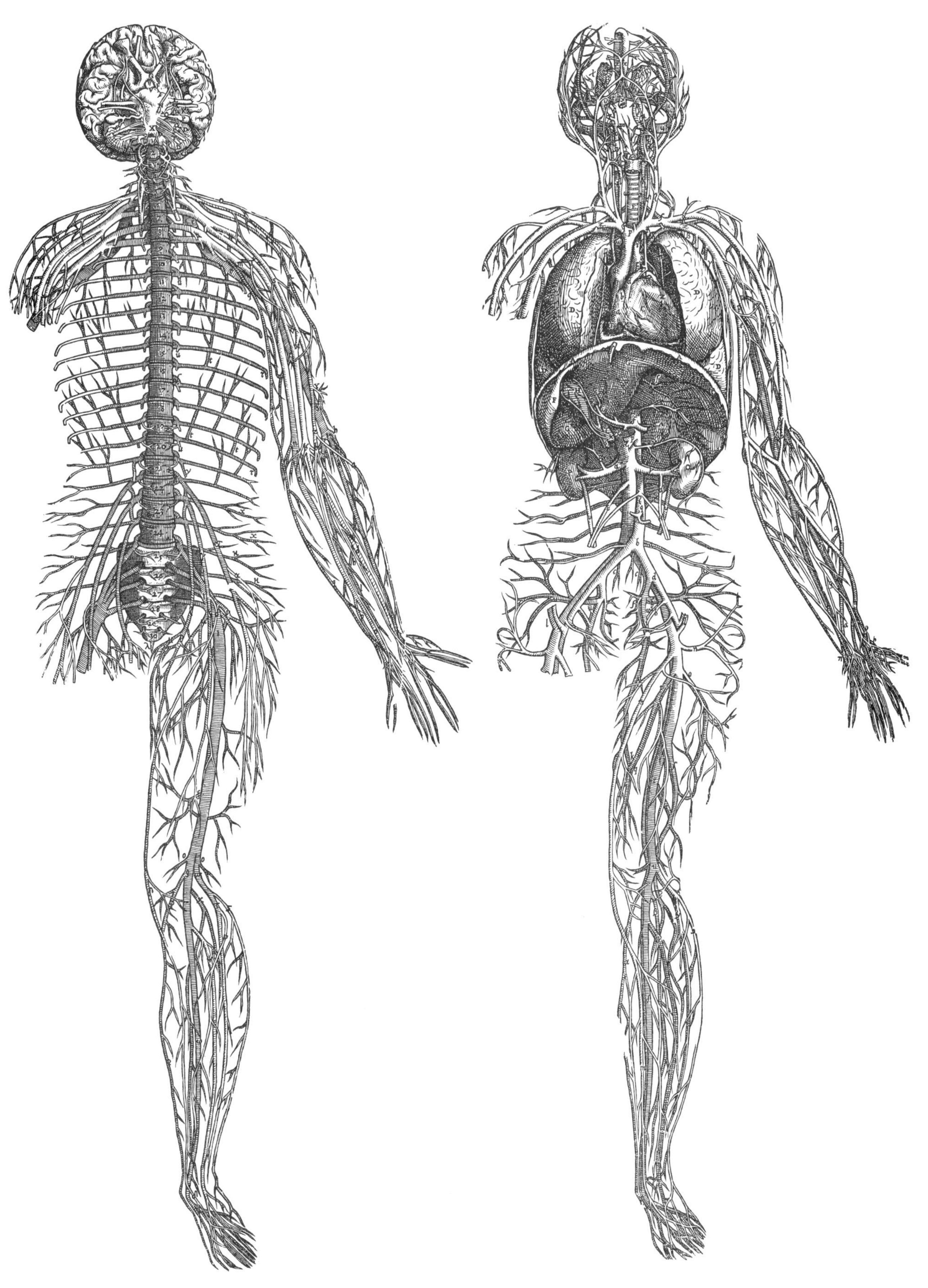

Vessels and Nerves

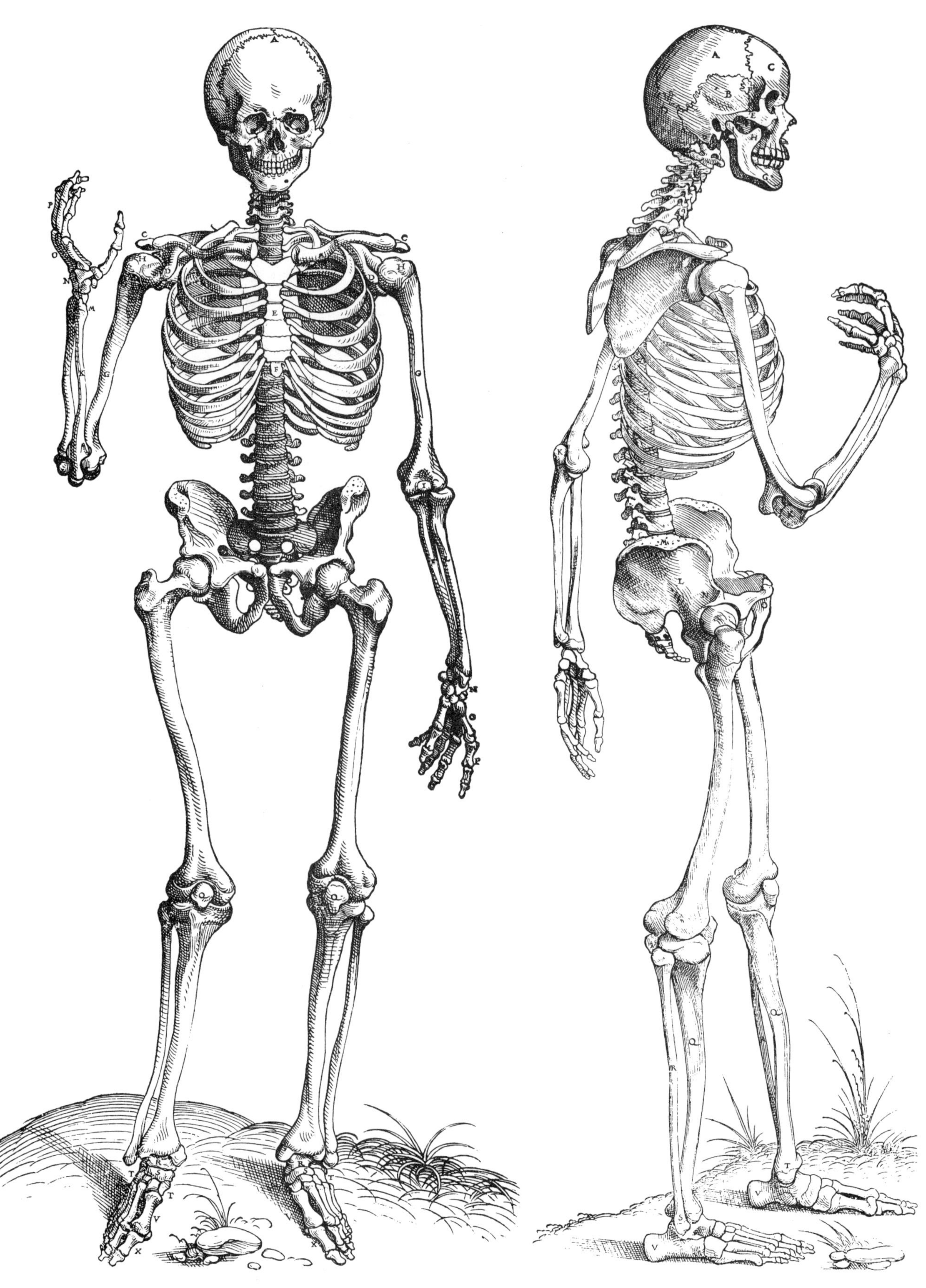

Left: The Skeleton, front view. *Right:* The Skeleton, side view.

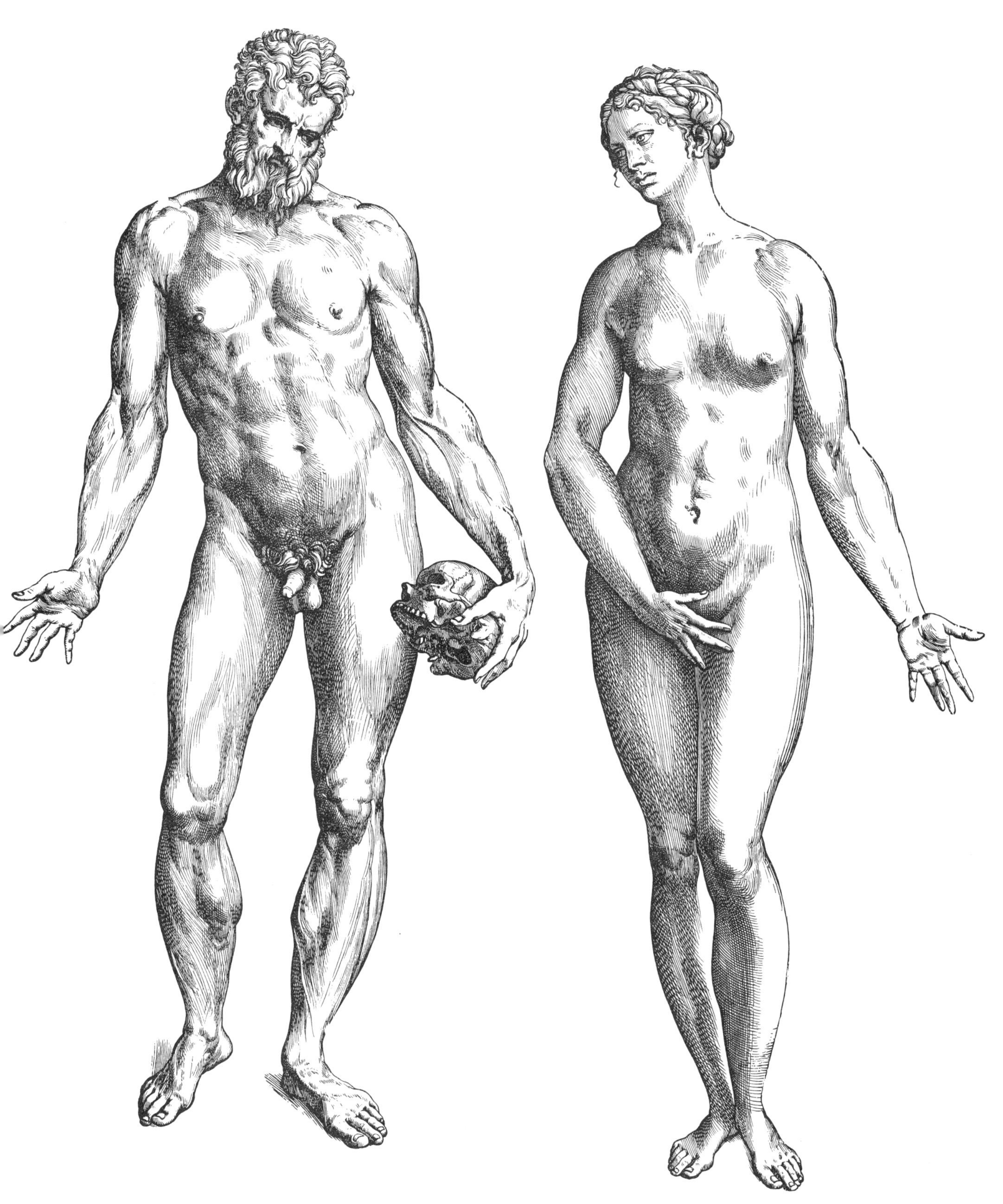

Male and Female Nudes

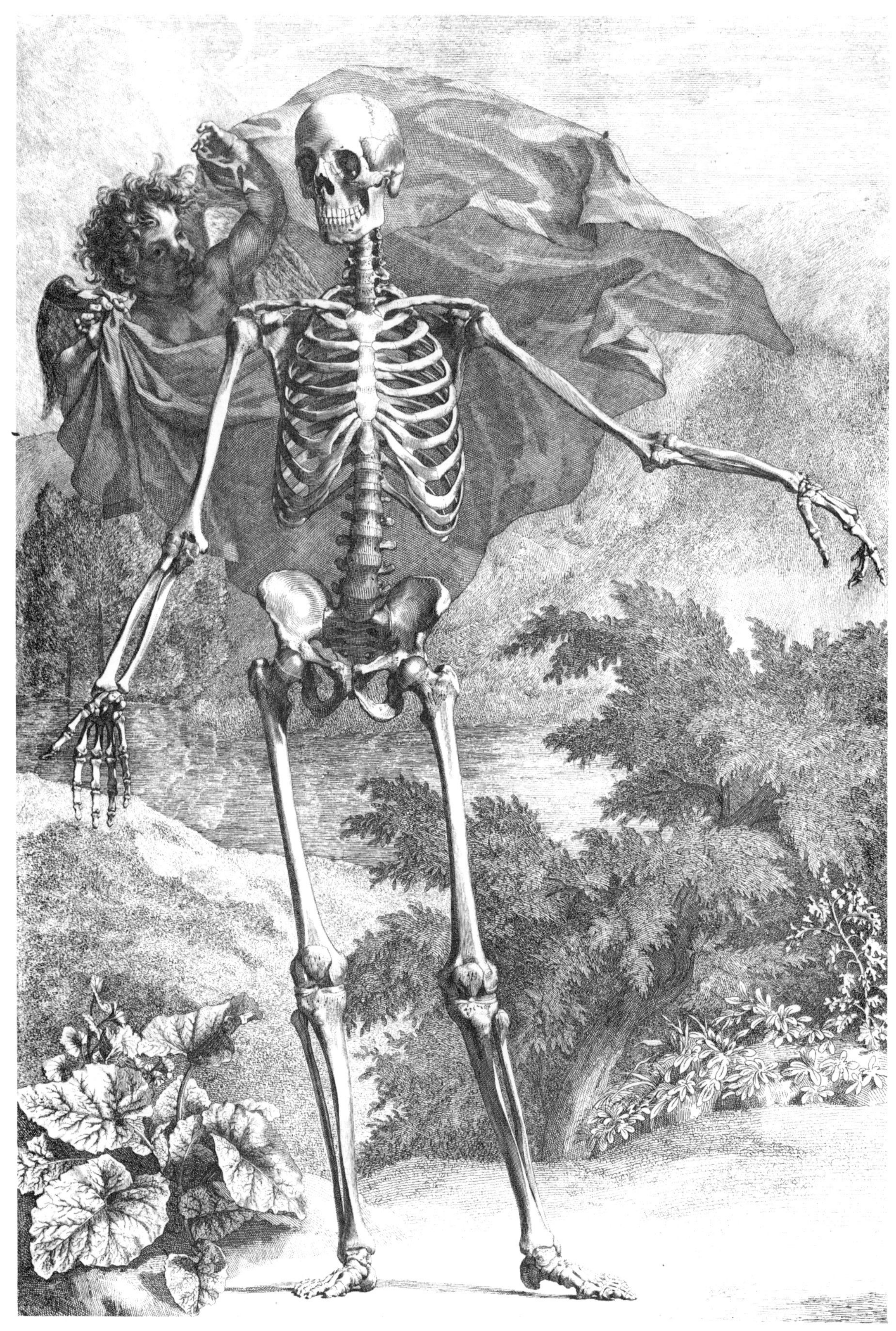

The Skeleton, front view

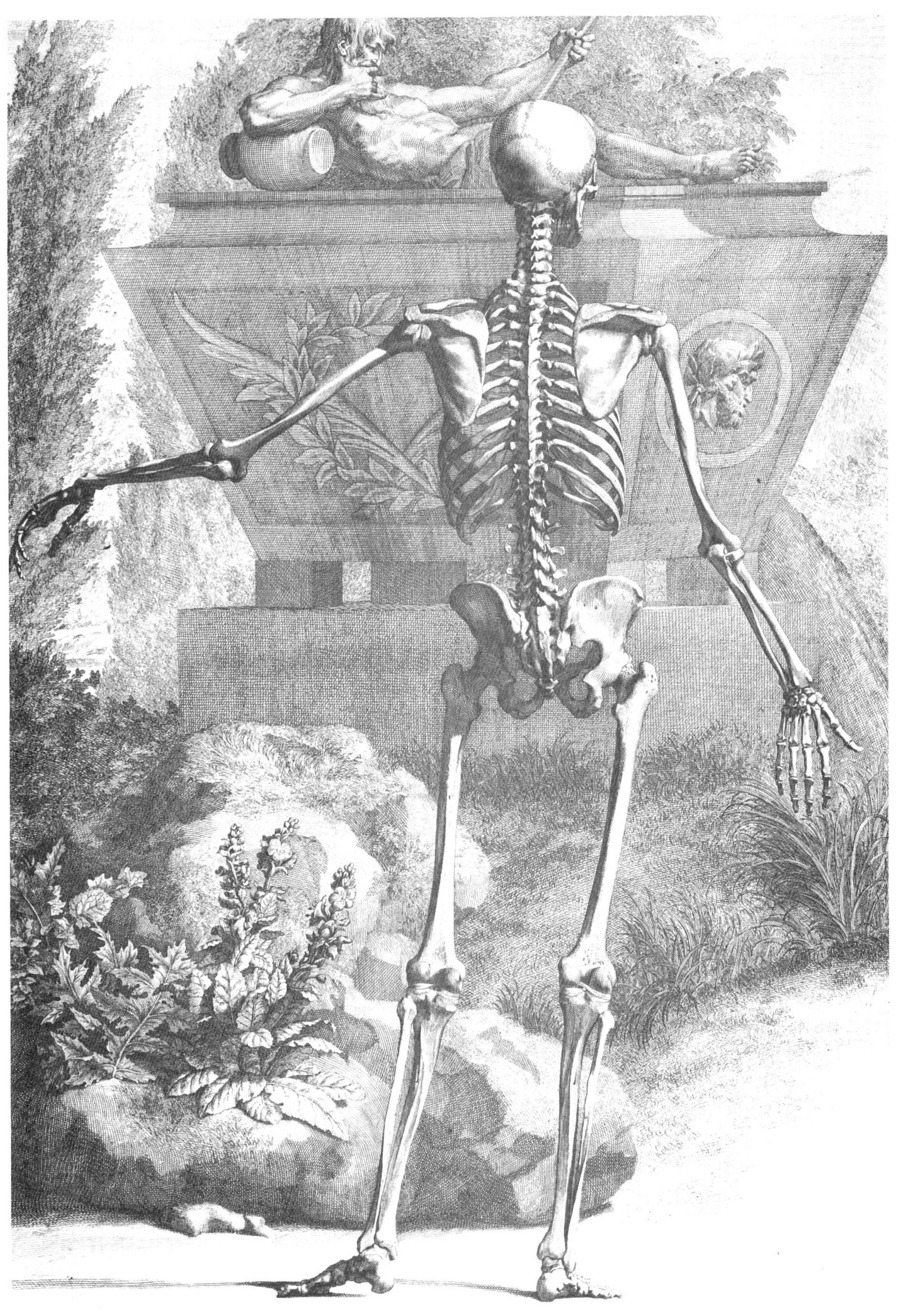

The Skeleton, back view

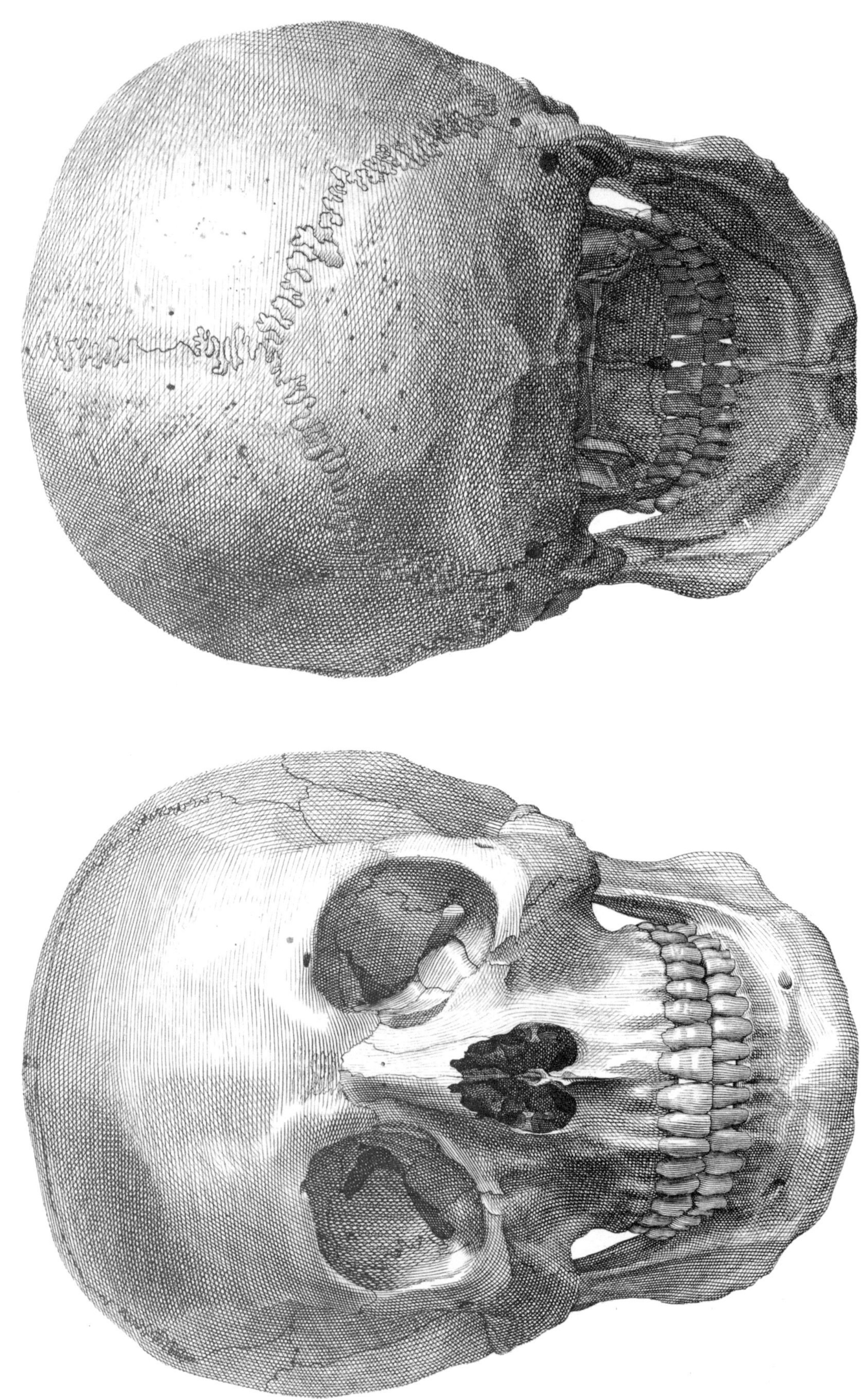

The Skull, front and back views

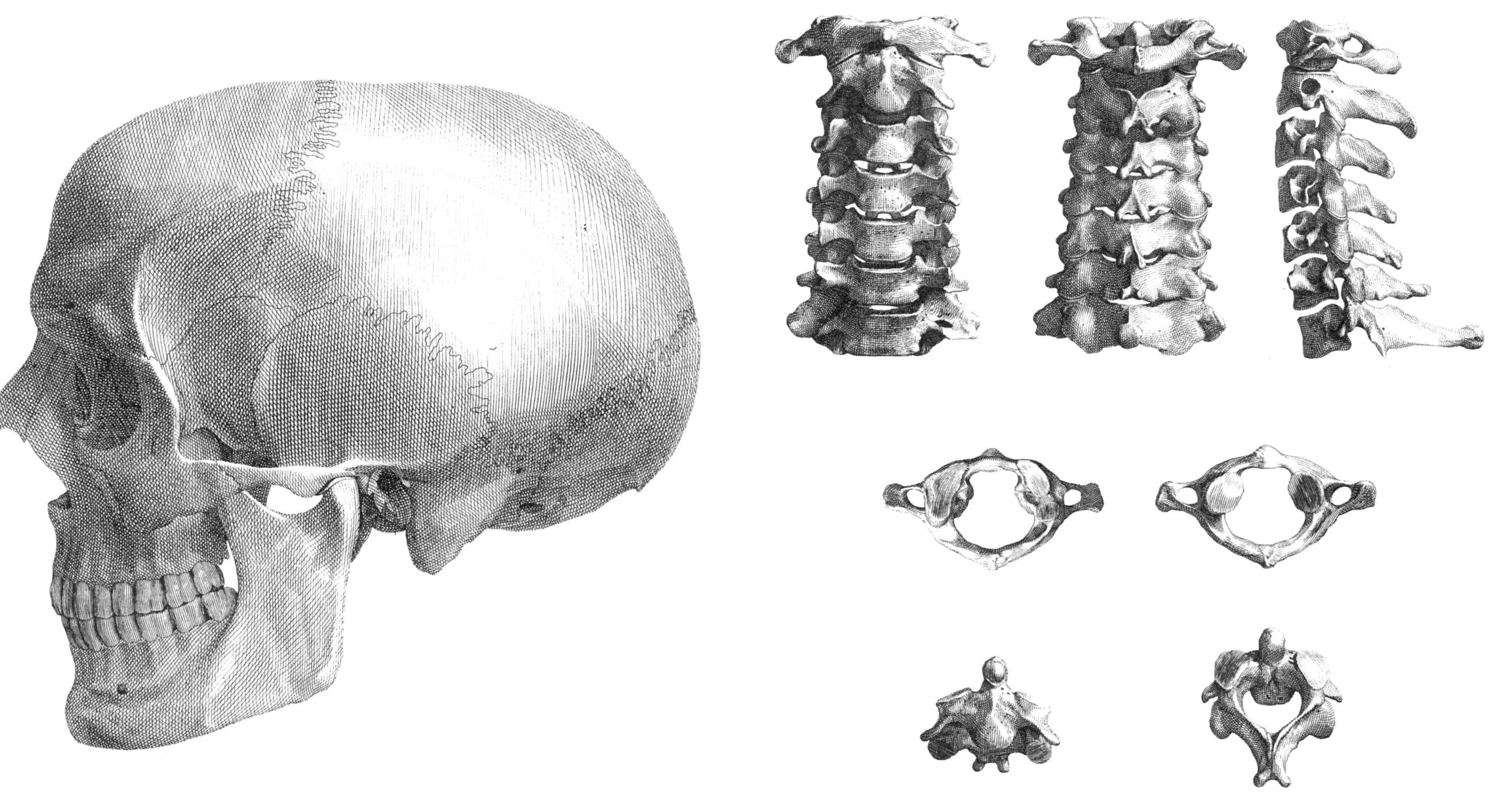

Left: The Skull, side view. *Right:* Cervical Vertebrae.

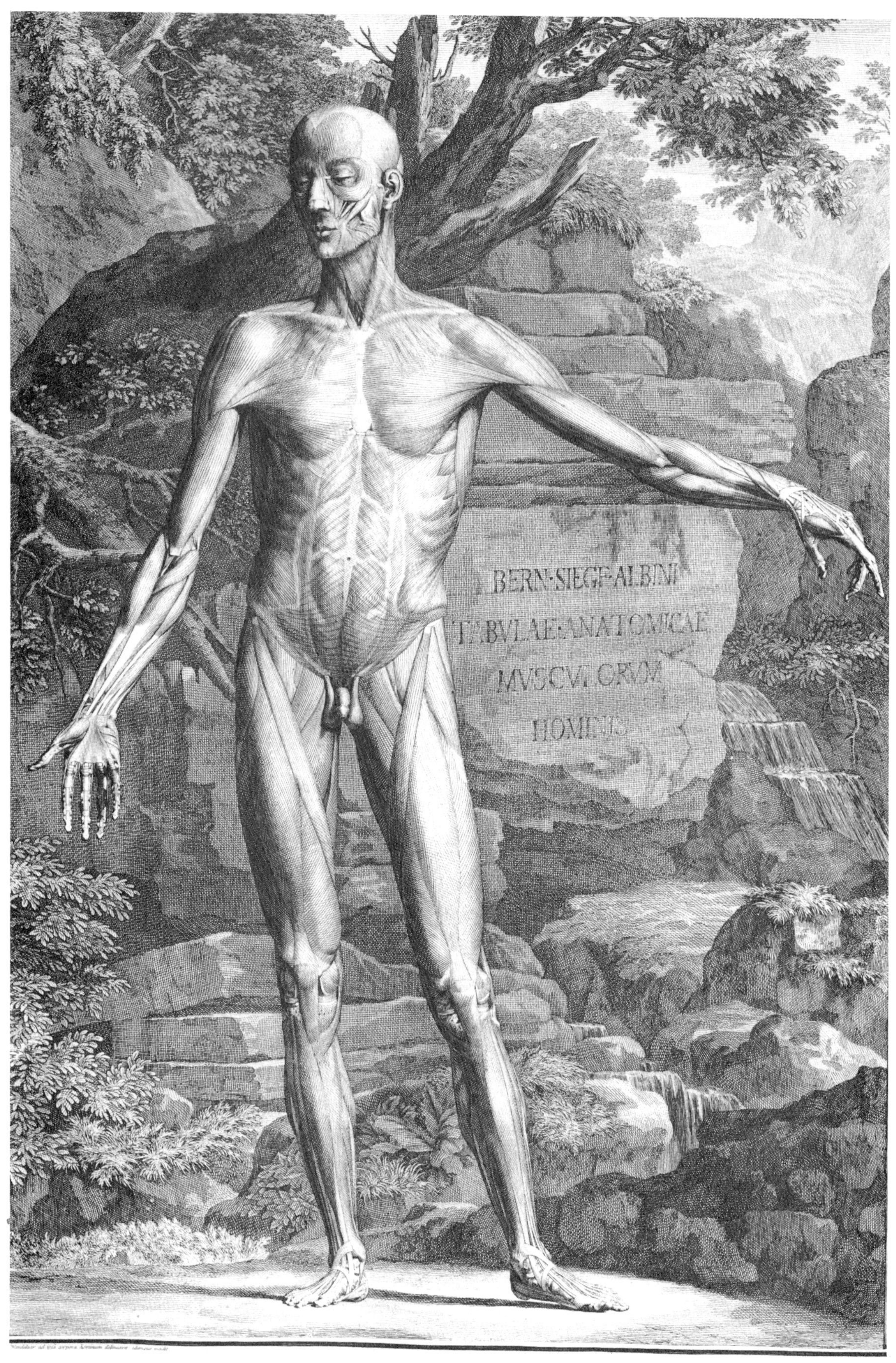

The Outermost Order of Muscles, front view

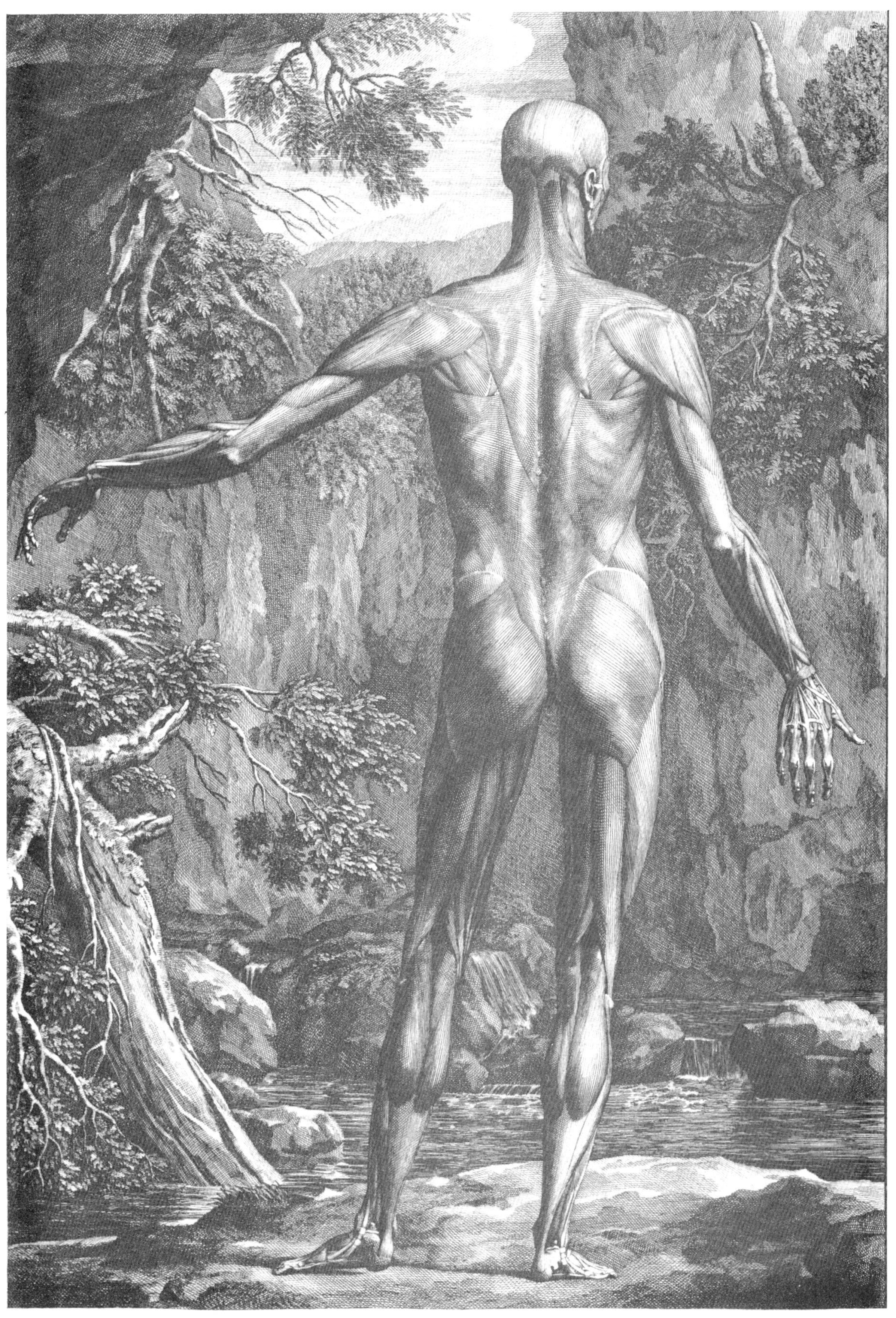

The Outermost Order of Muscles, back view

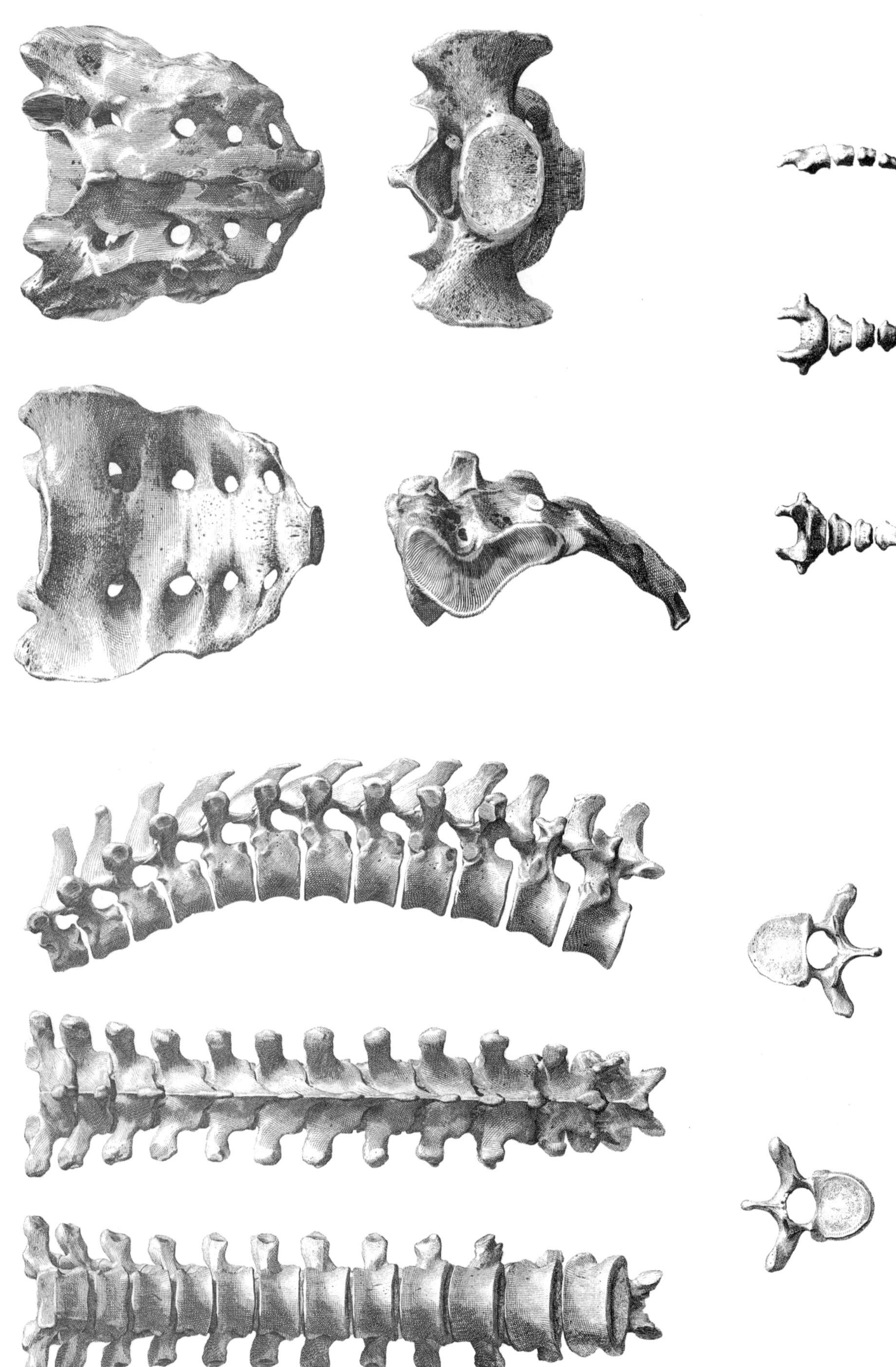

Left: The Vertebral Column—Thoracic Vertebrae. *Right:* Sacrum and Coccyx.

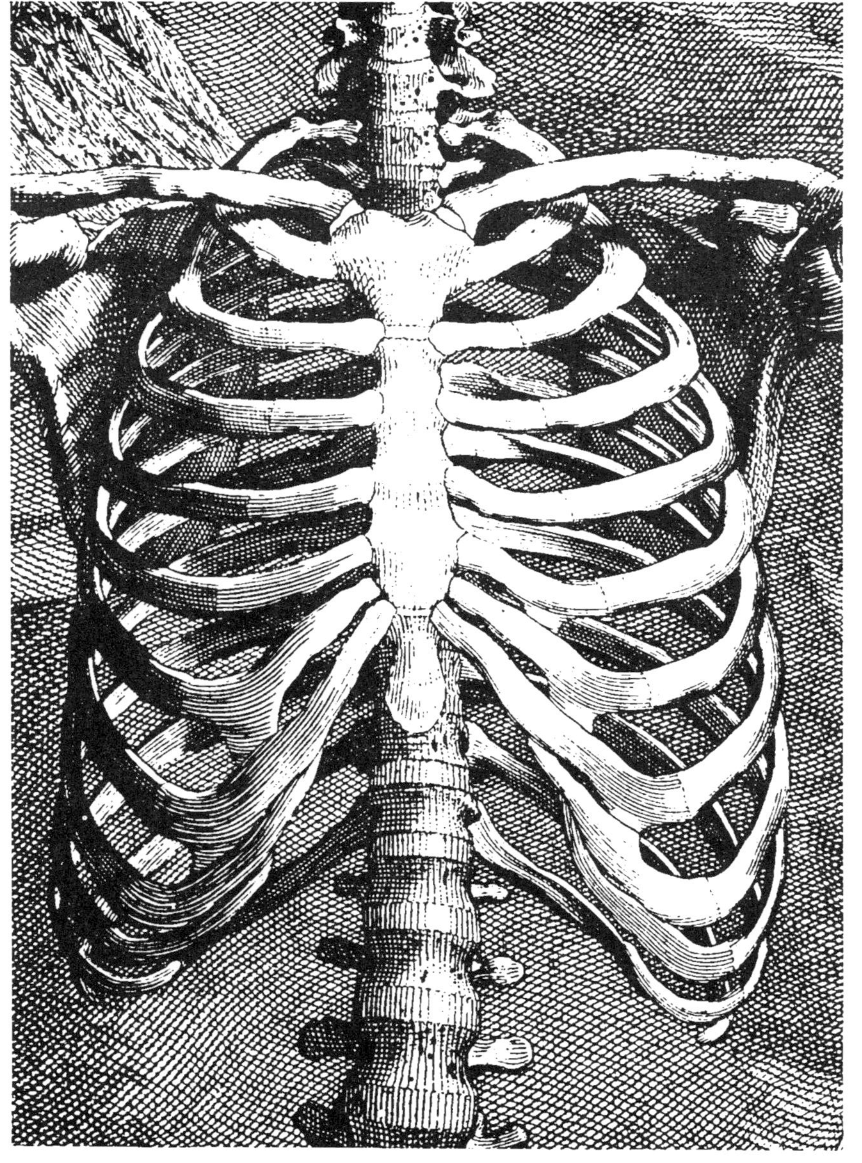

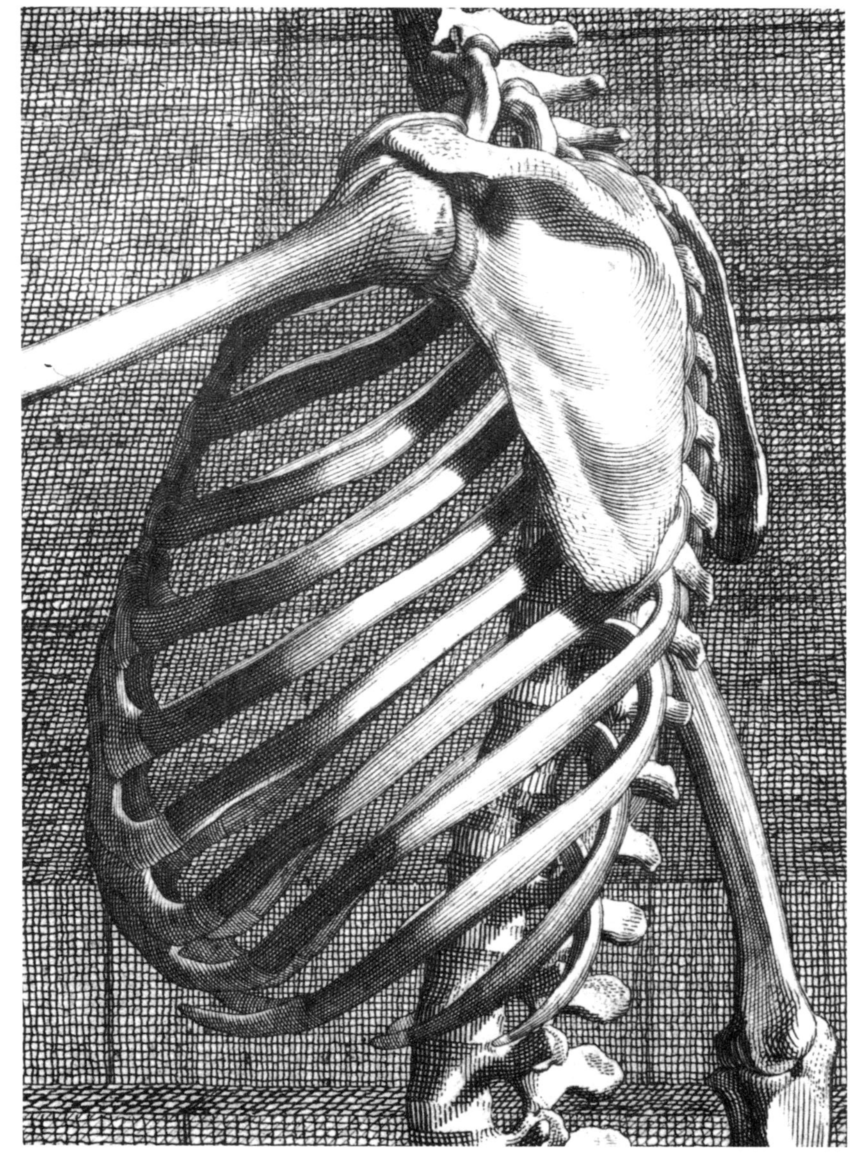

Left: The Rib Cage, front view. *Right:* The Rib Cage, side view.

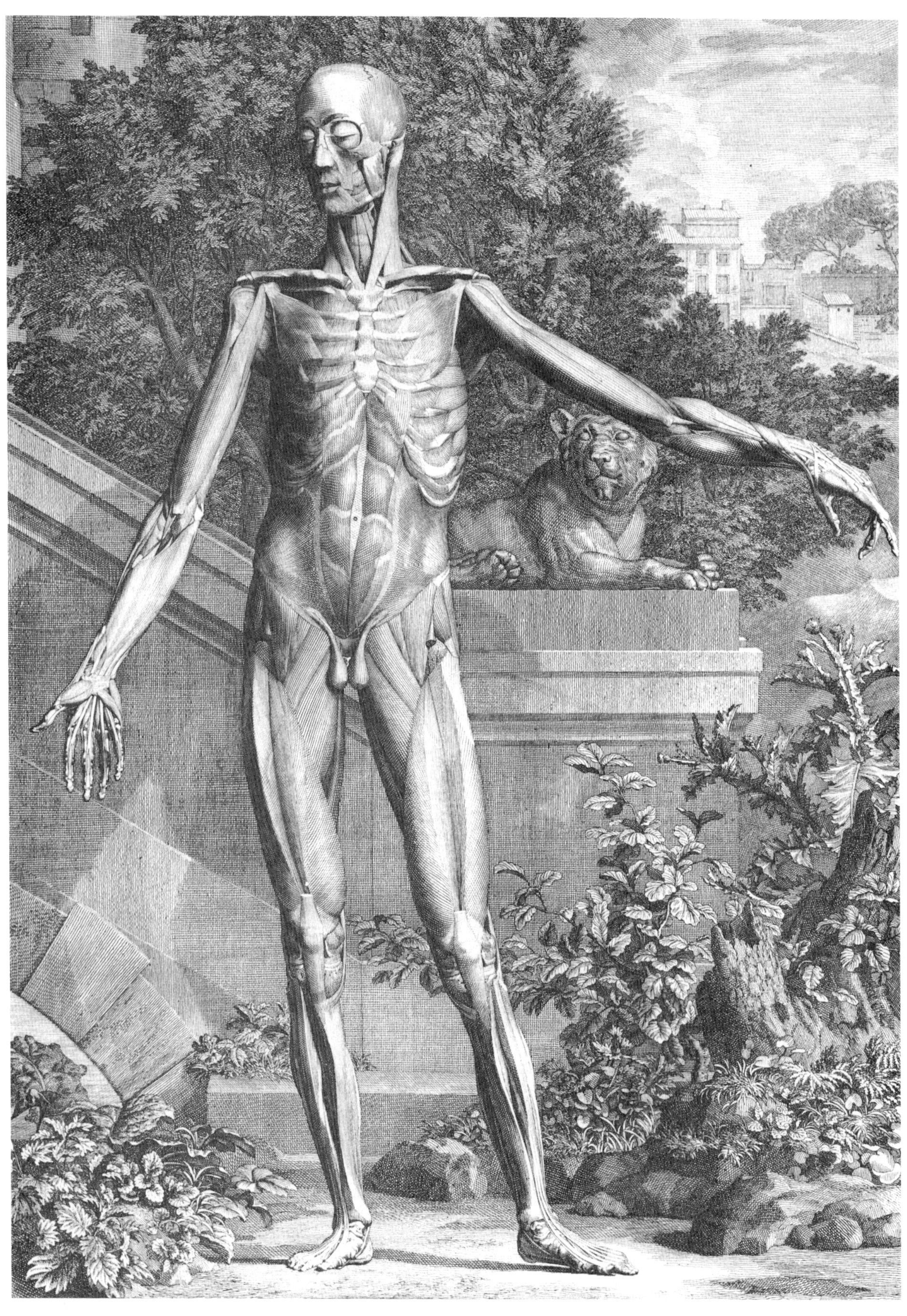

The Second Order of Muscles, front view

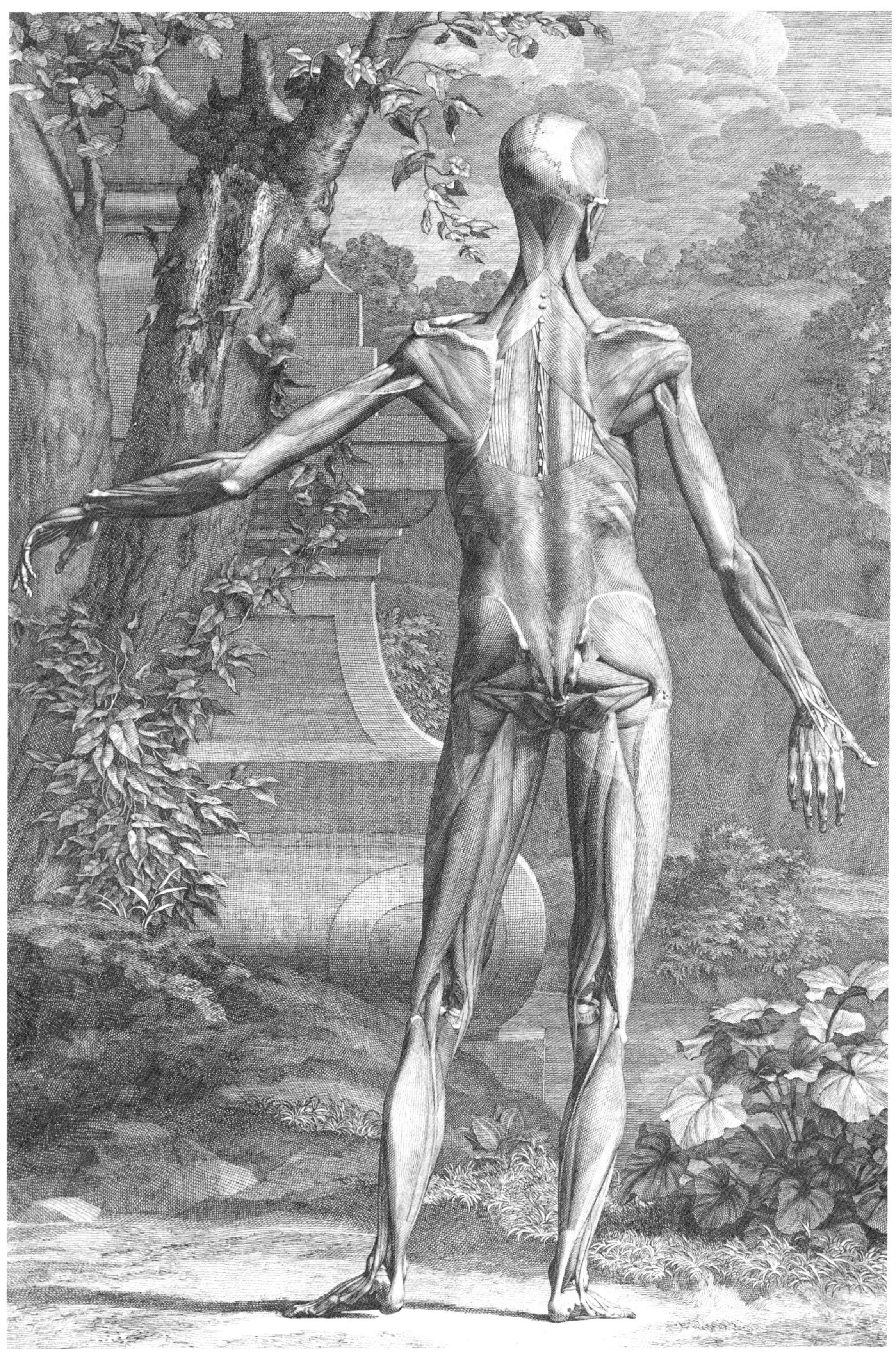

The Second Order of Muscles, back view

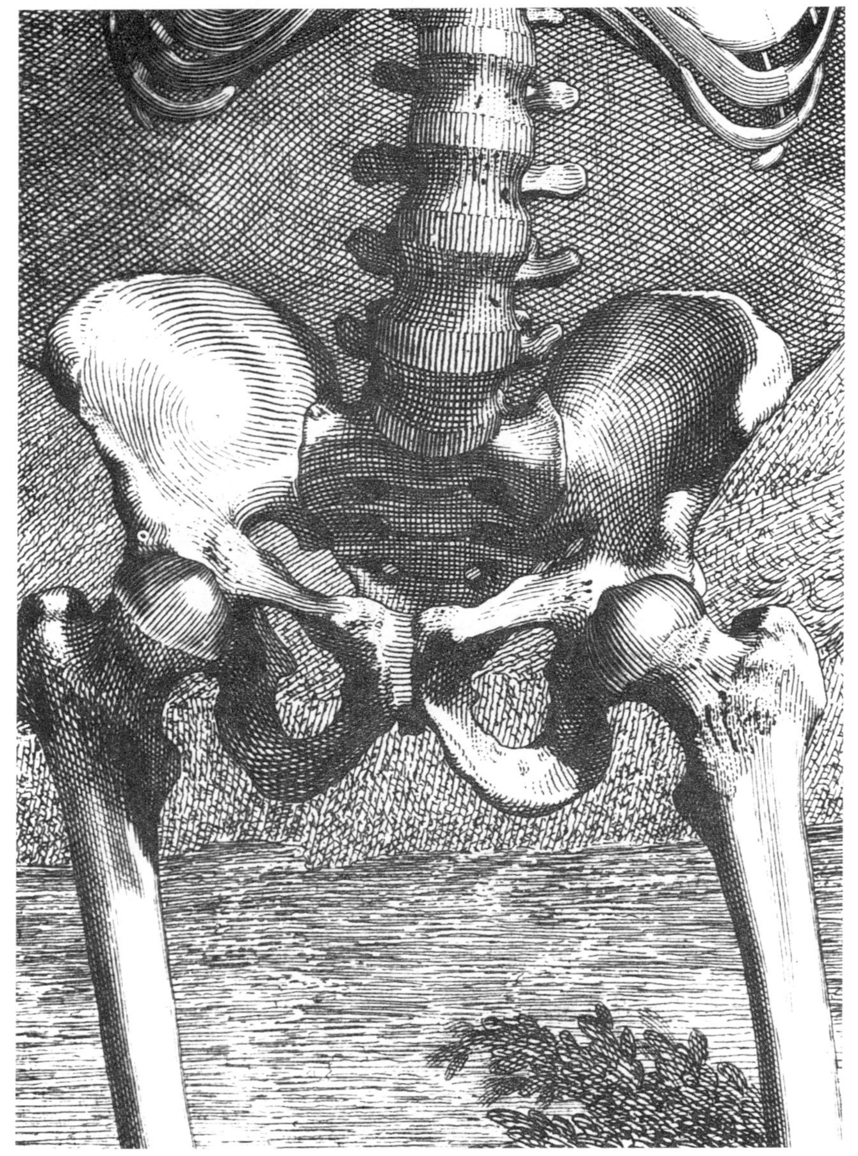

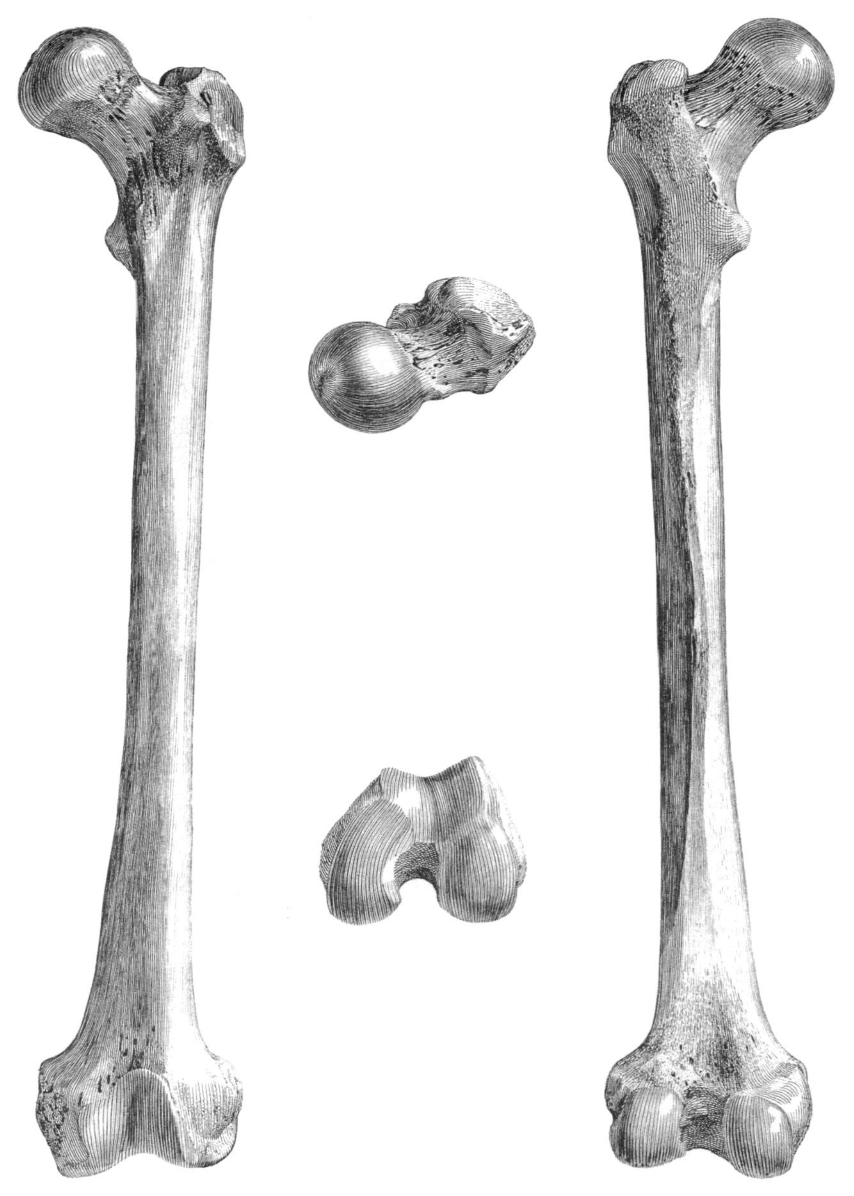

Left: The Pelvis, front view. *Right:* The Femur.

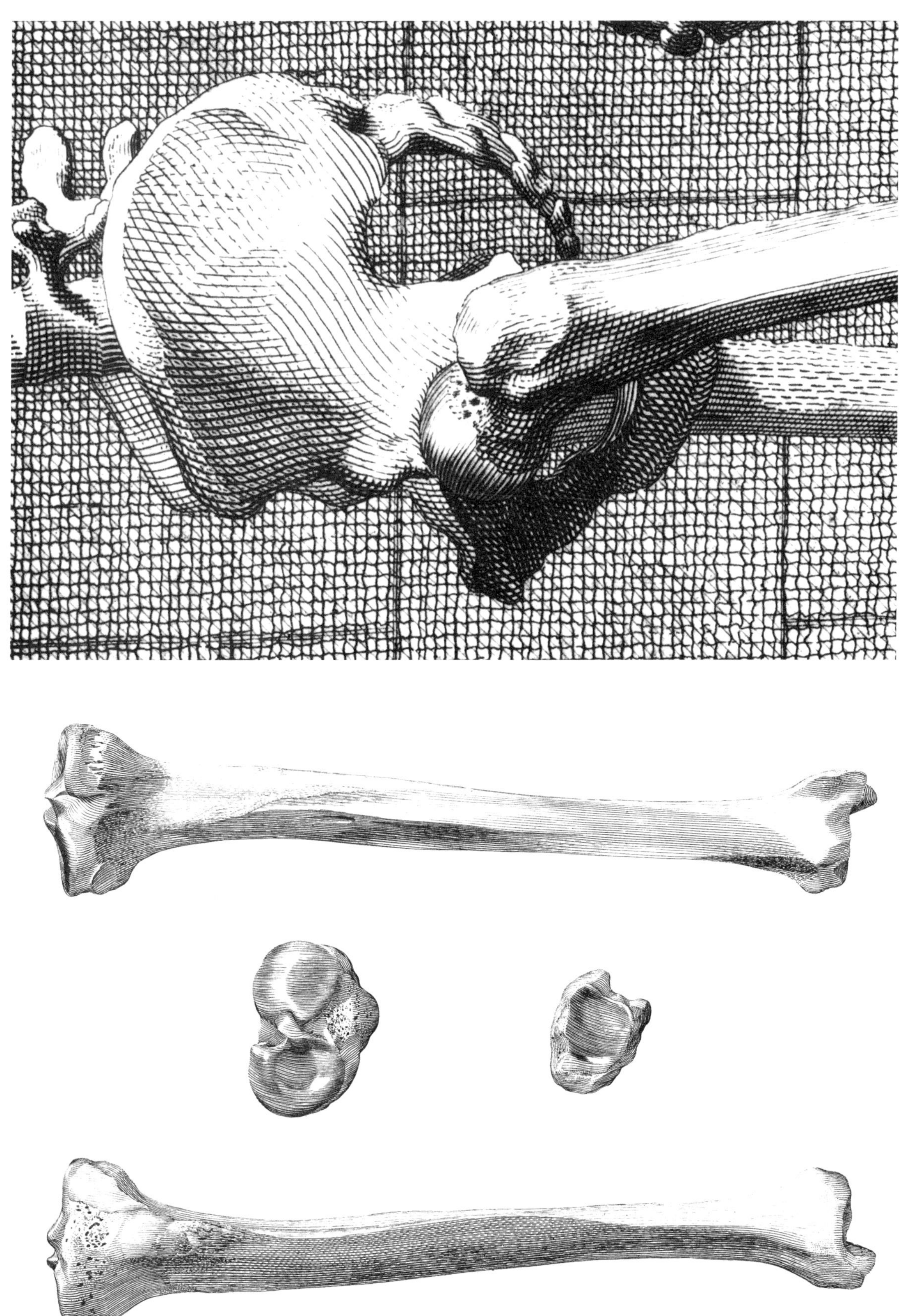

Left: The Bones of the Lower Leg: Tibia. *Right:* The Pelvis.

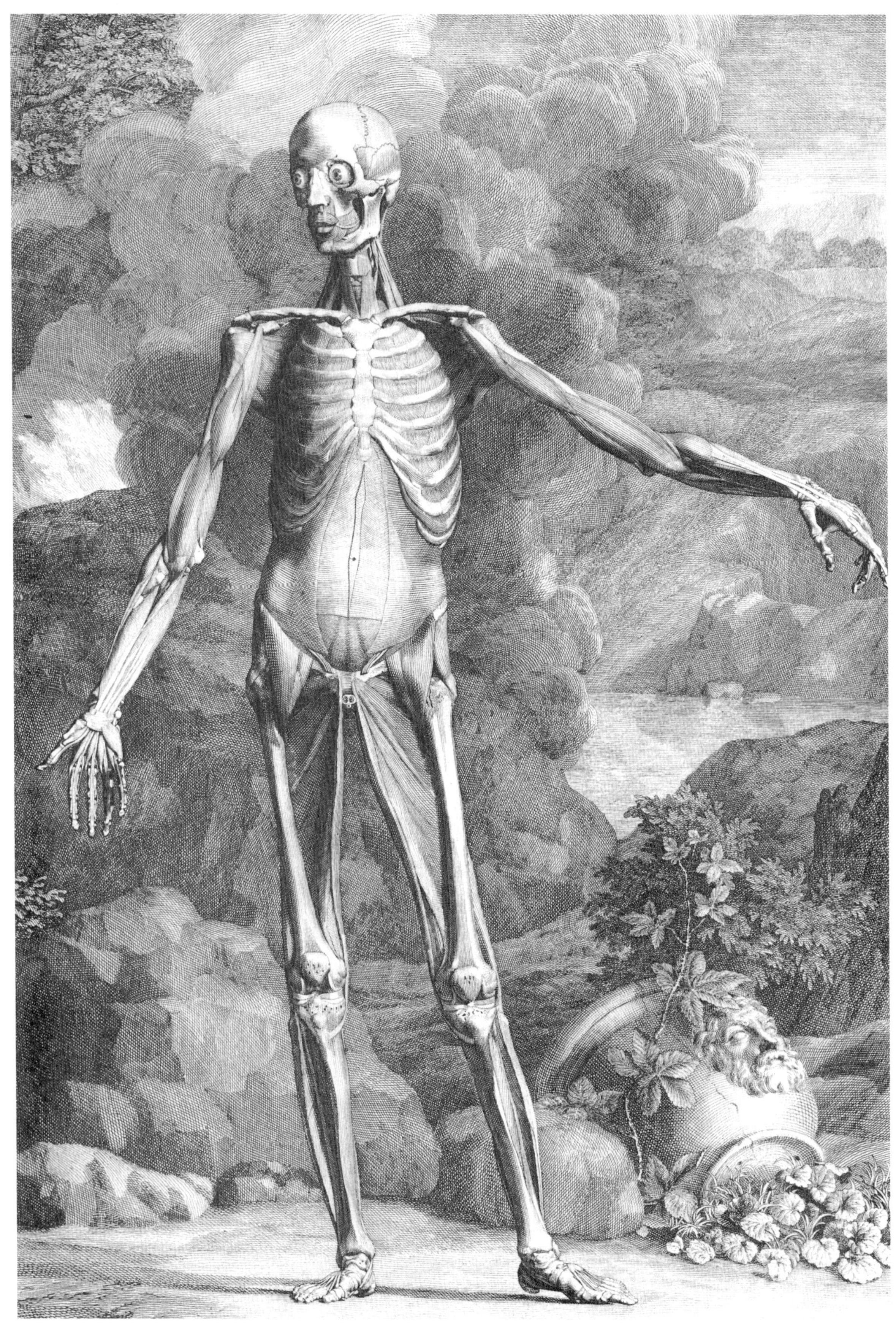

The Third Order of Muscles, front view

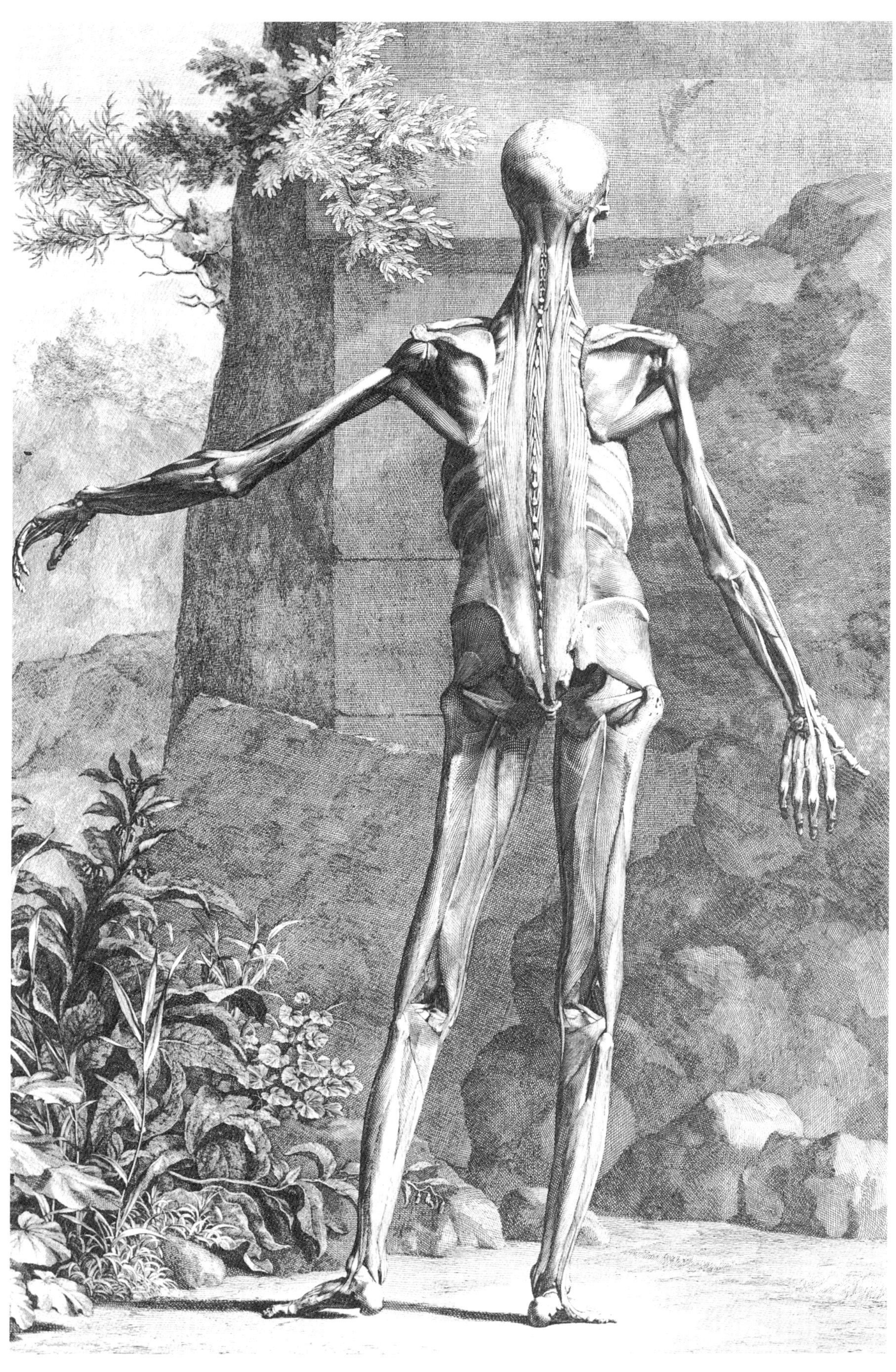

The Third Order of Muscles, back view

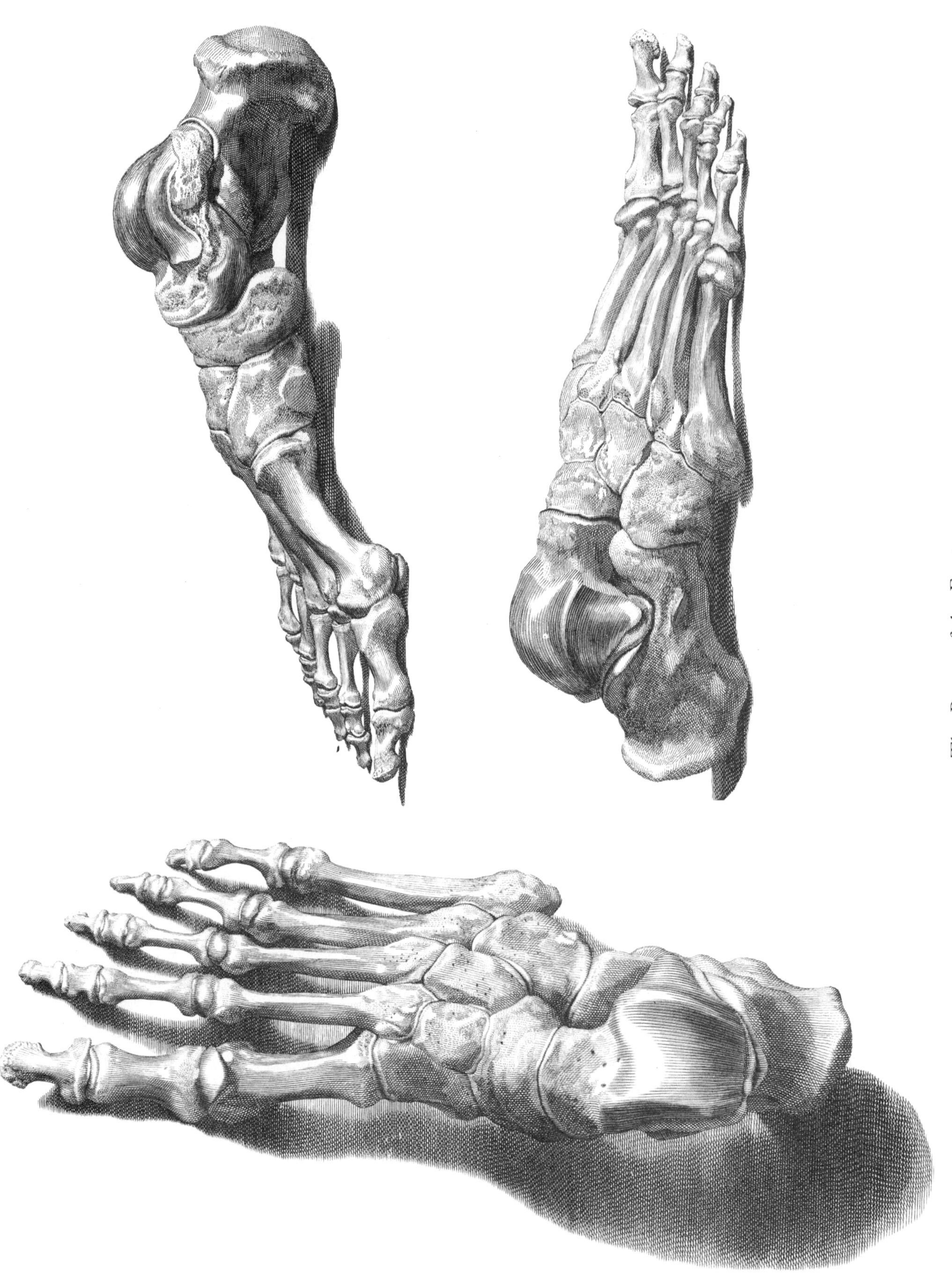

The Bones of the Foot

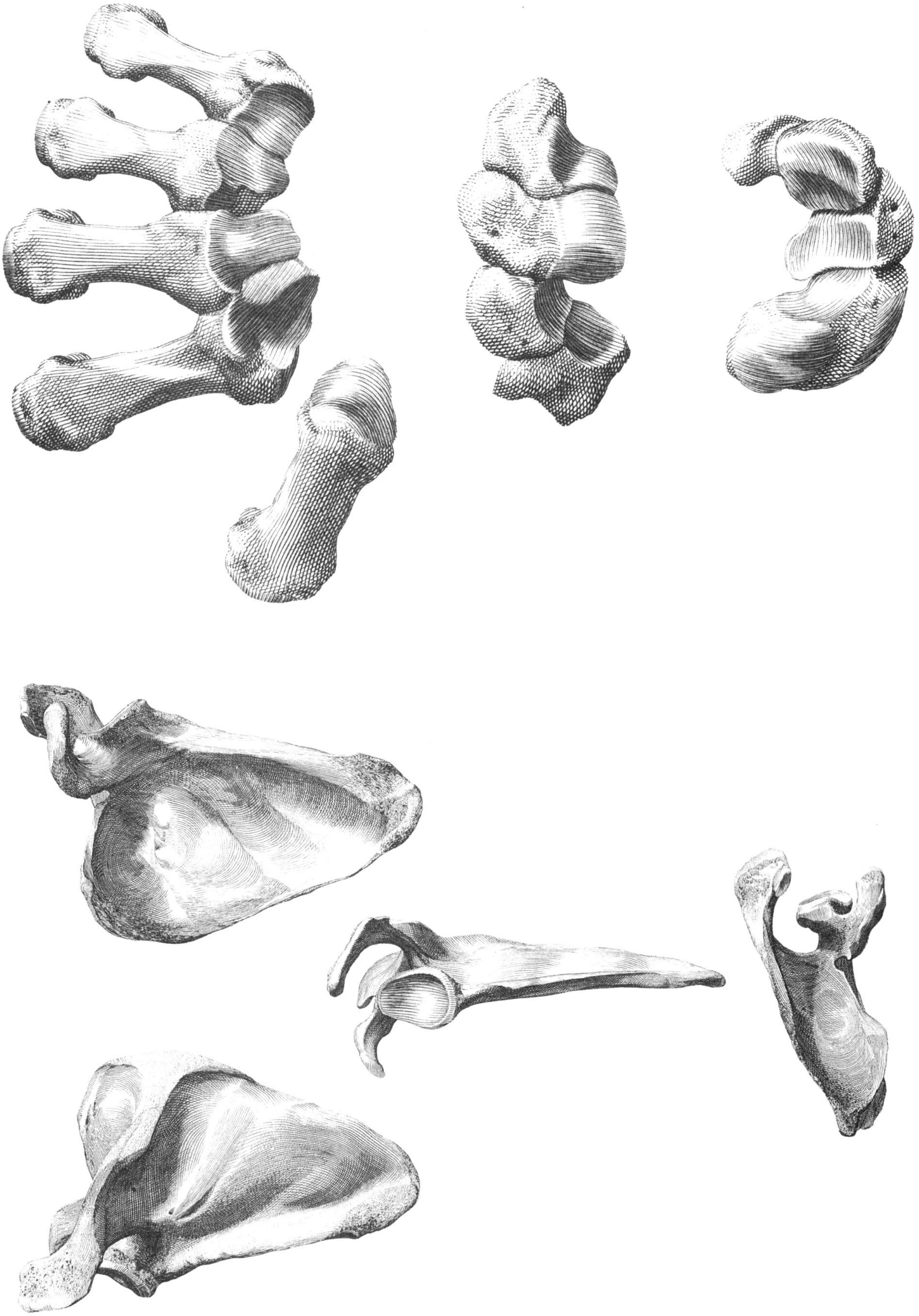

Left: The Bones of the Shoulder Blade. *Right:* The Bones of the Hand.

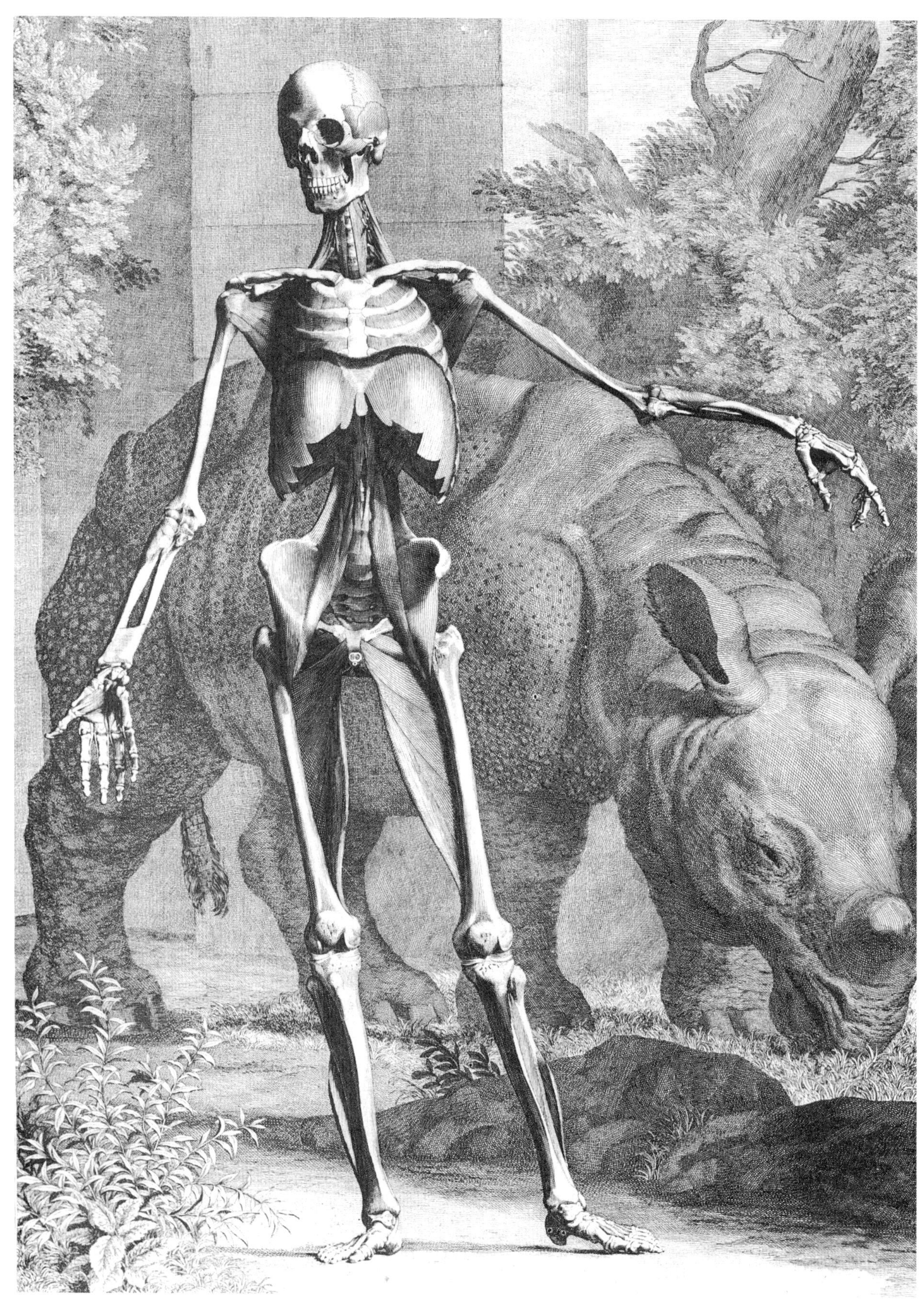

The Fourth Order of Muscles, front view

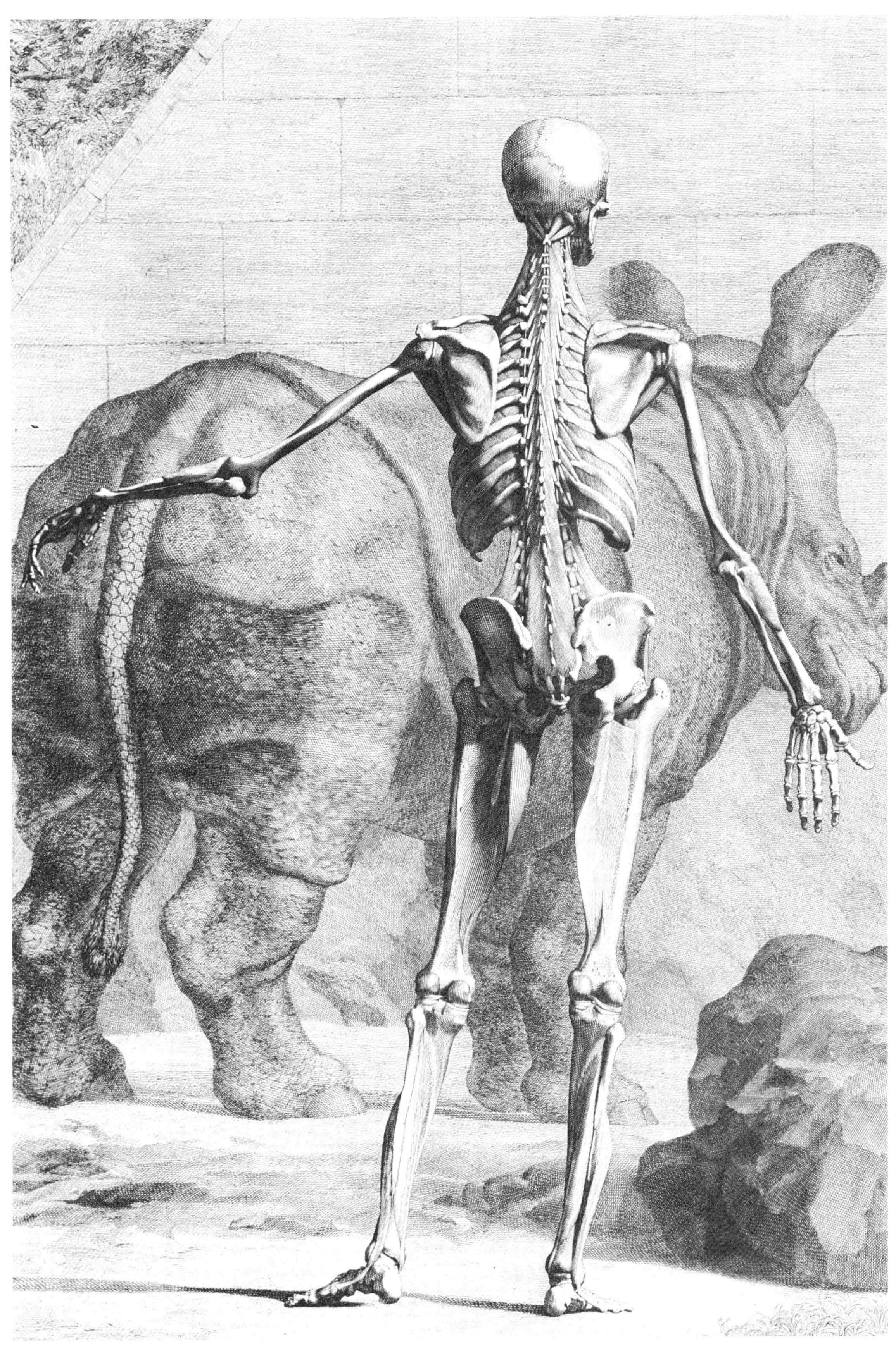

The Fourth Order of Muscles, back view

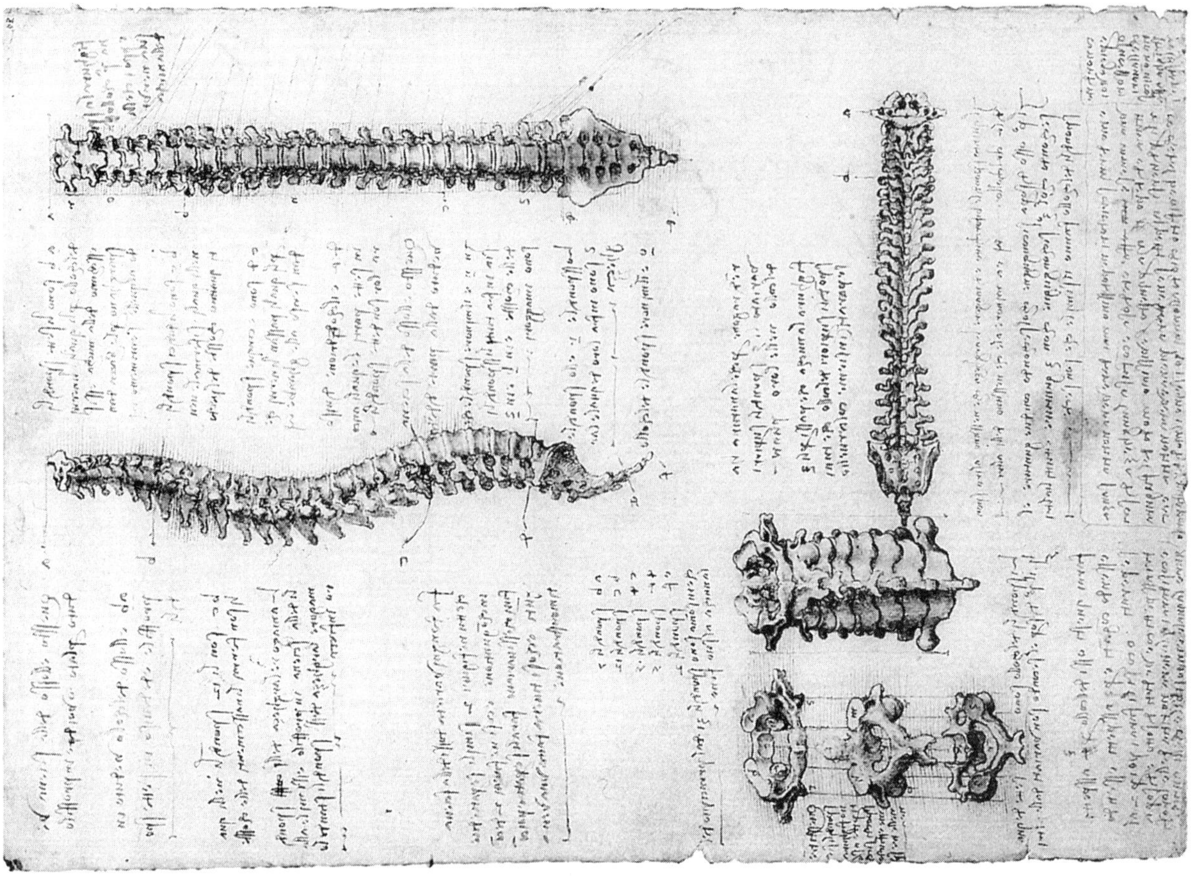

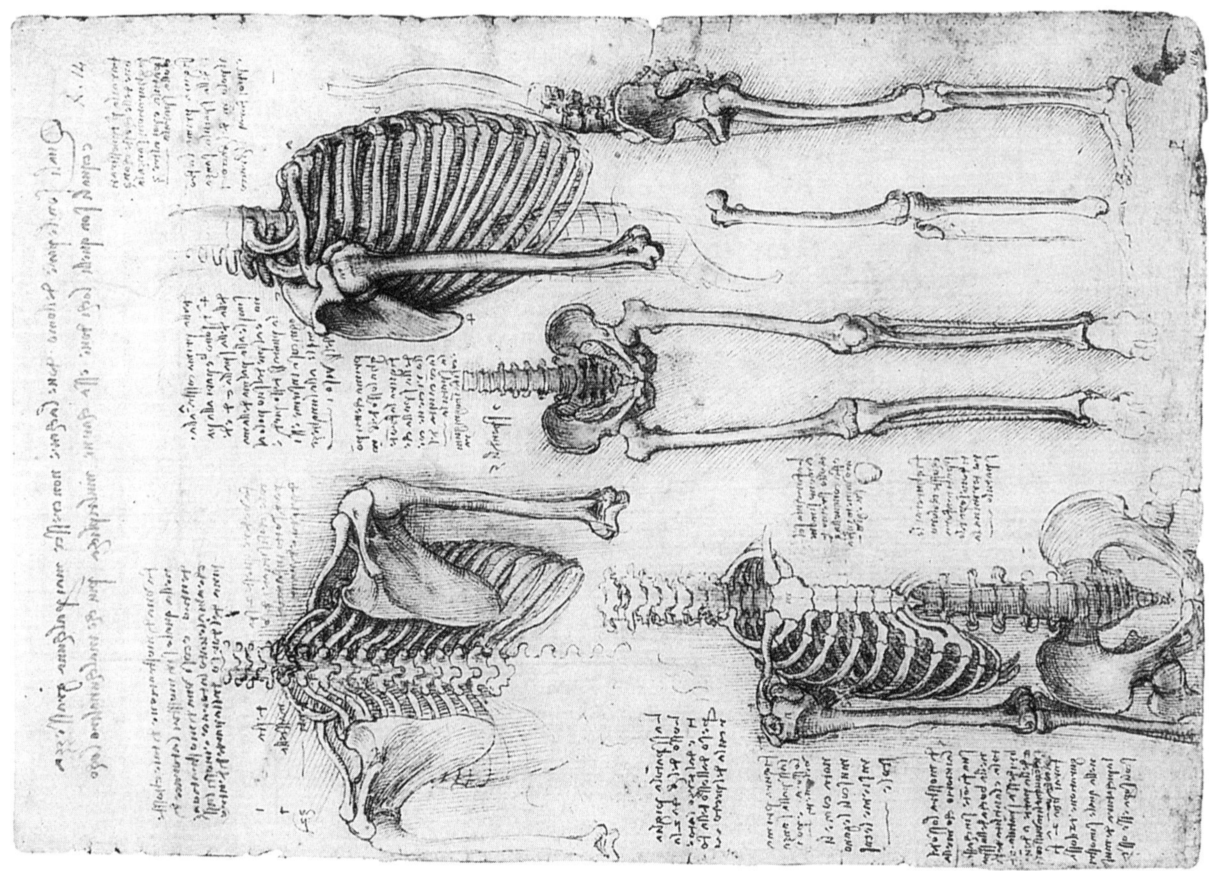

Left: The Skeleton. *Right:* The Vertebral Column.

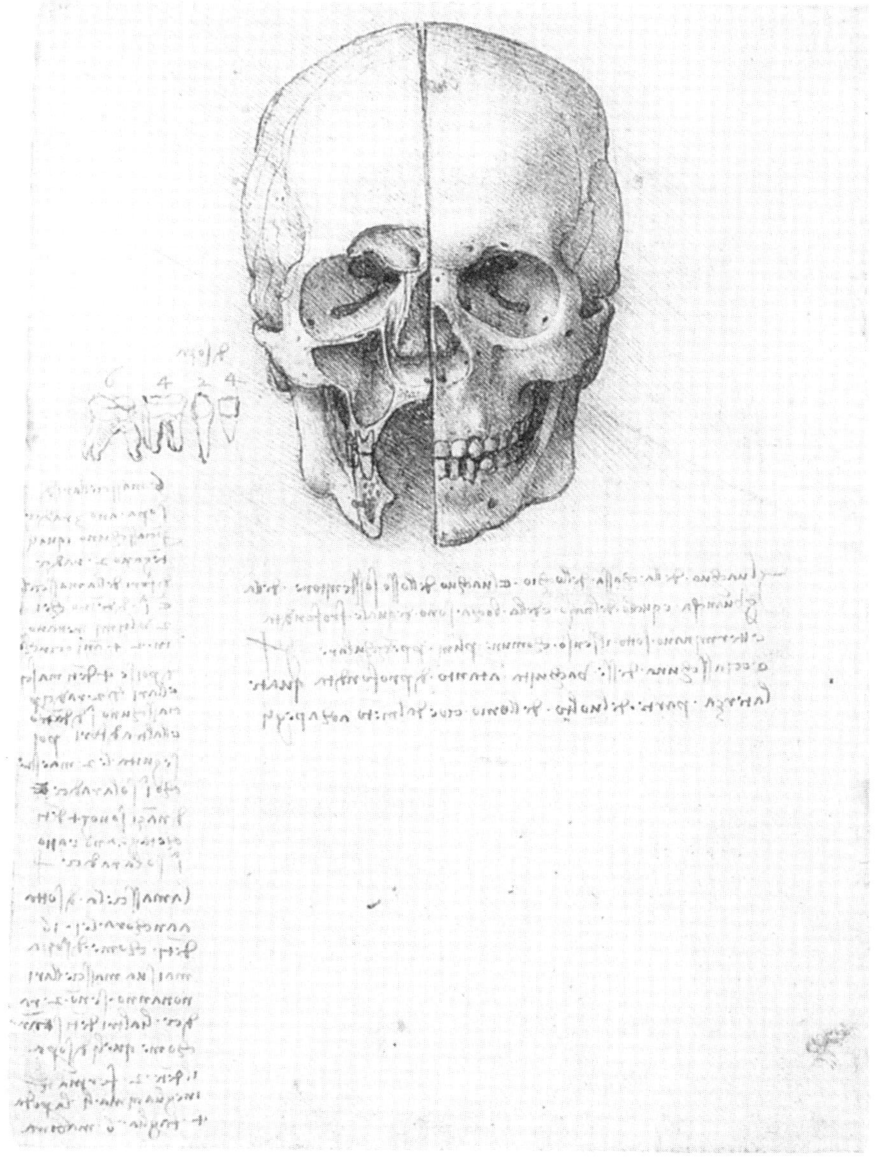

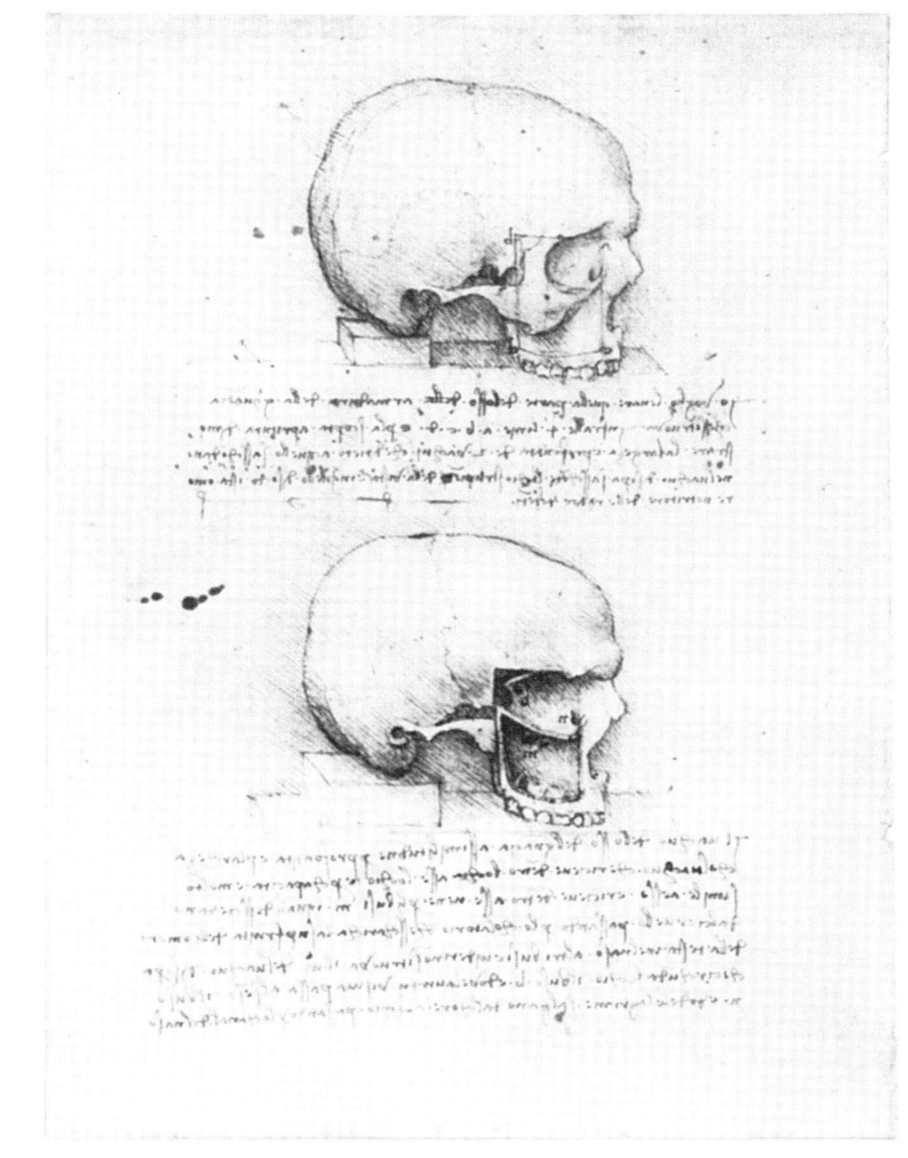

Left: The Skull, front view. *Right:* The Skull, side view.

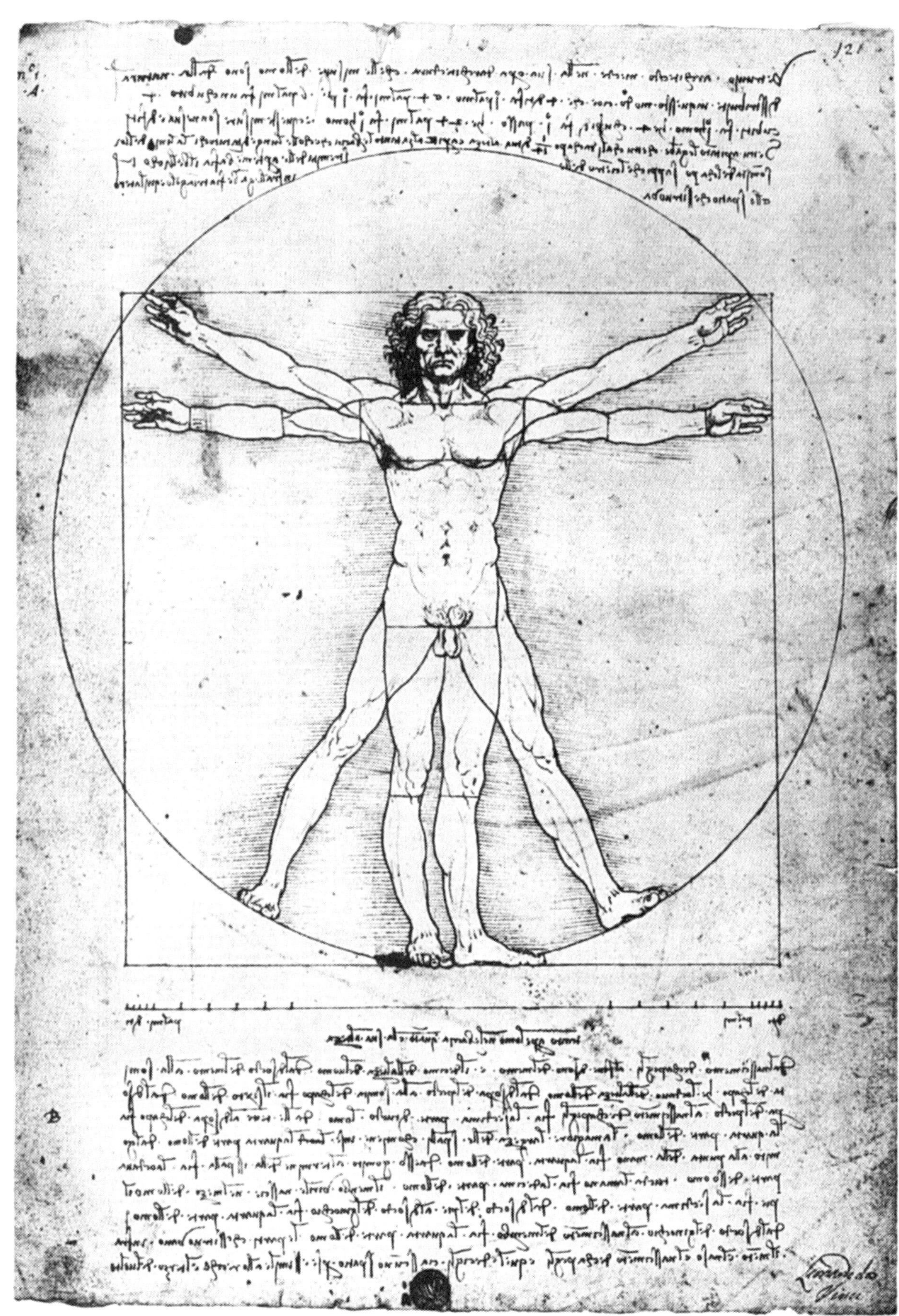

Diagram of Human Proportions

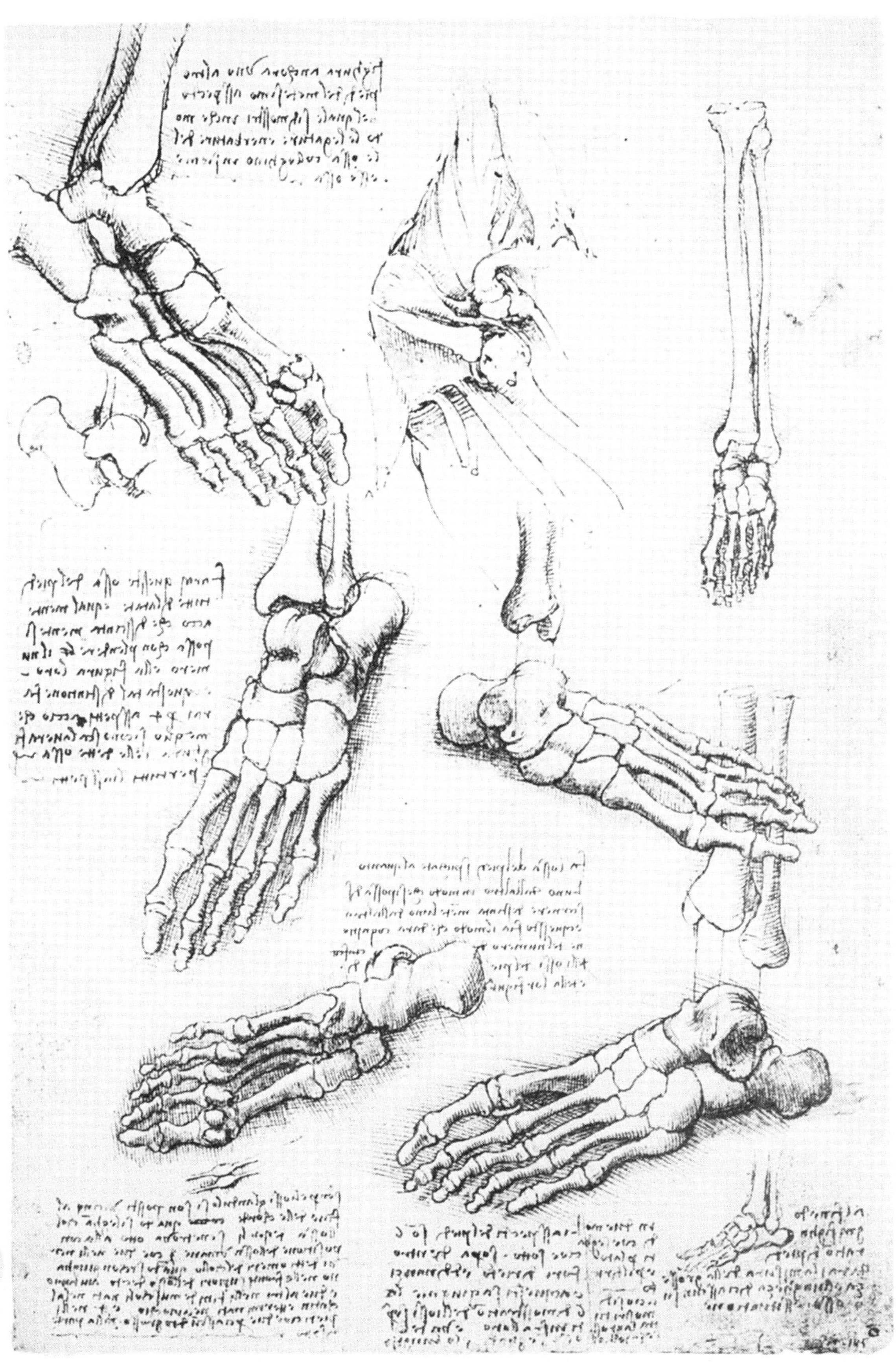

The Bones of the Foot

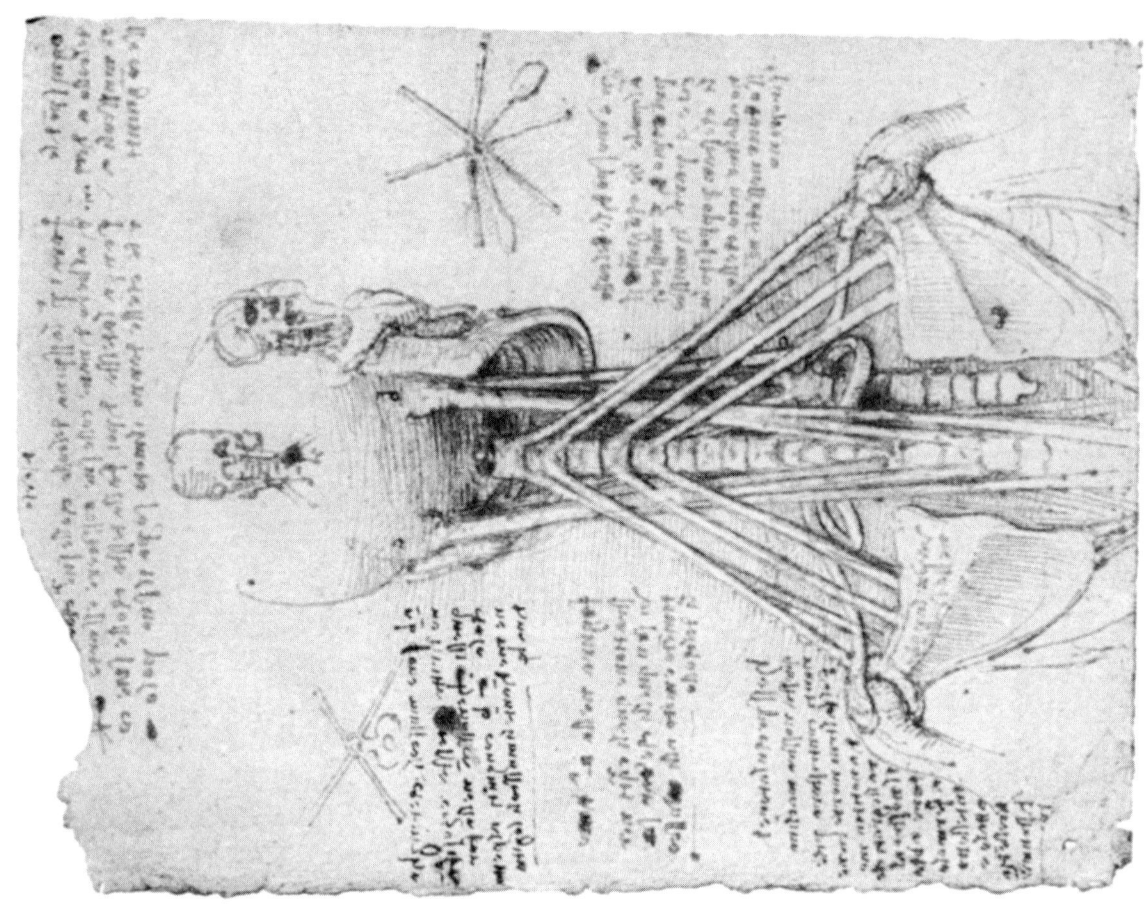

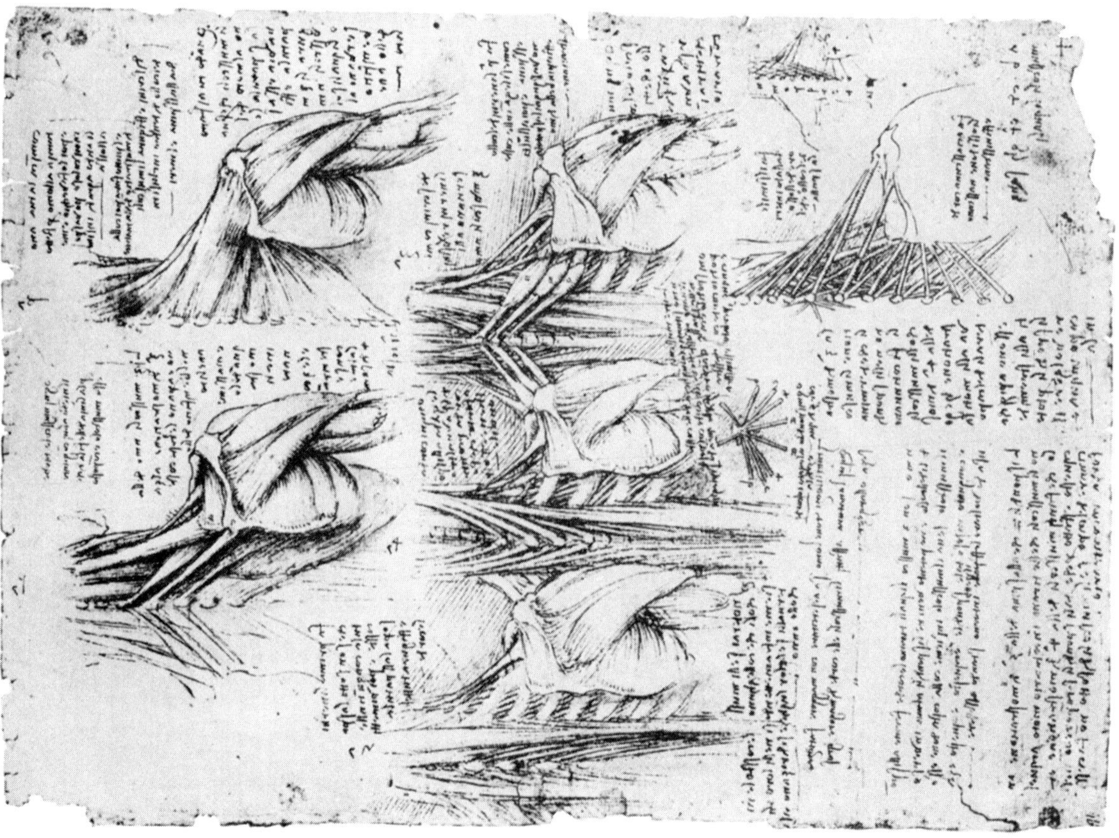

Muscles of the Trunk

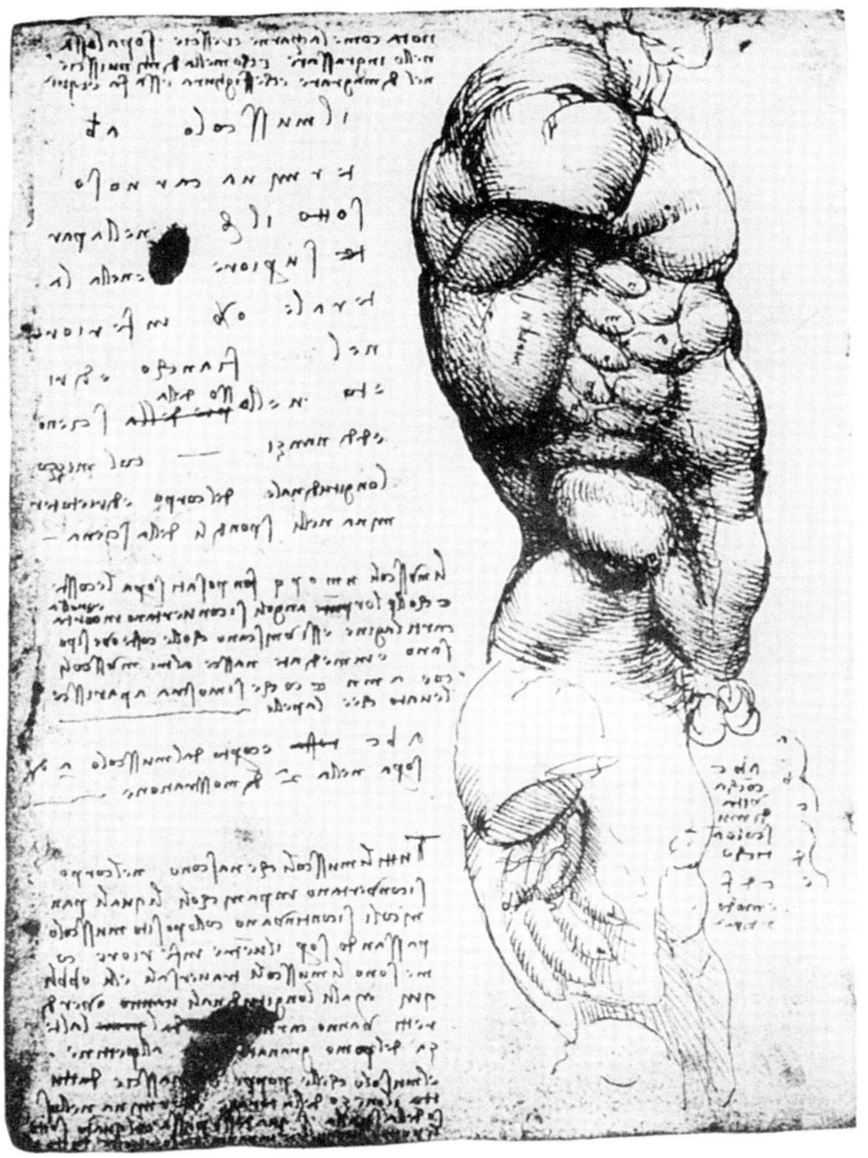

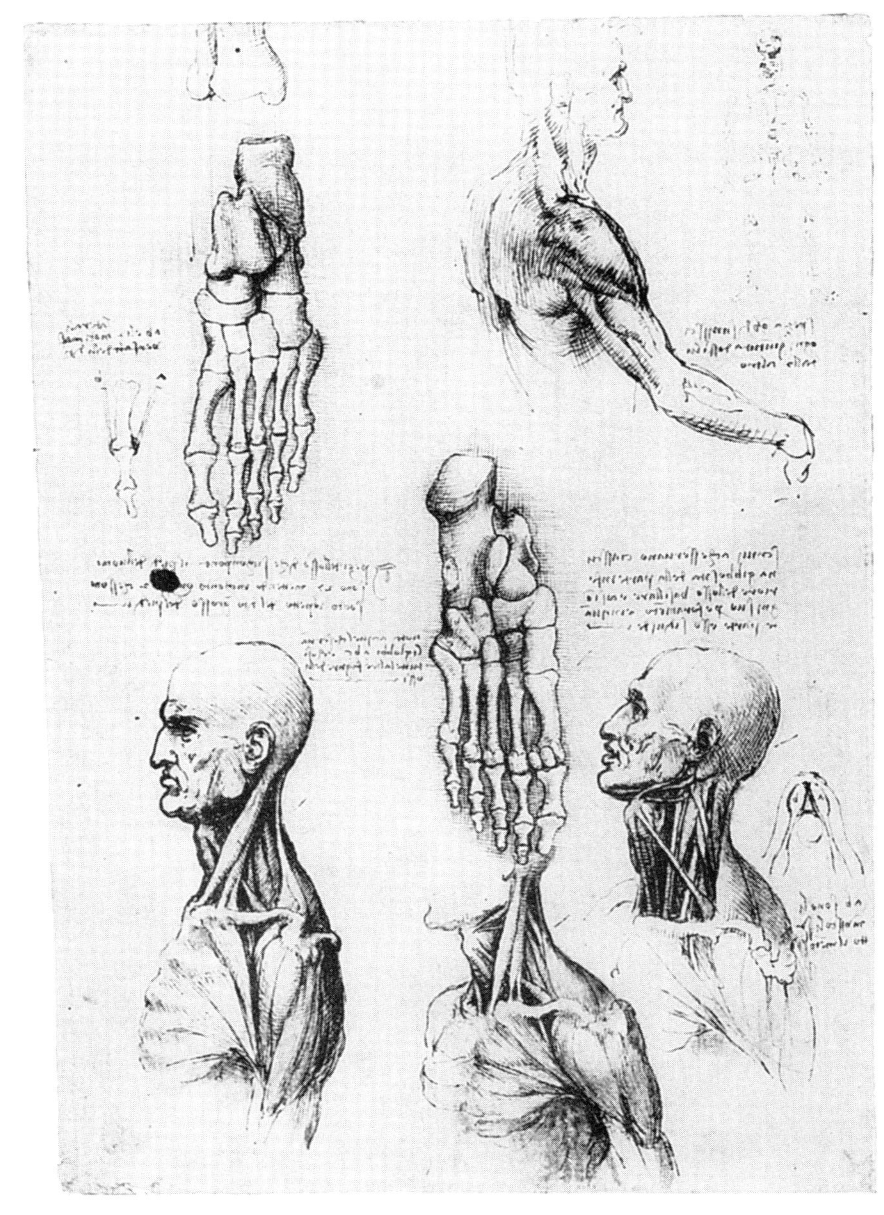

Left: Muscles of the Trunk. *Right:* Muscles of the Head and Neck.

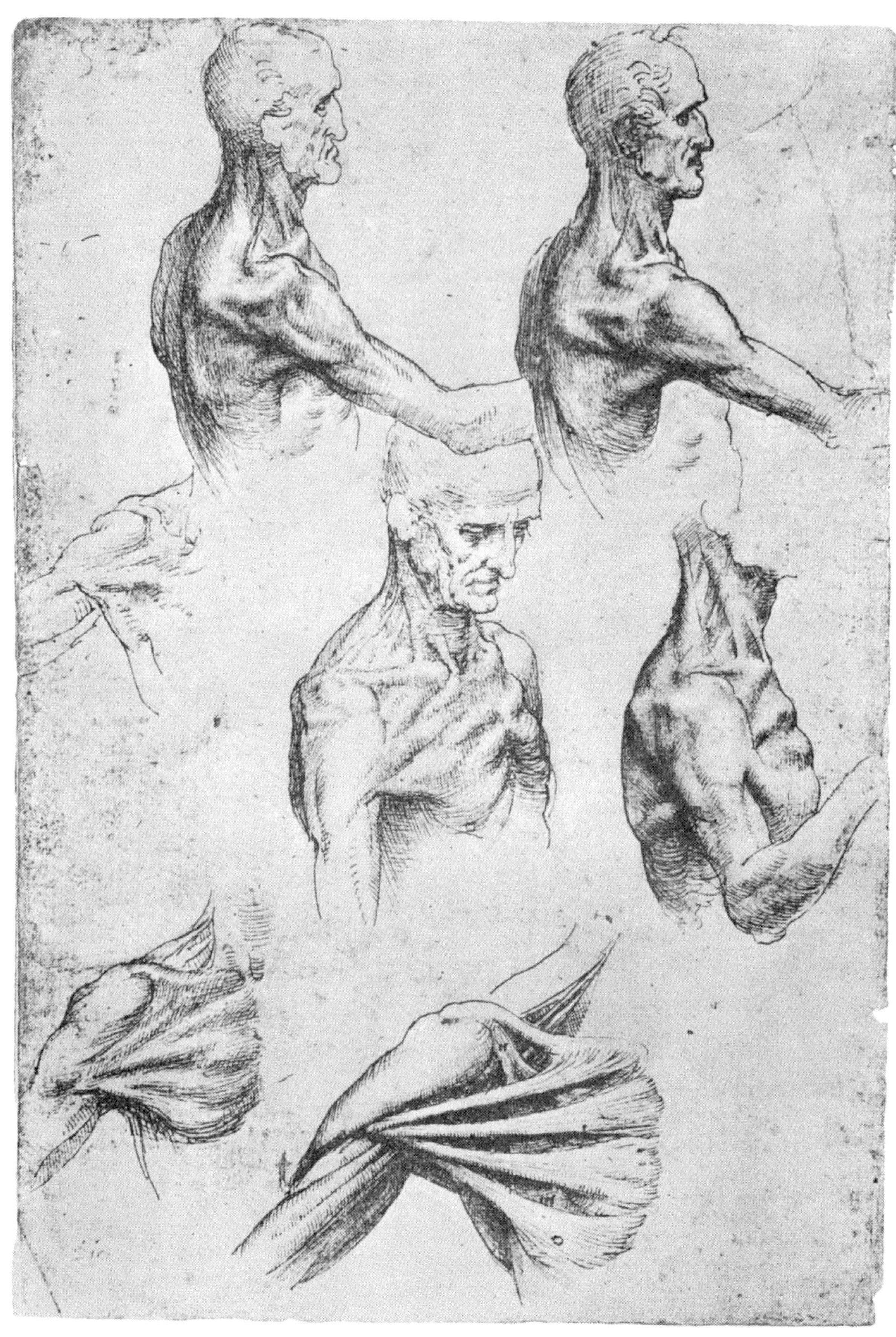

The Muscles of the Shoulder and Chest

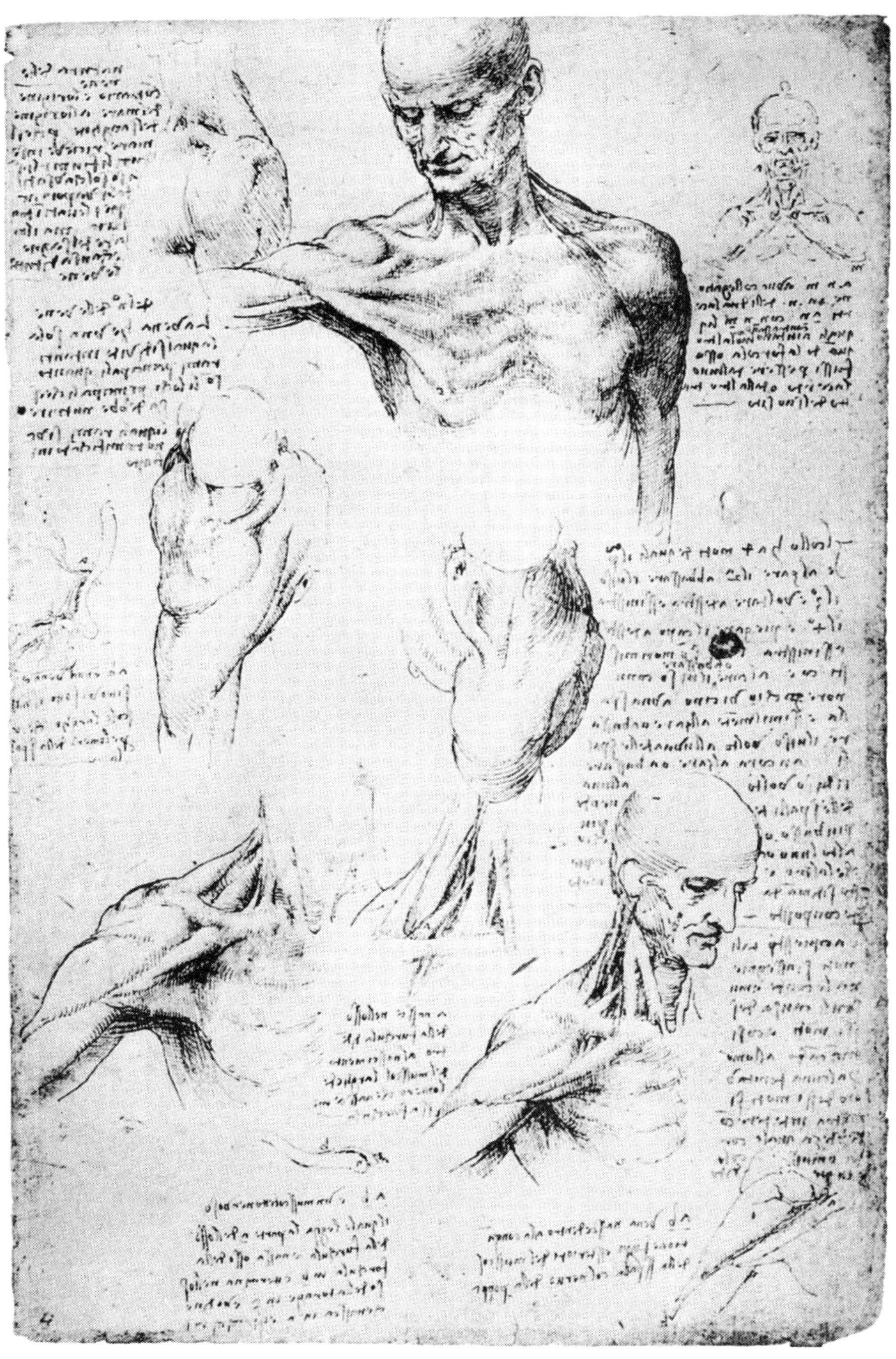

Muscles of the Shoulder Region

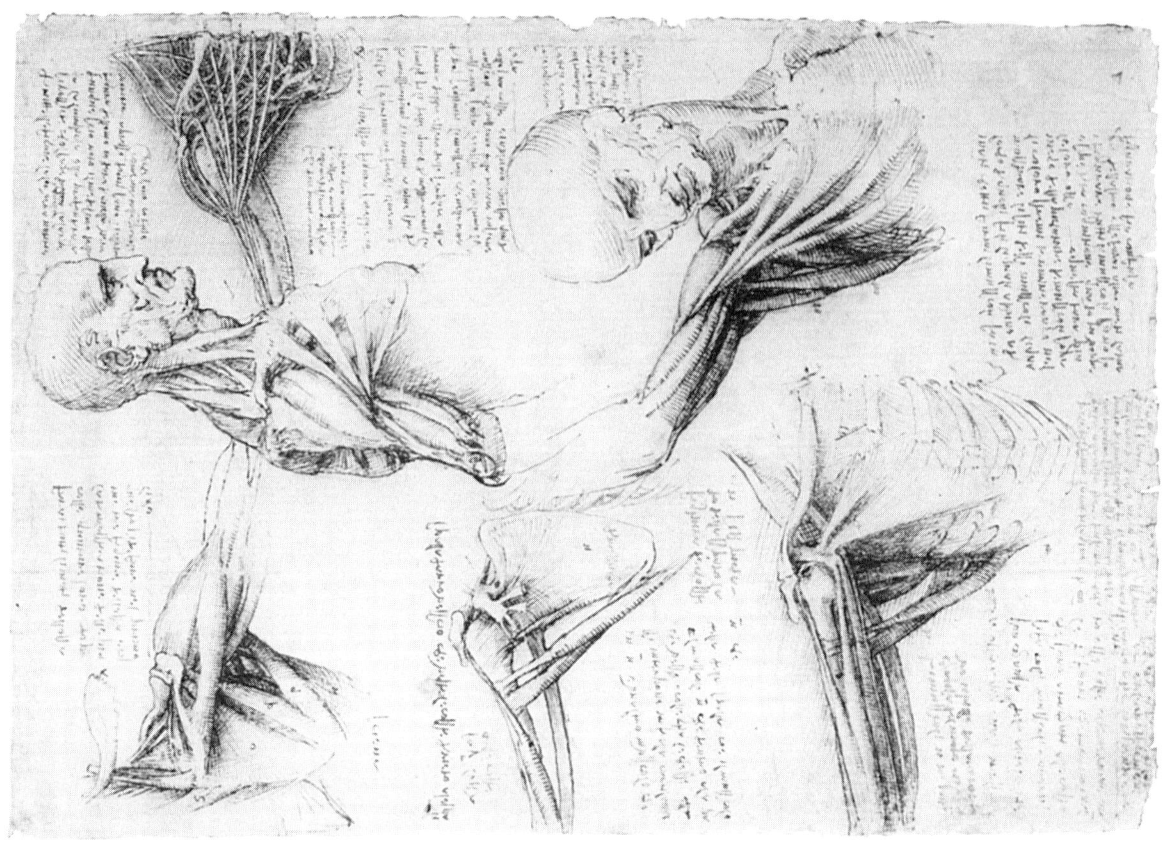

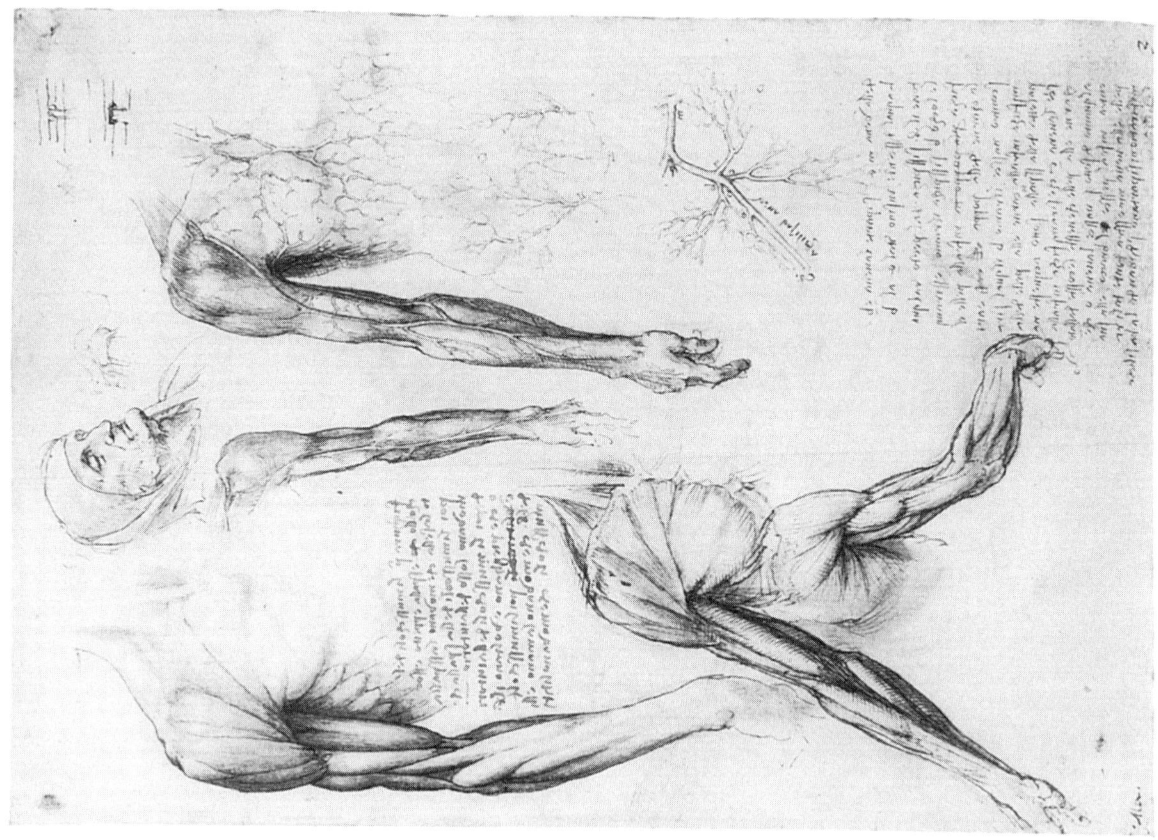

Muscles of the Shoulder Region

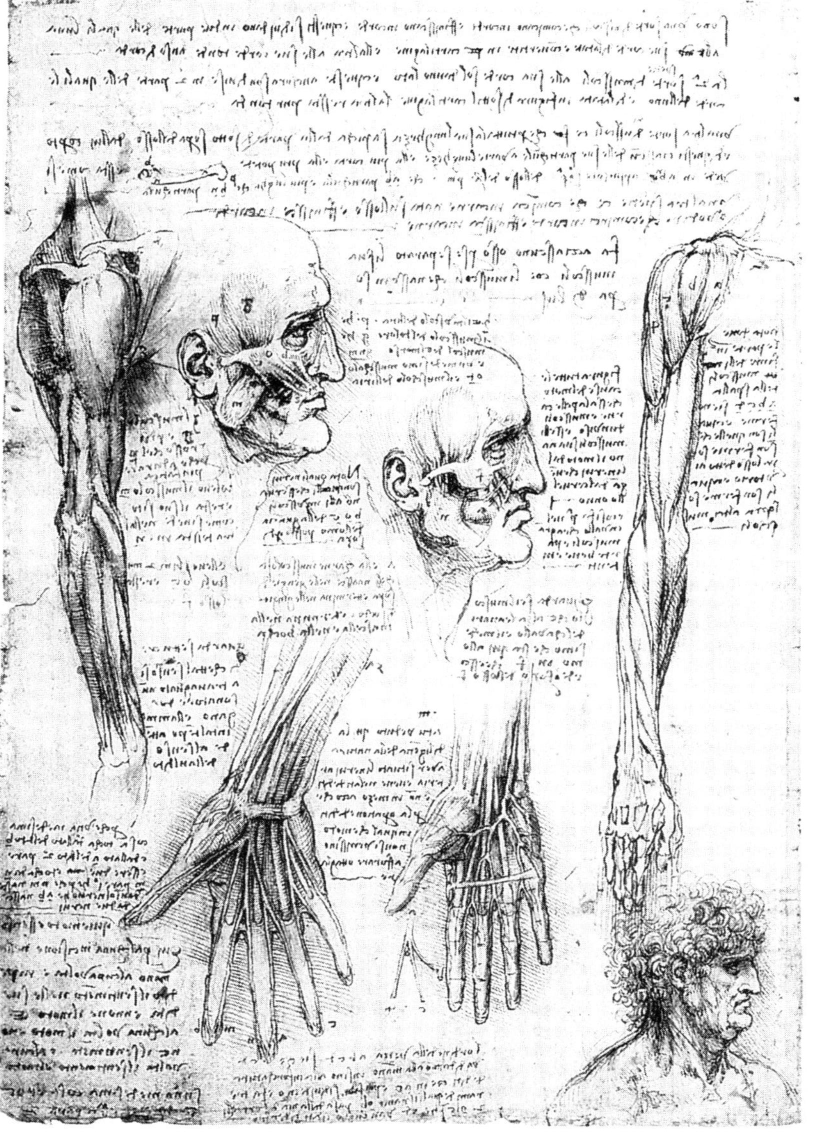

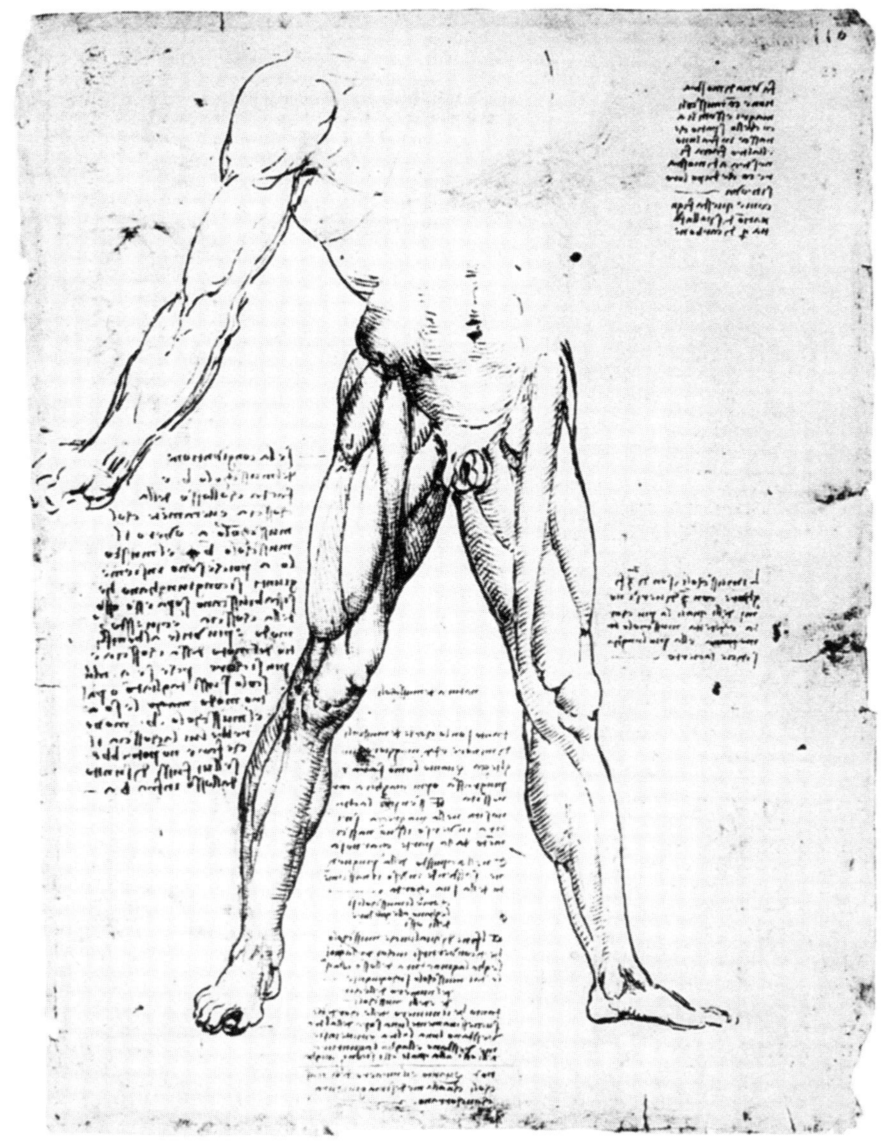

Left: Muscles of the Upper Extremity. *Right:* Muscles of the Lower Extremity.

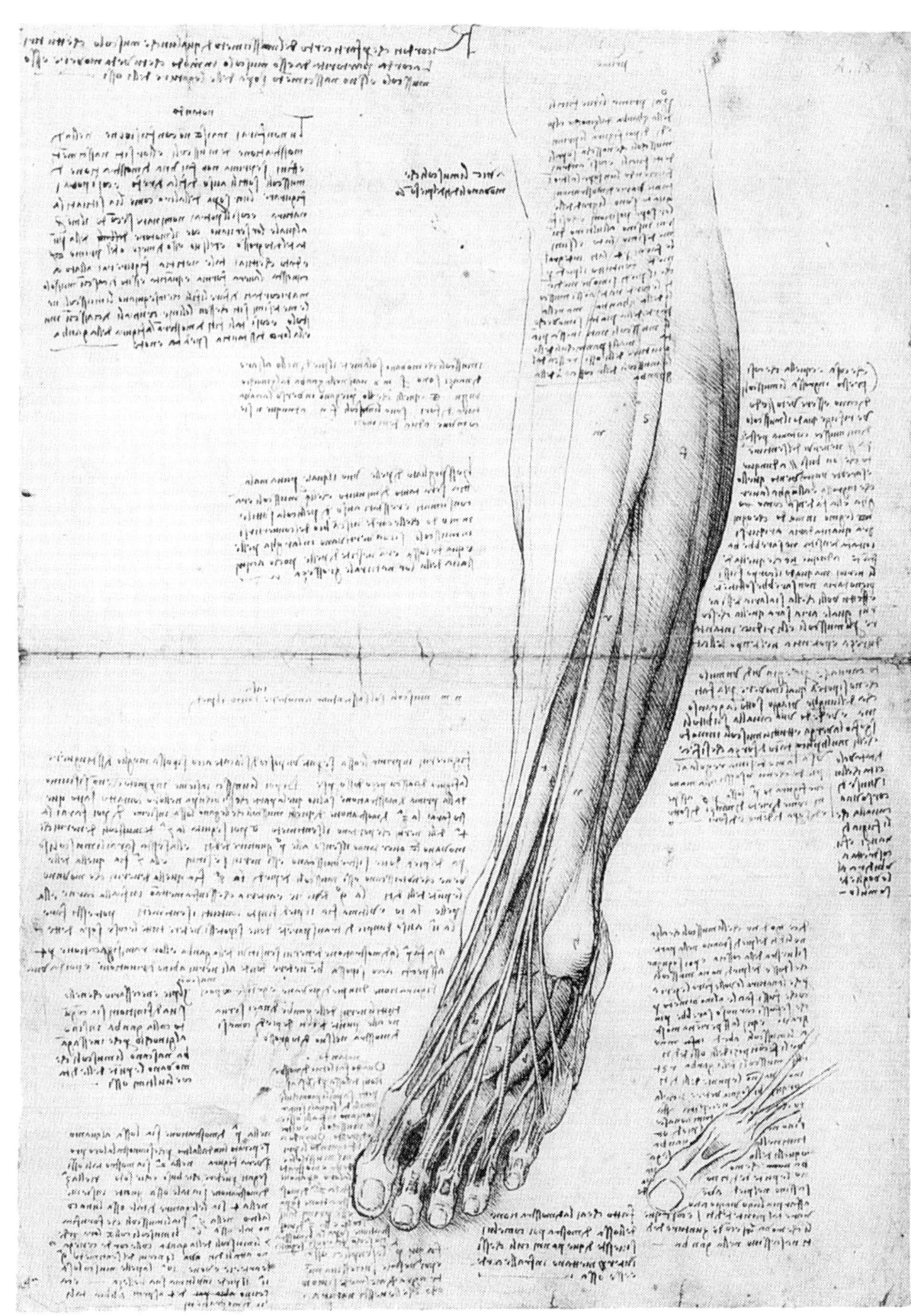

Muscles of the Lower Leg

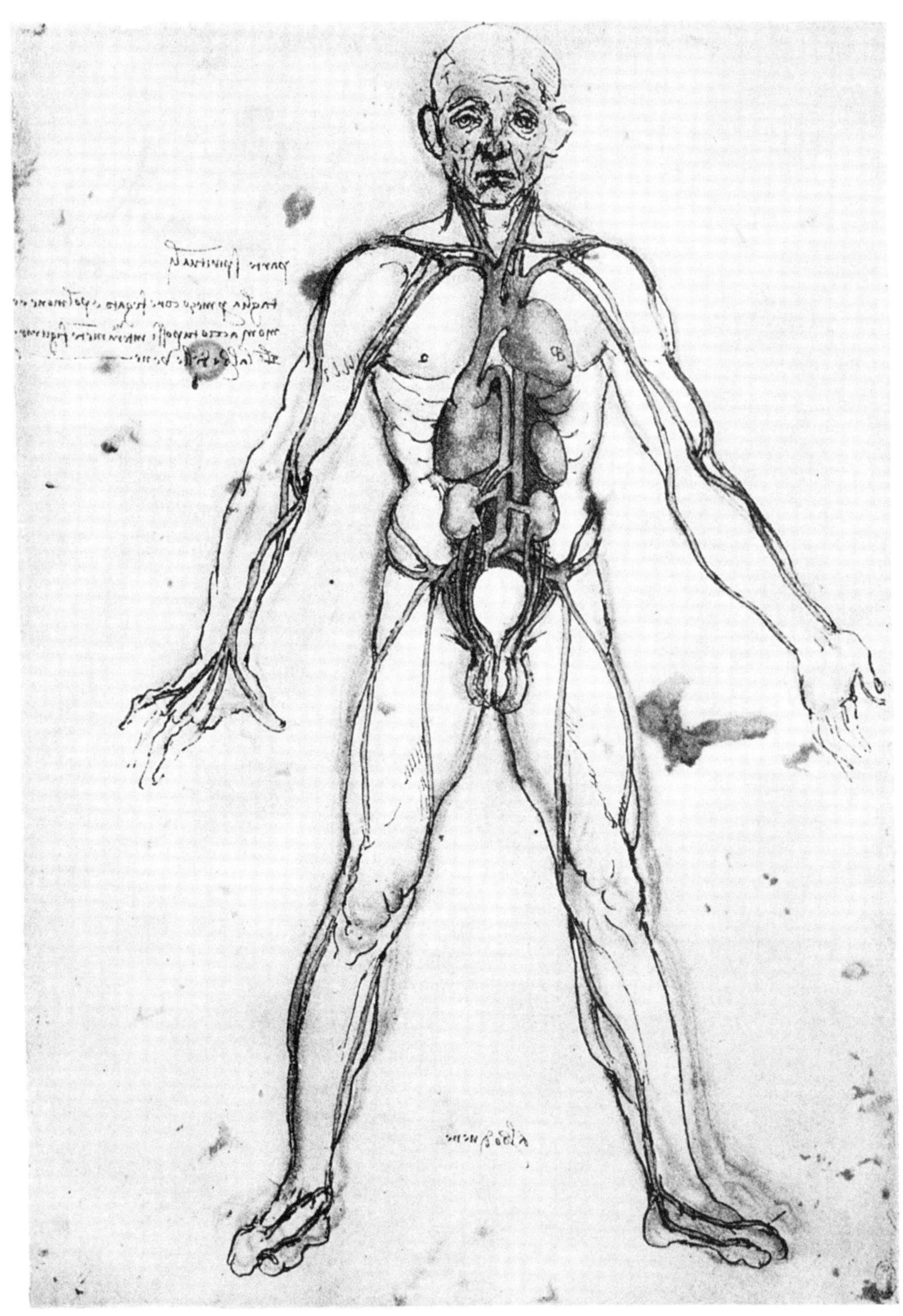

Cardiovascular System

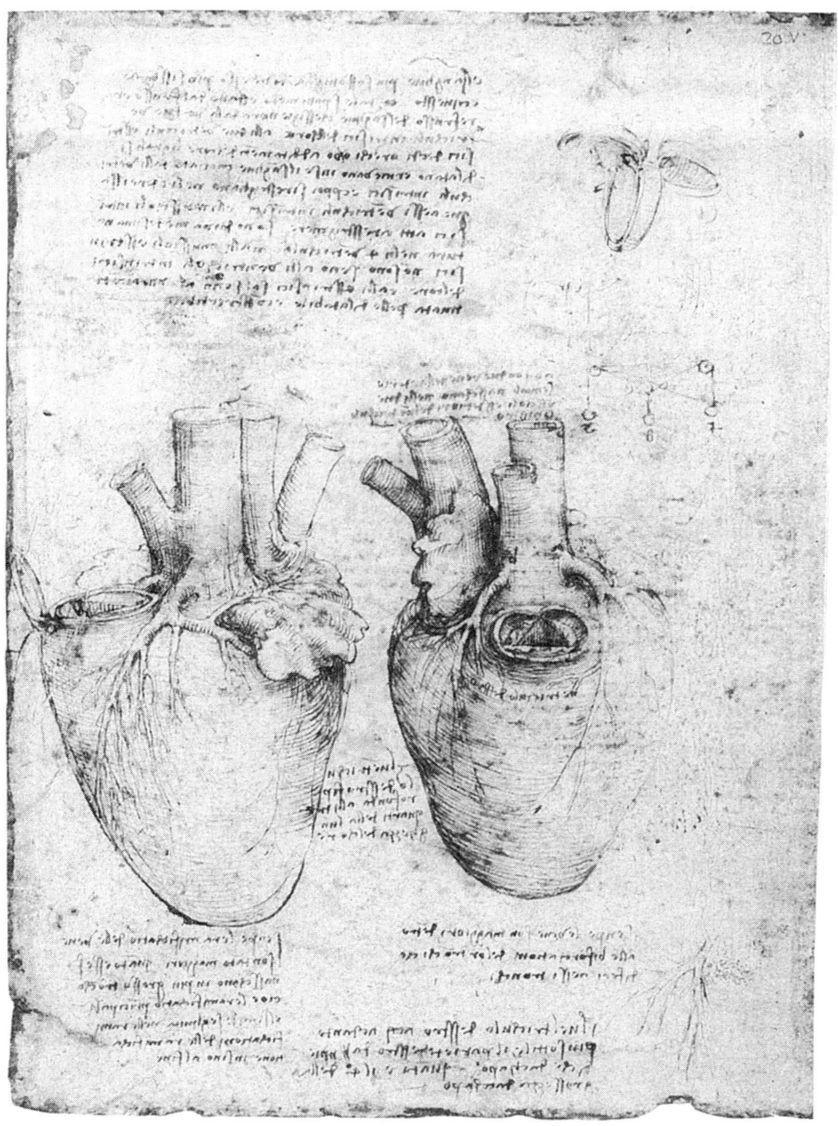

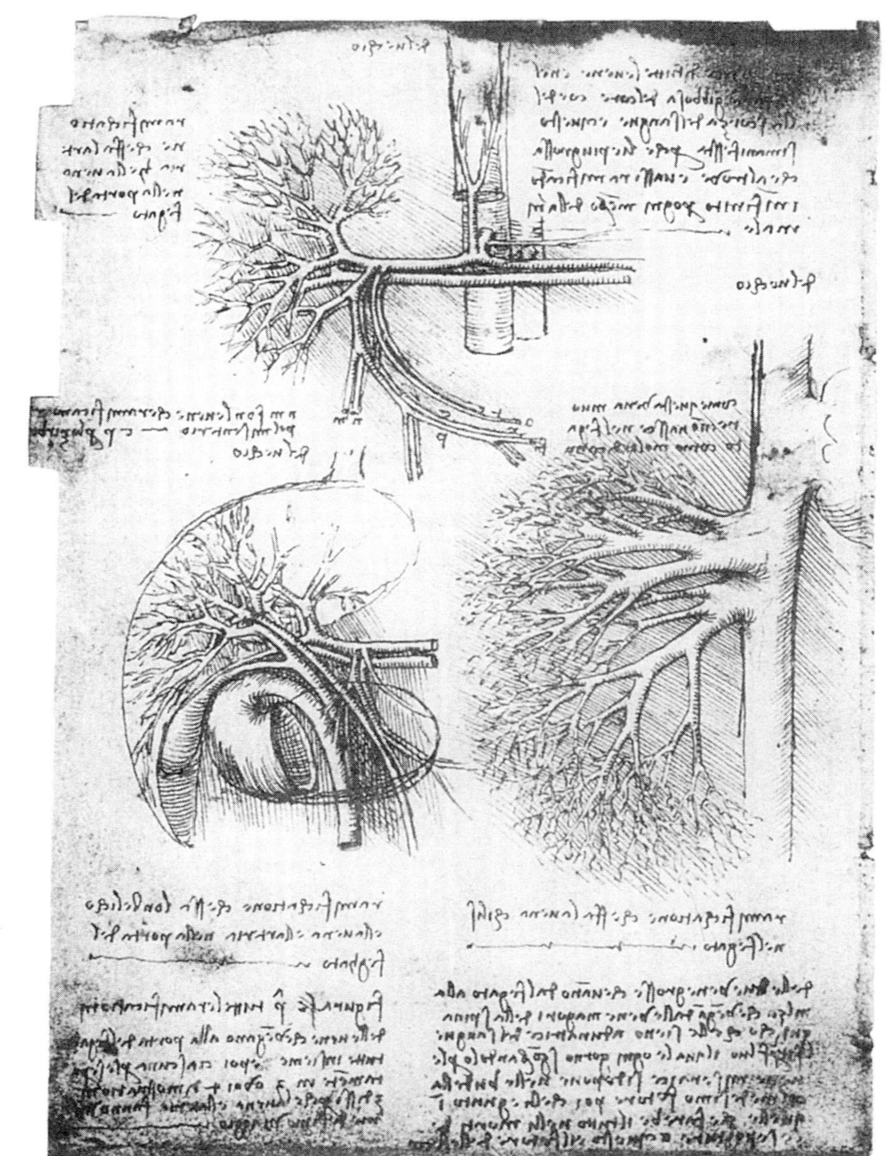

Left: The Heart. *Right:* Cardiovascular System.

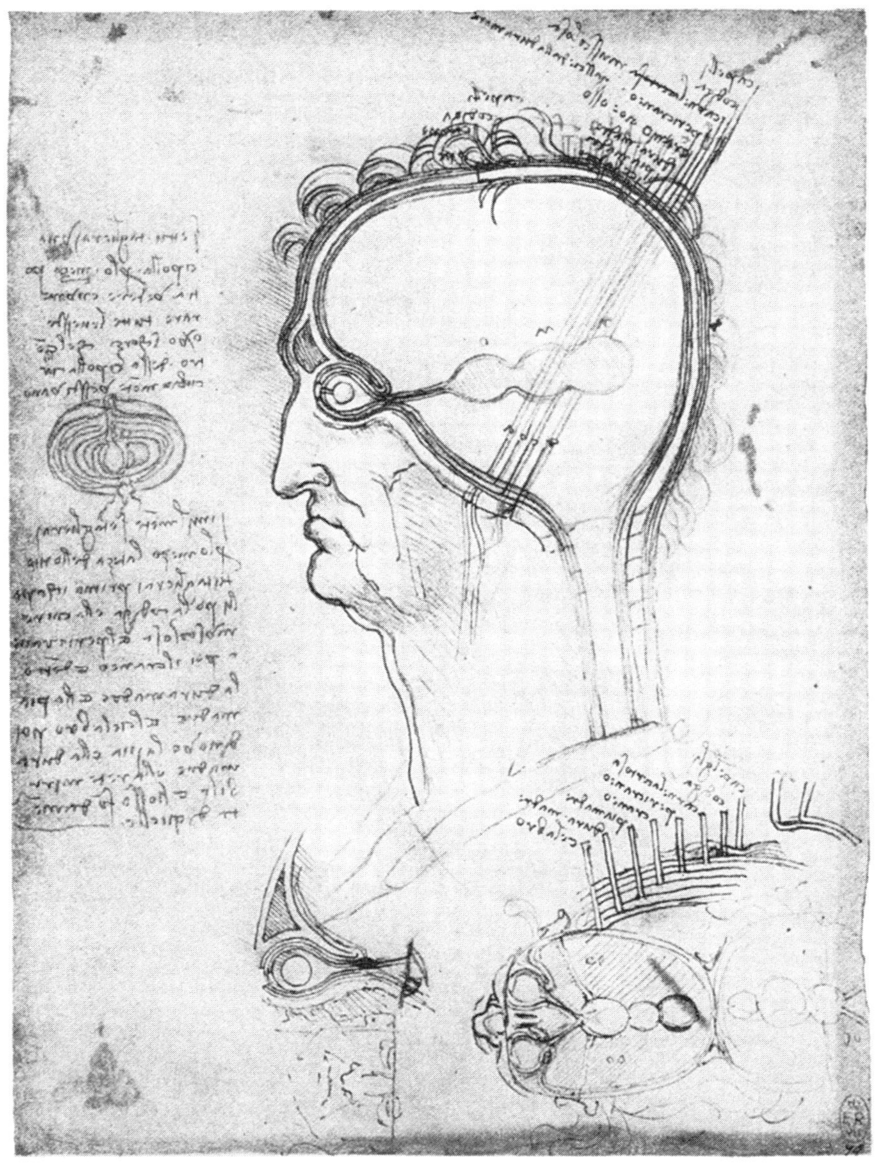

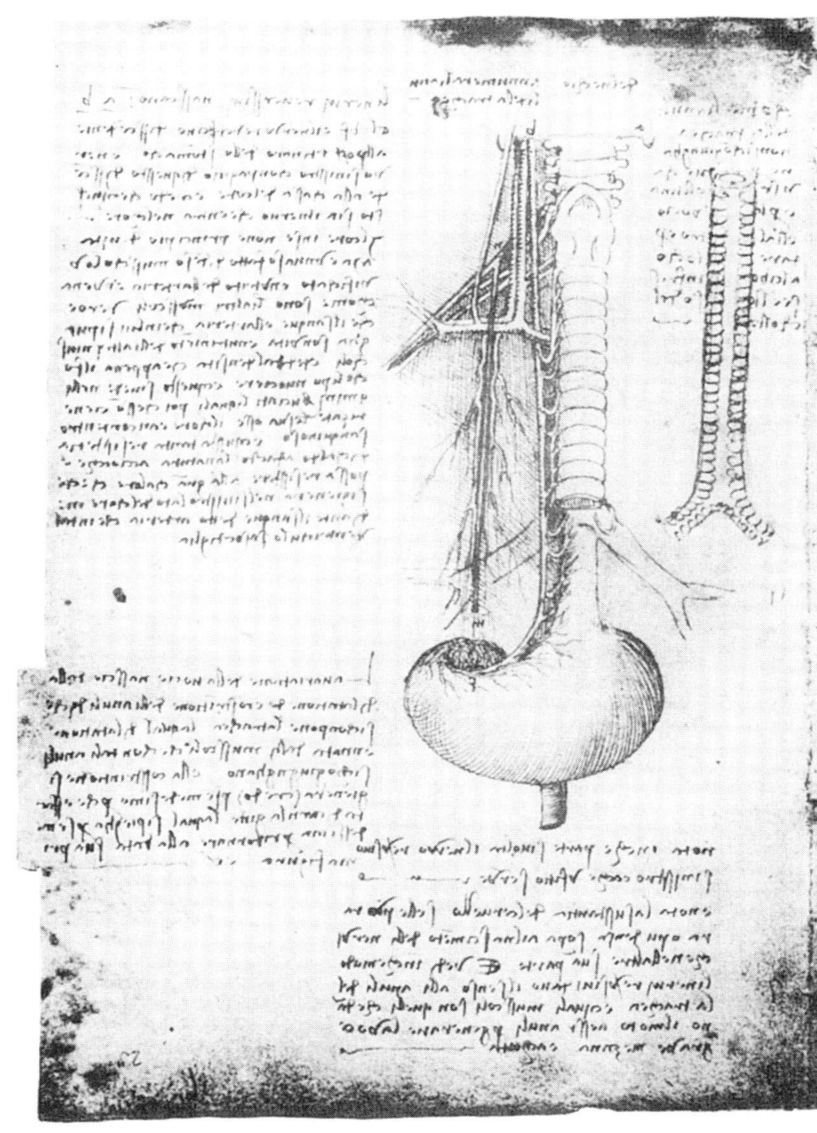

Central Nervous System and Cranial Nerves

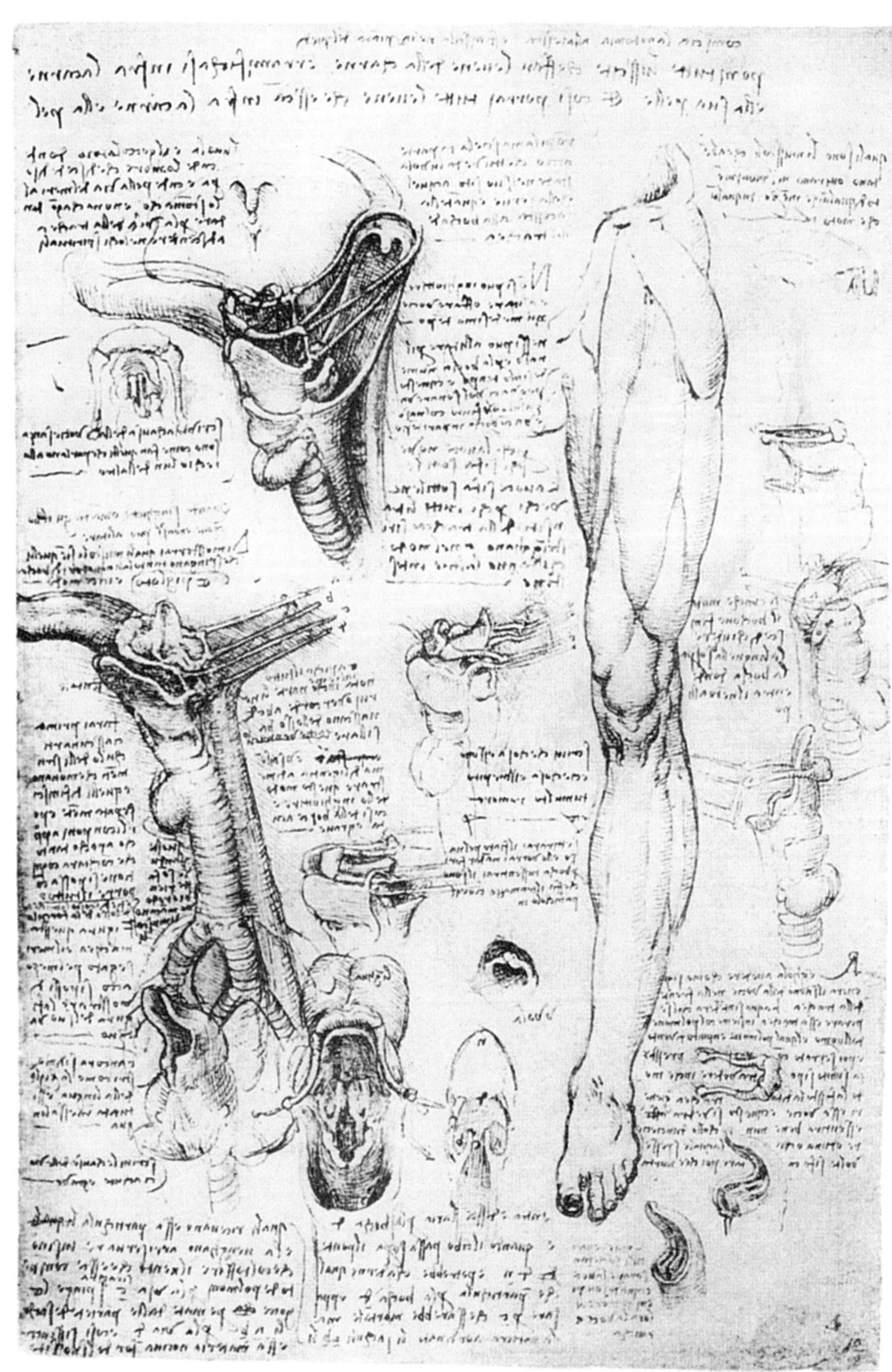

Respiratory System and Muscles of the Lower Extremity

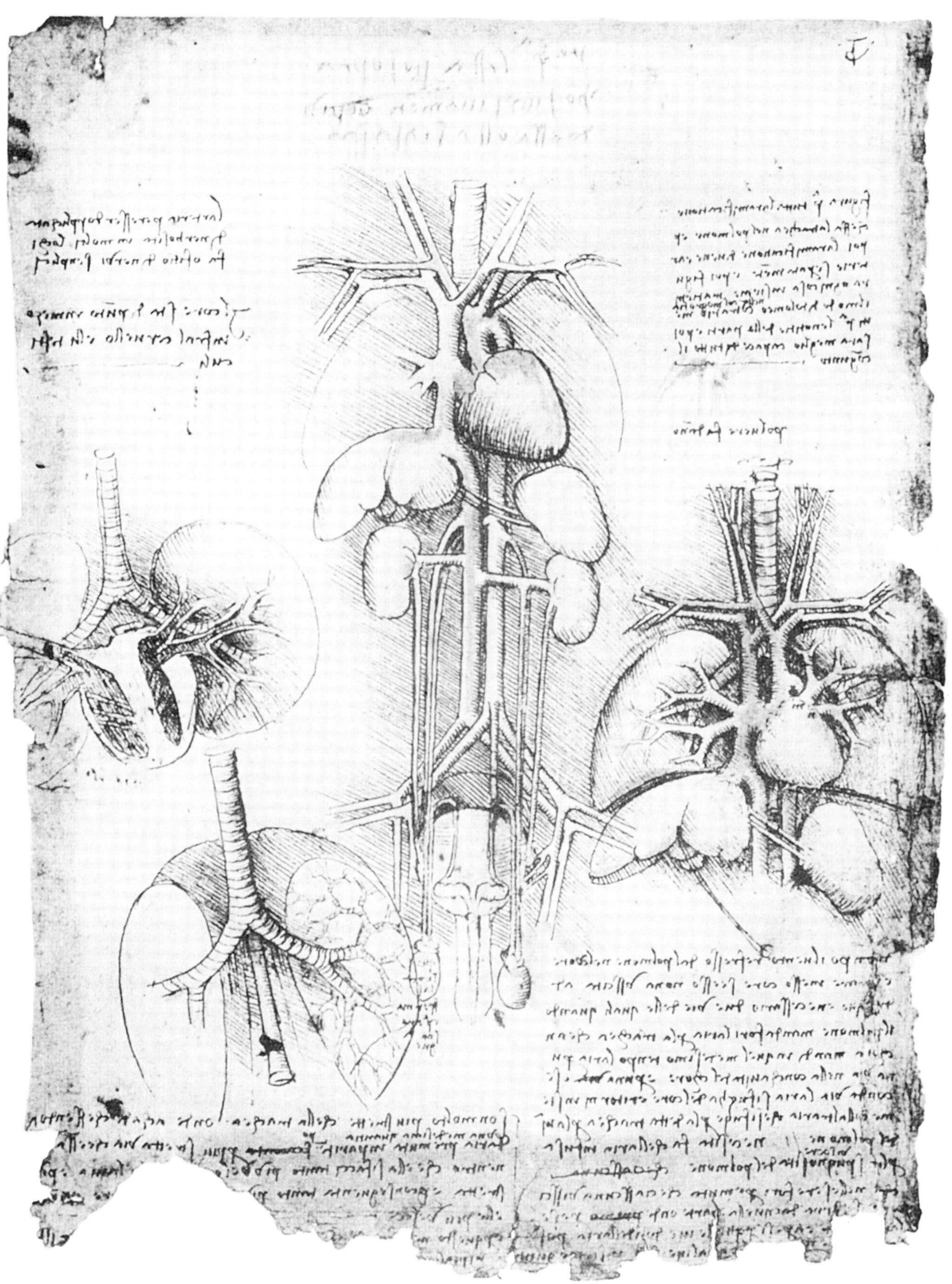

Respiratory System

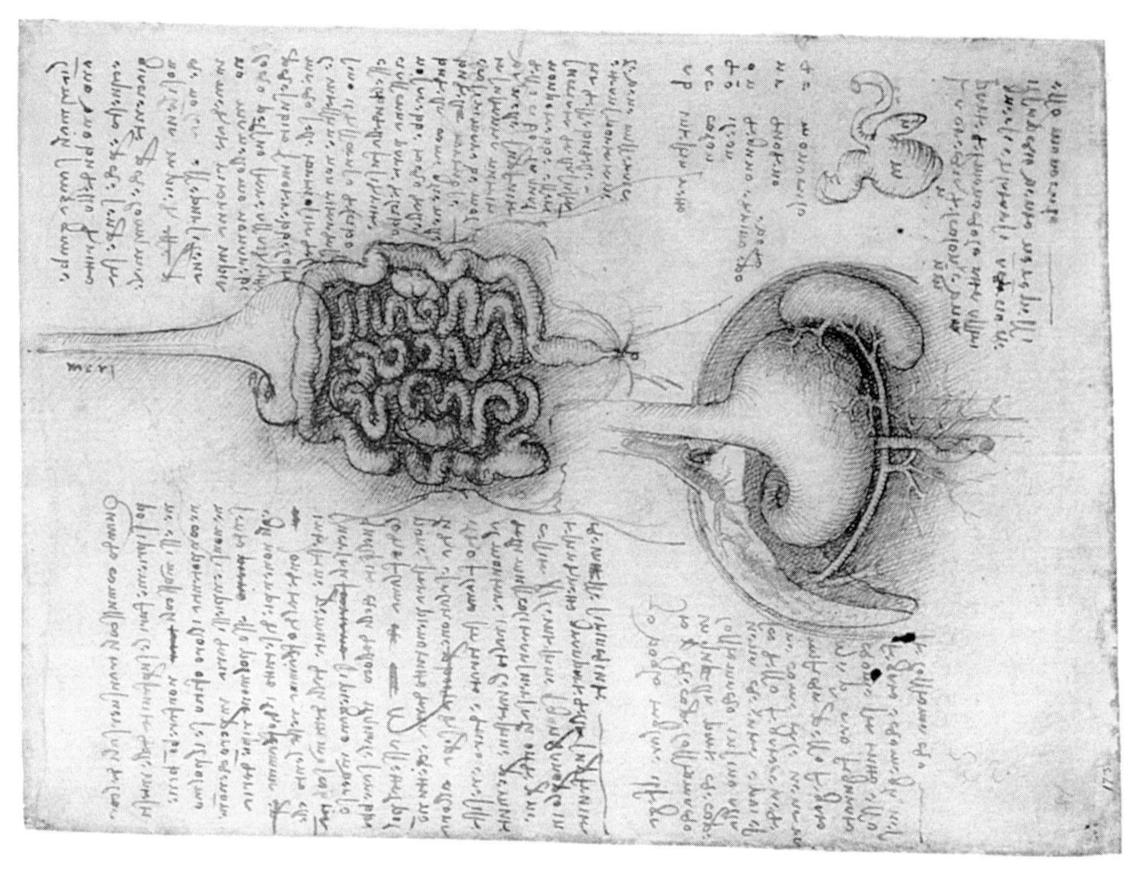

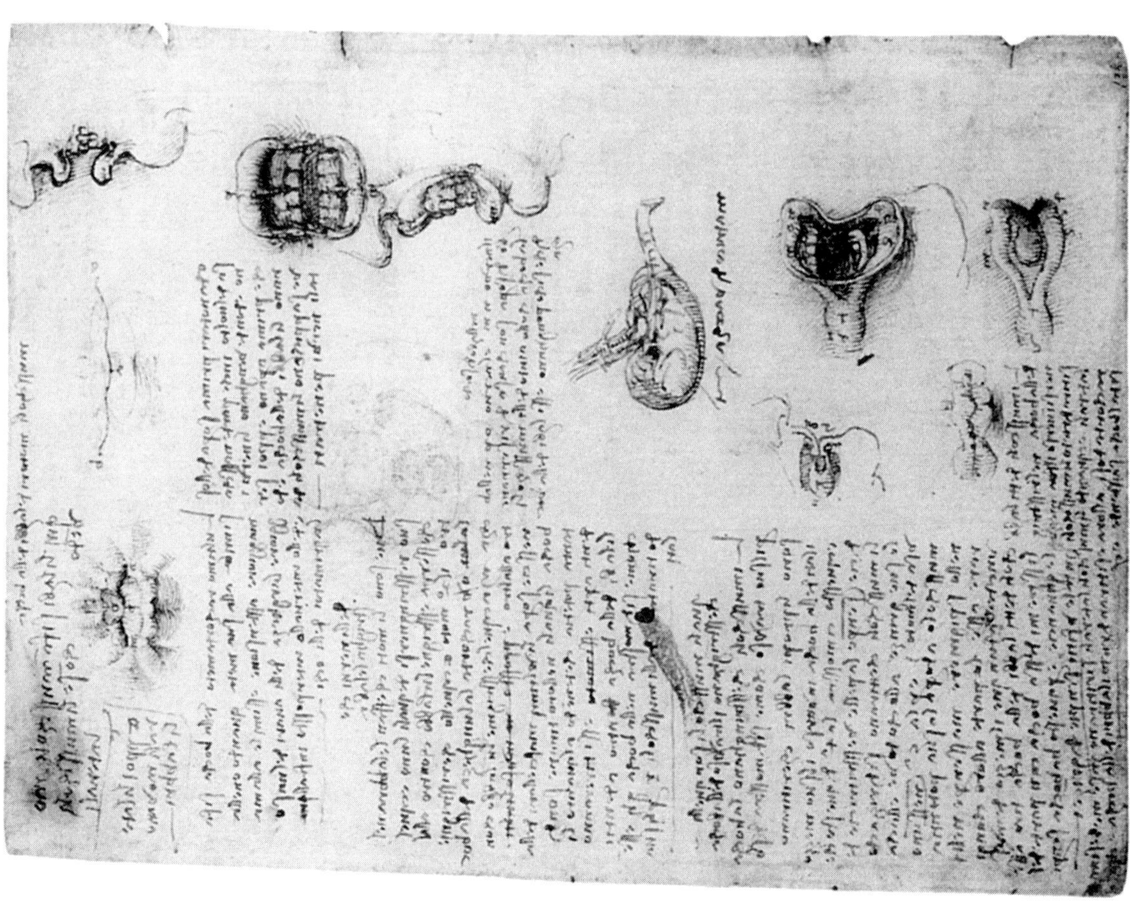

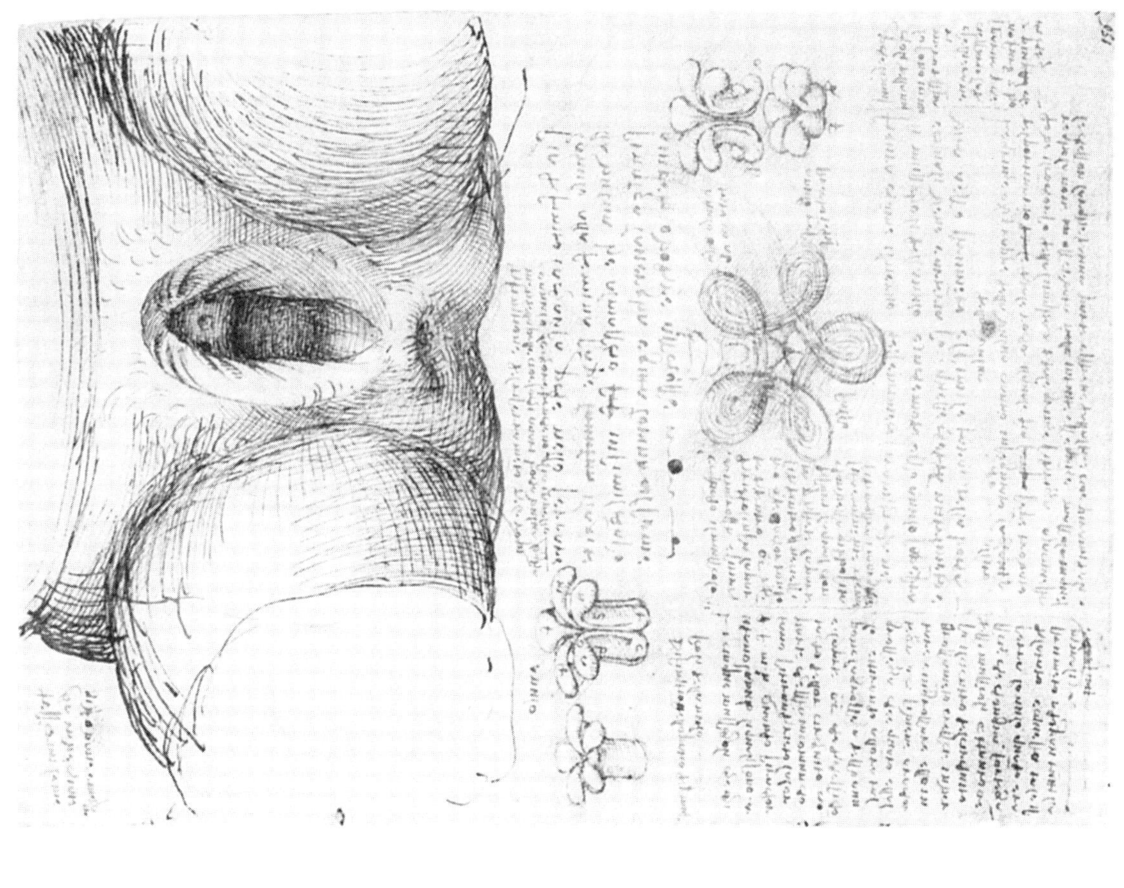

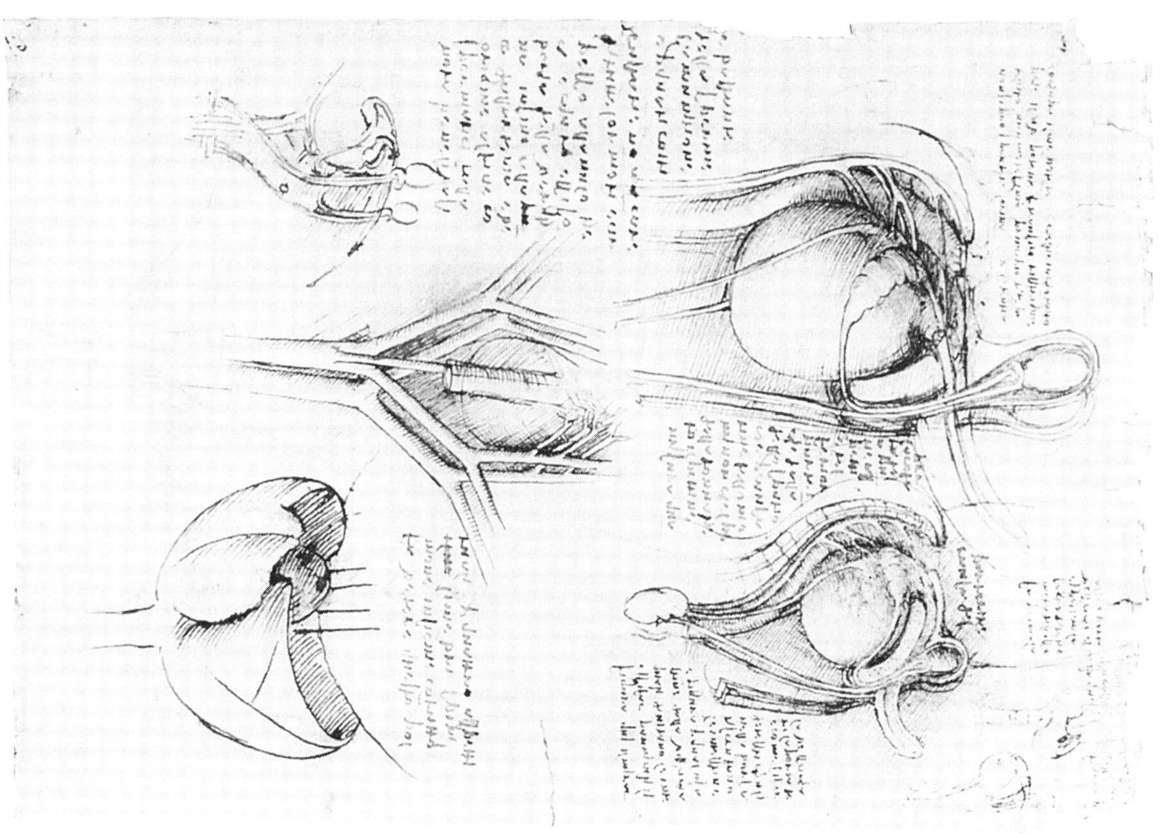

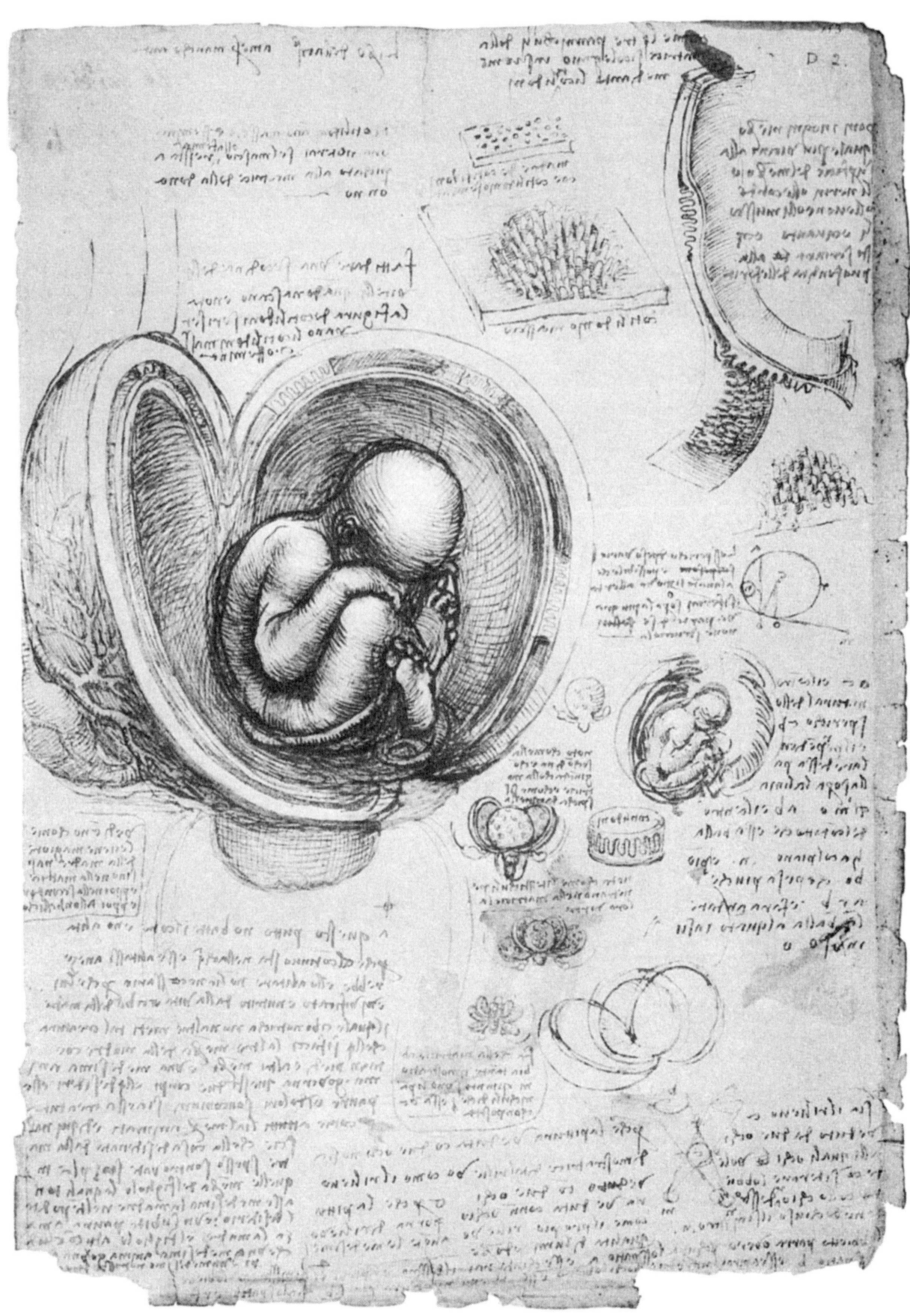

Embryology

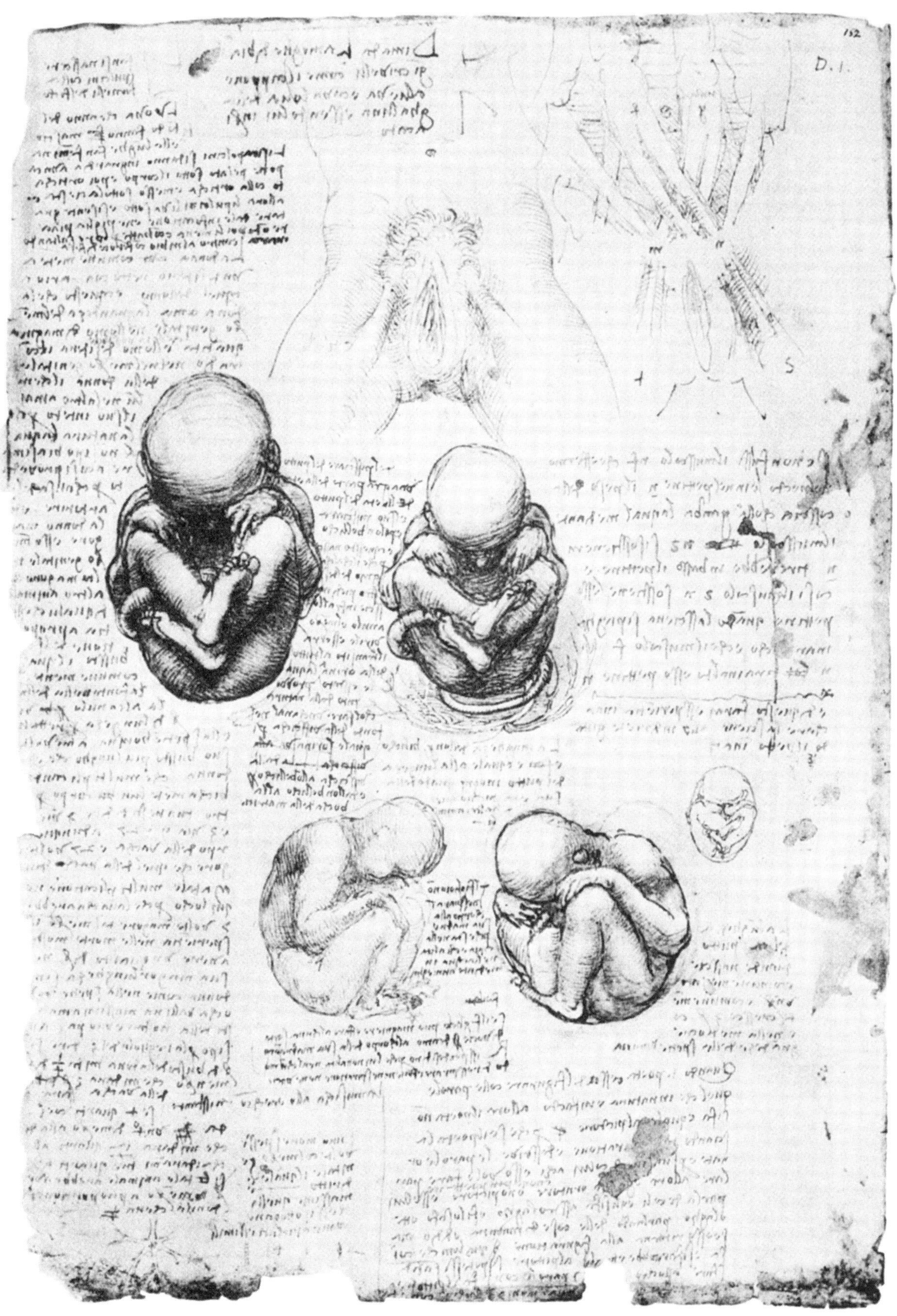

Embryology

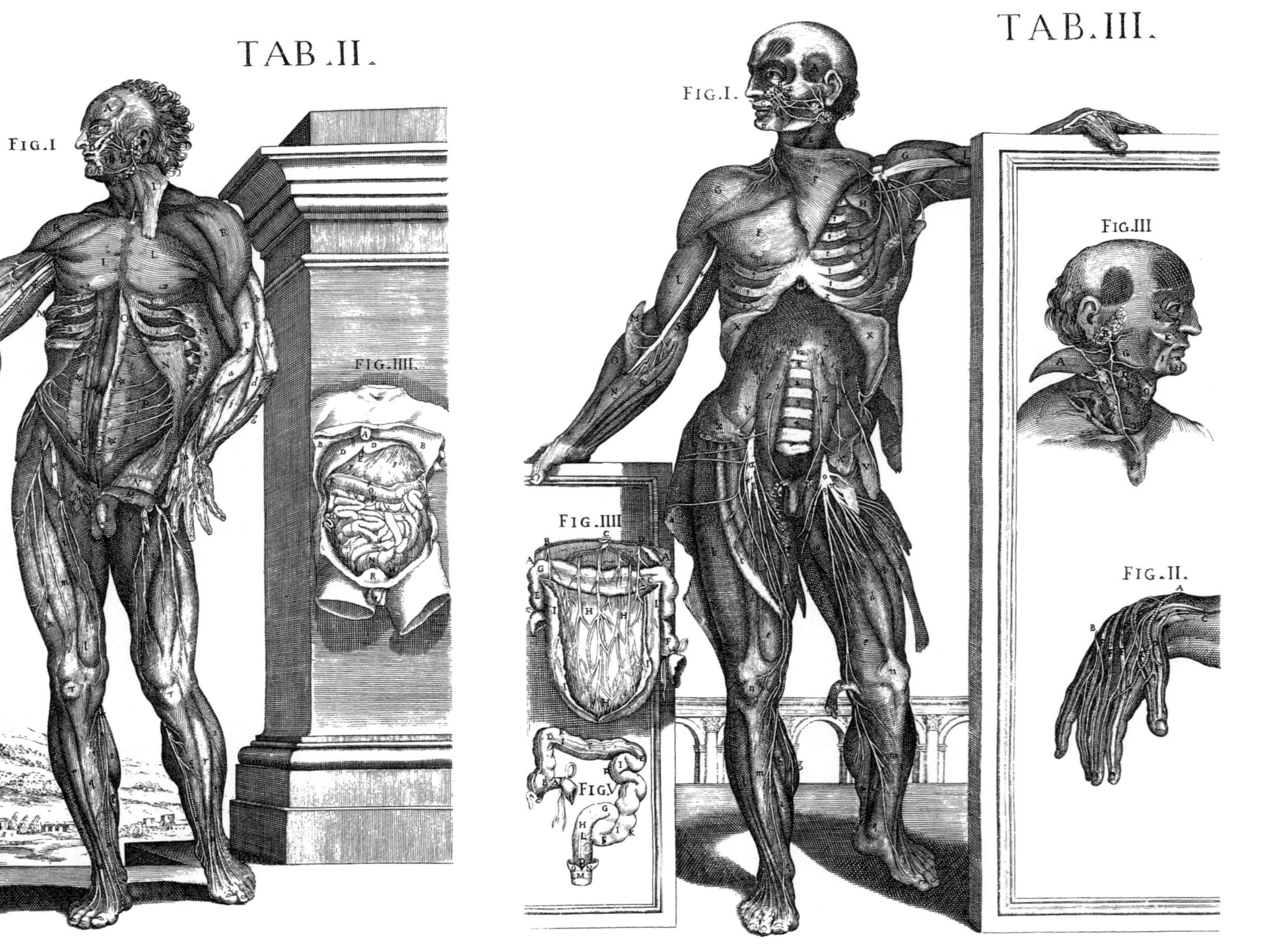

Left: Blood Vessels and Nerves. *Right:* Nerves.

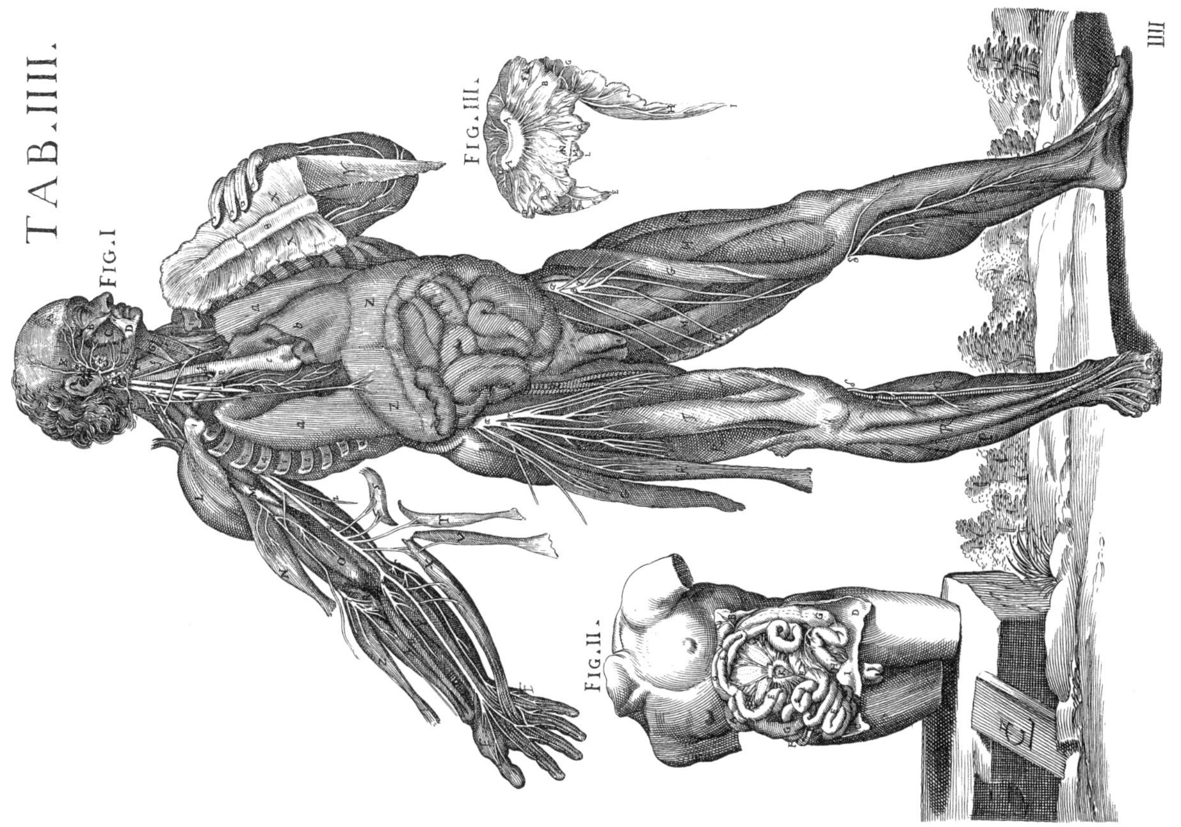

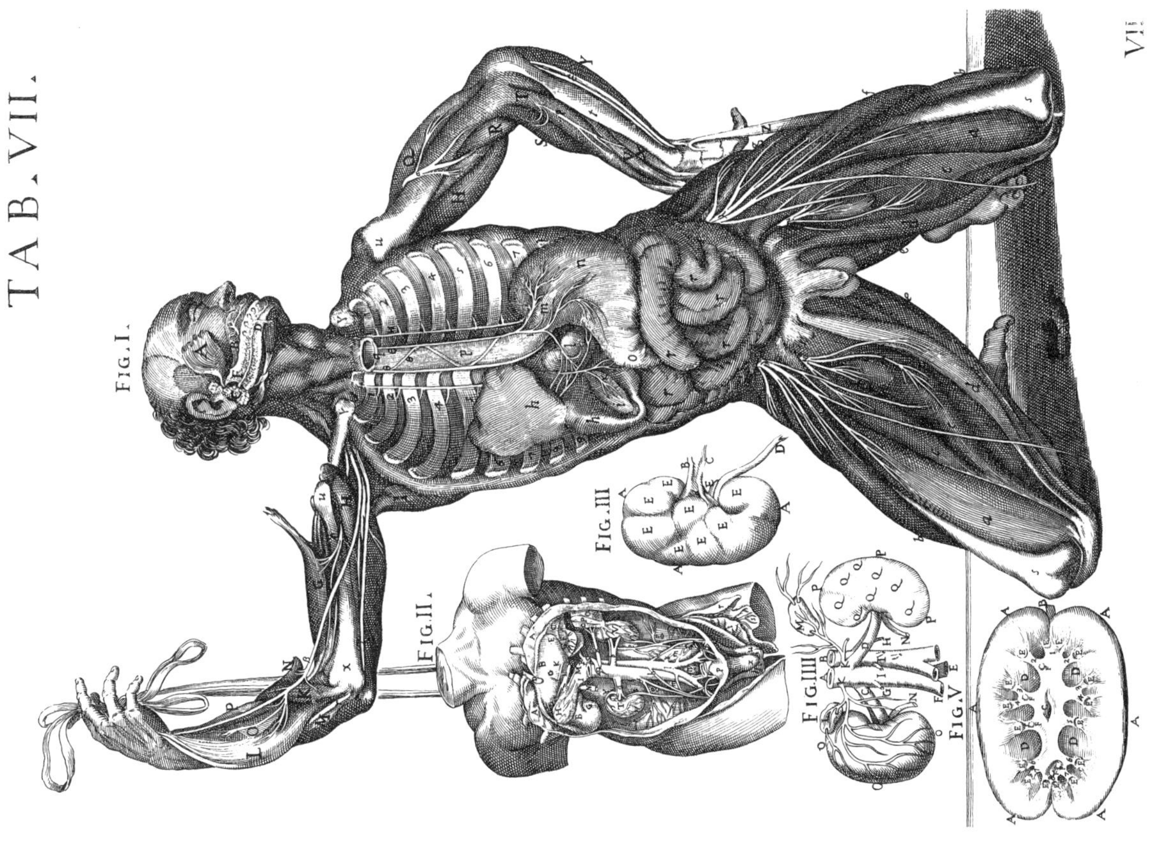

Left: Nerves of the Thorax and Abdomen. *Right:* Nerves of the Limbs and Thorax.

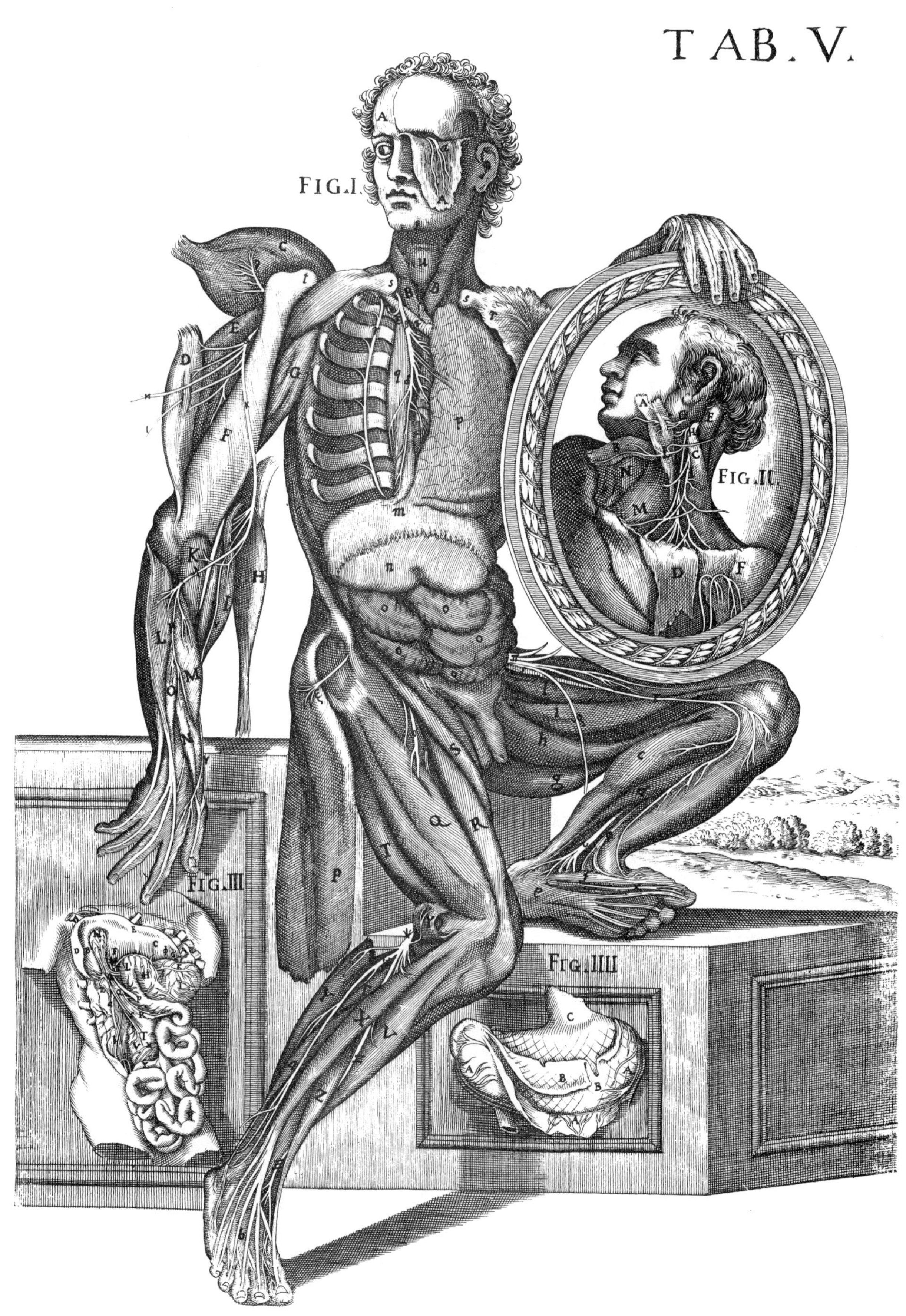

Nerves of the Limbs and Thorax

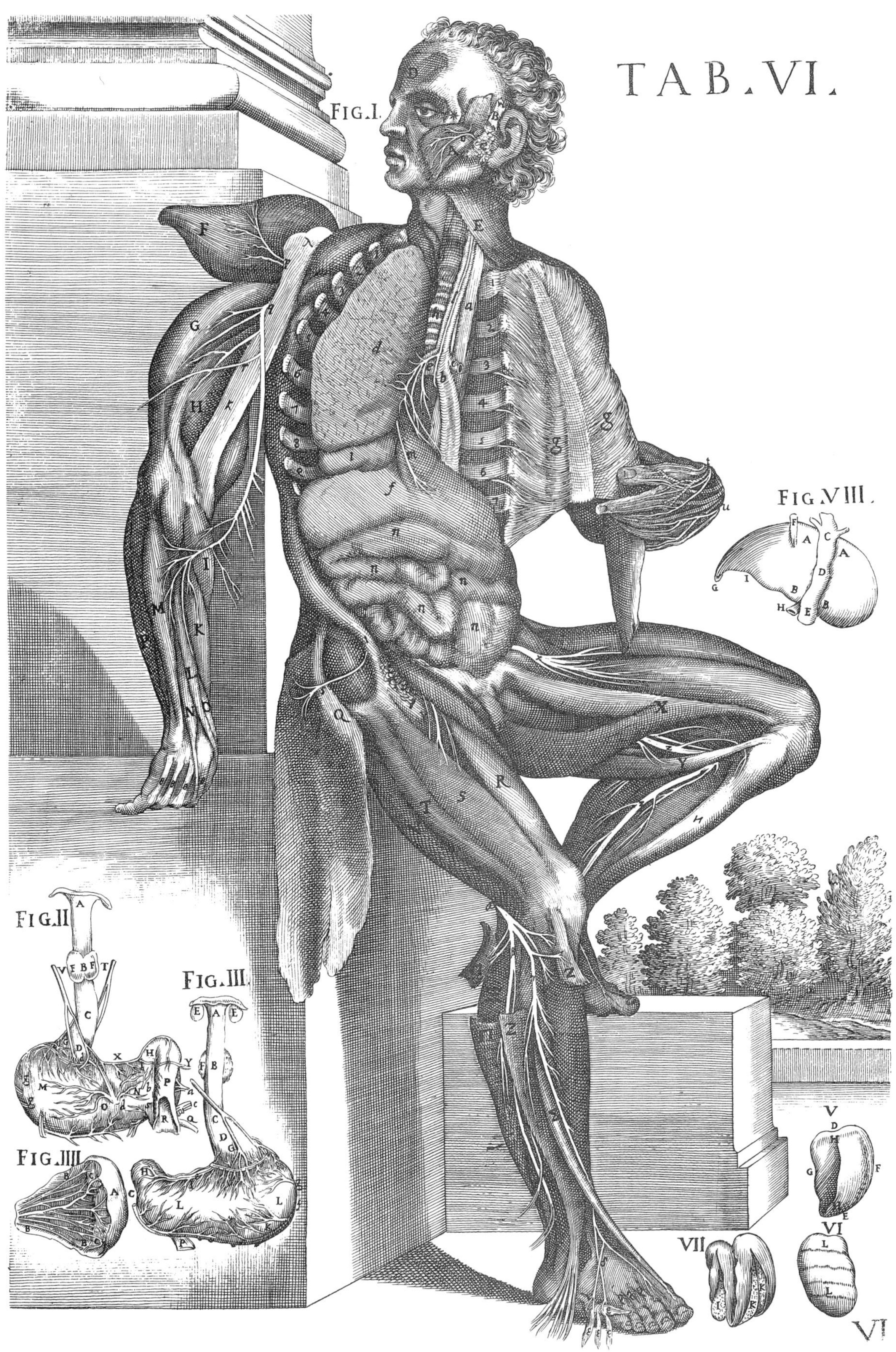

Nerves of the Limbs and Thorax

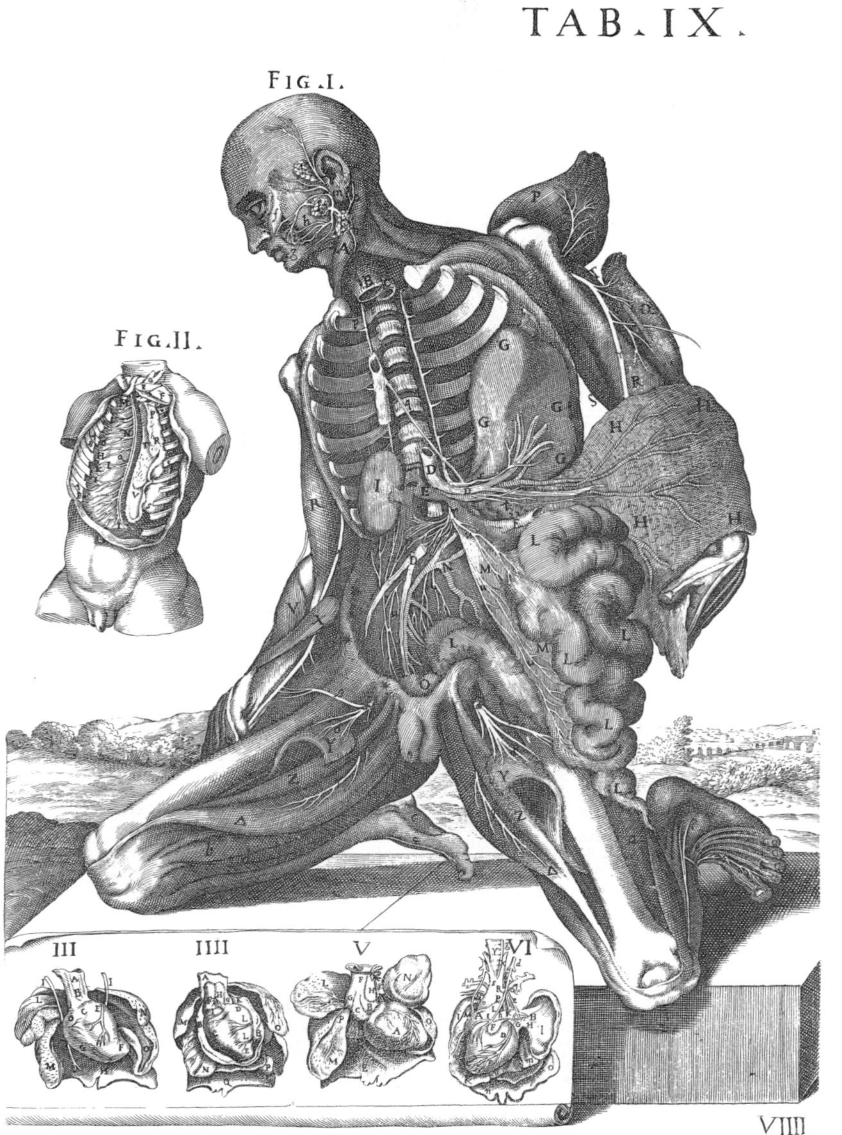

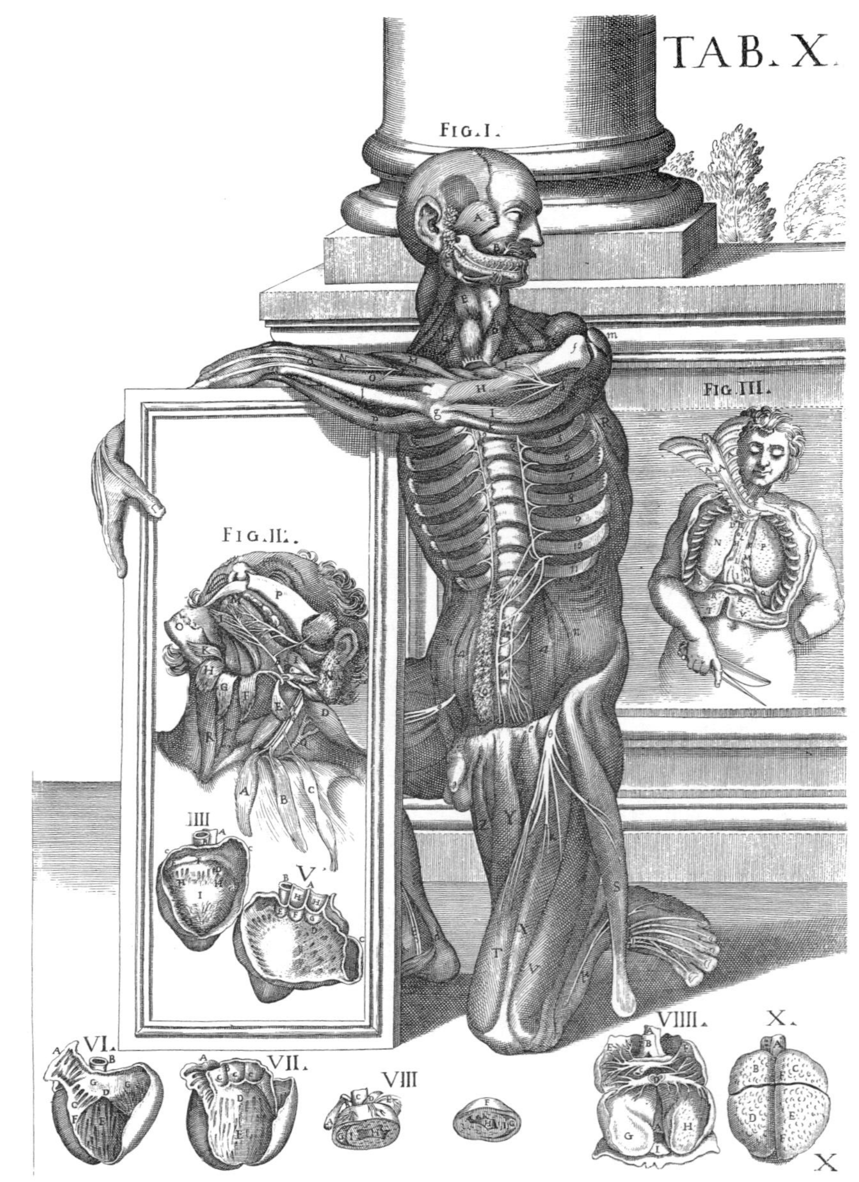

Left: Blood Vessels and Nerves. *Right:* Nerves.

TAB. XI.

XI.

TAB. XII.

XII.

Left: Nerves of the Thorax, Abdomen, and Limbs. *Right:* Spinal Nerves.

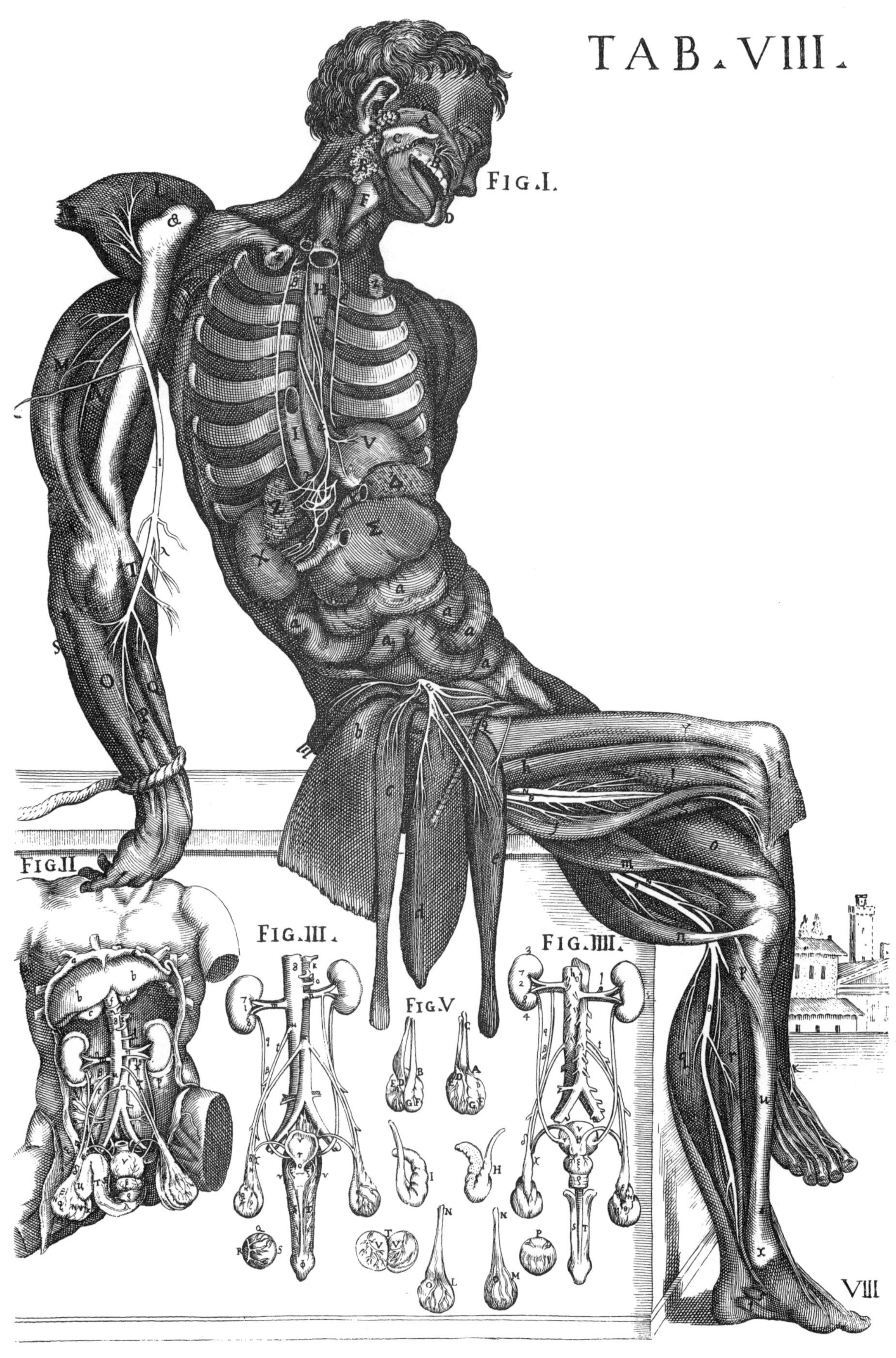

Nerves of the Limbs and Thorax

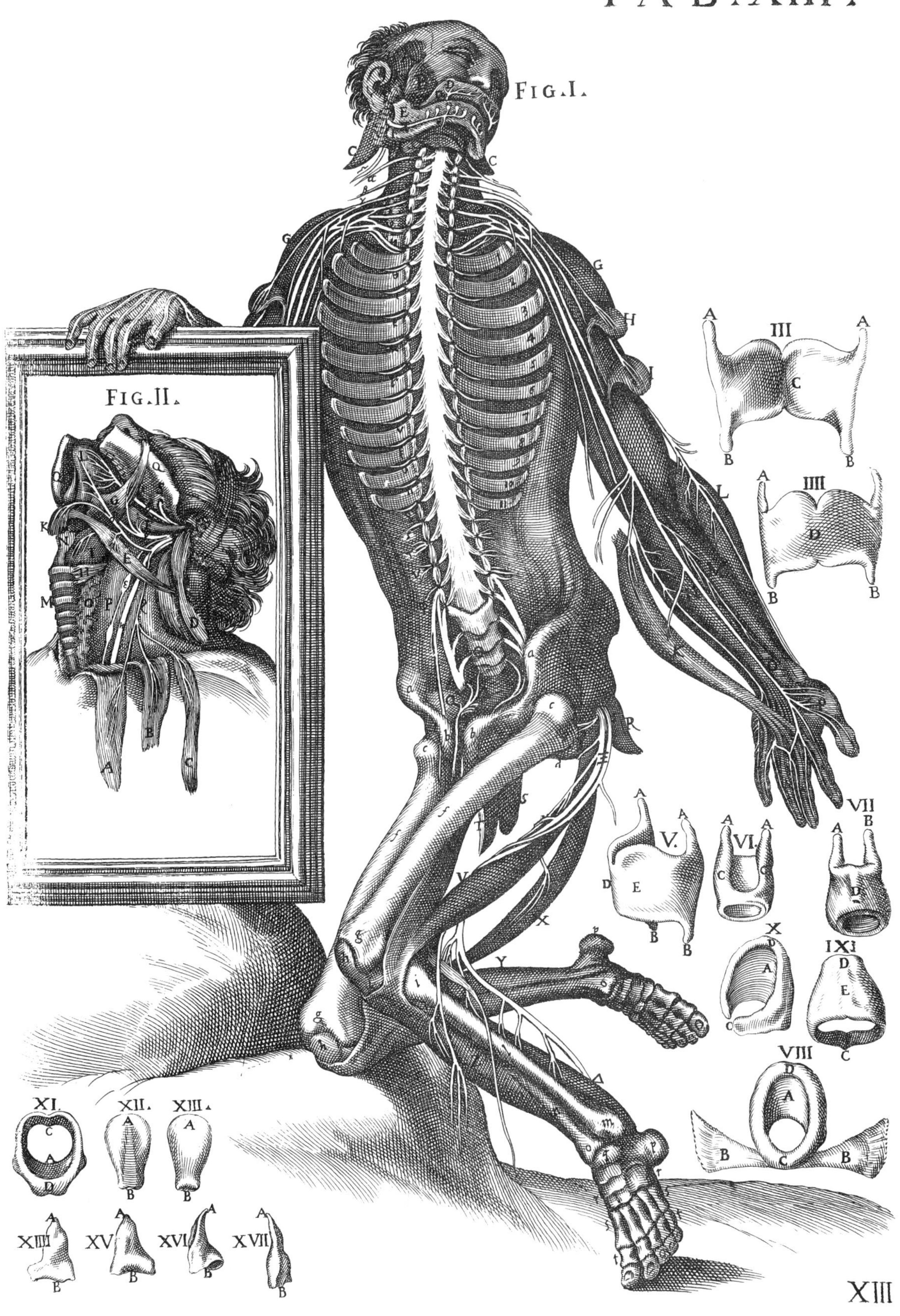

Spinal Cord and Nerves of the Neck and Limbs

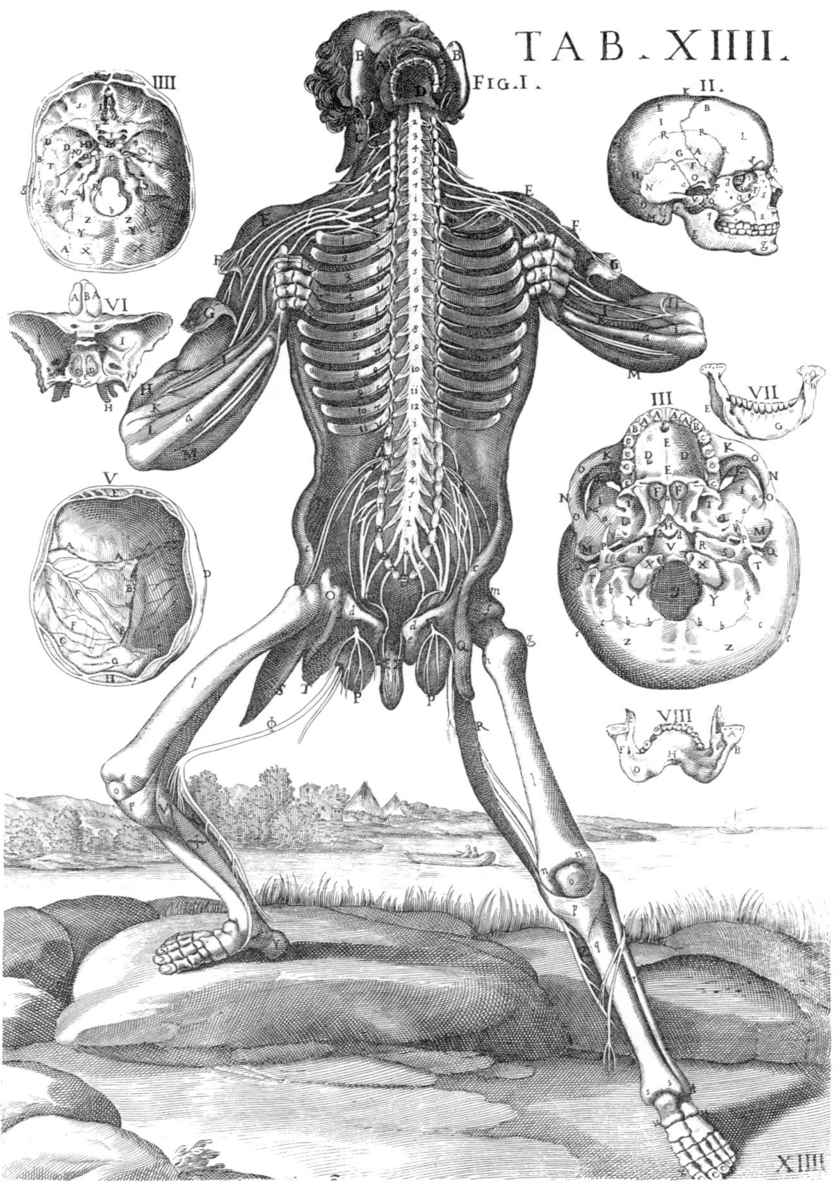

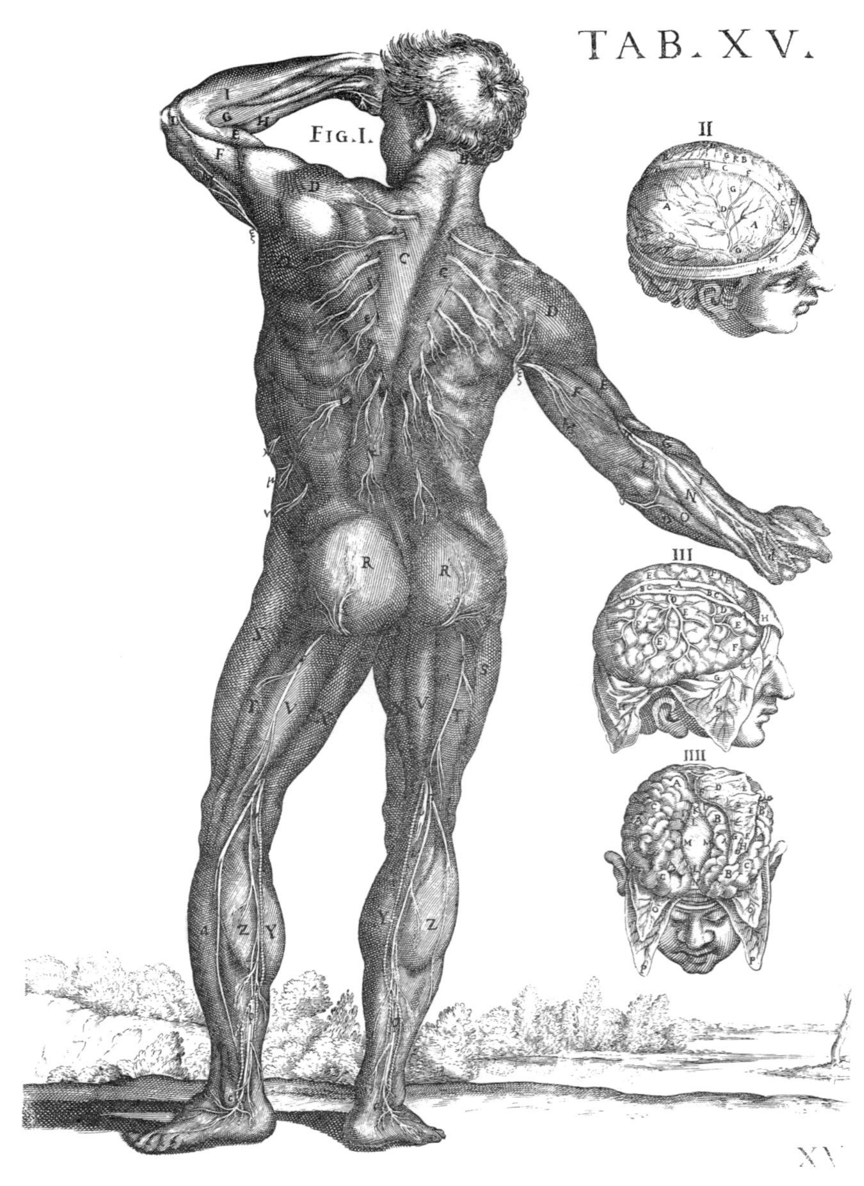

Left: Nerves of the Spinal Cord. *Right:* Nerves, back view.

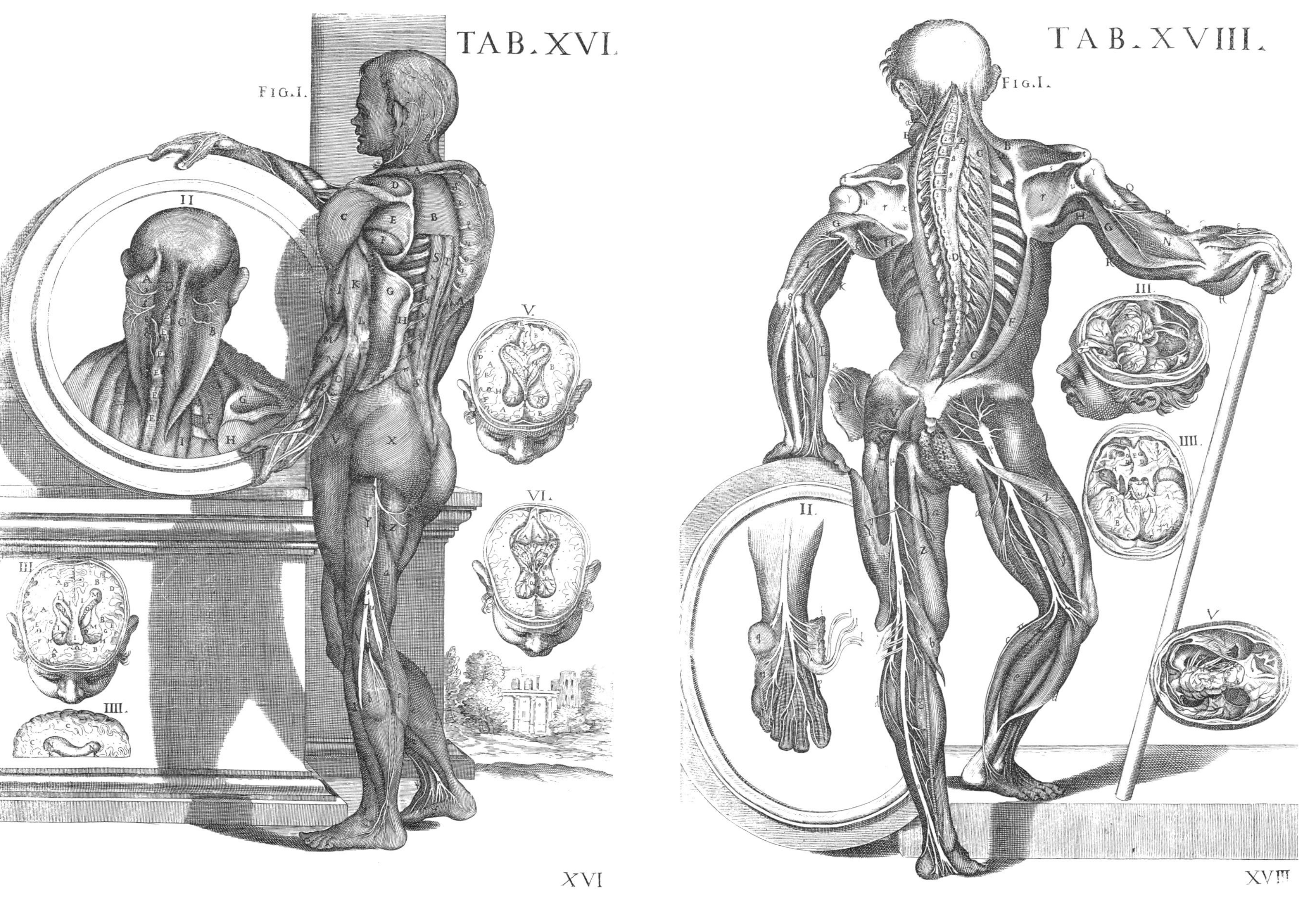

Left: Nerves, side view. *Right:* Nerves, back view.

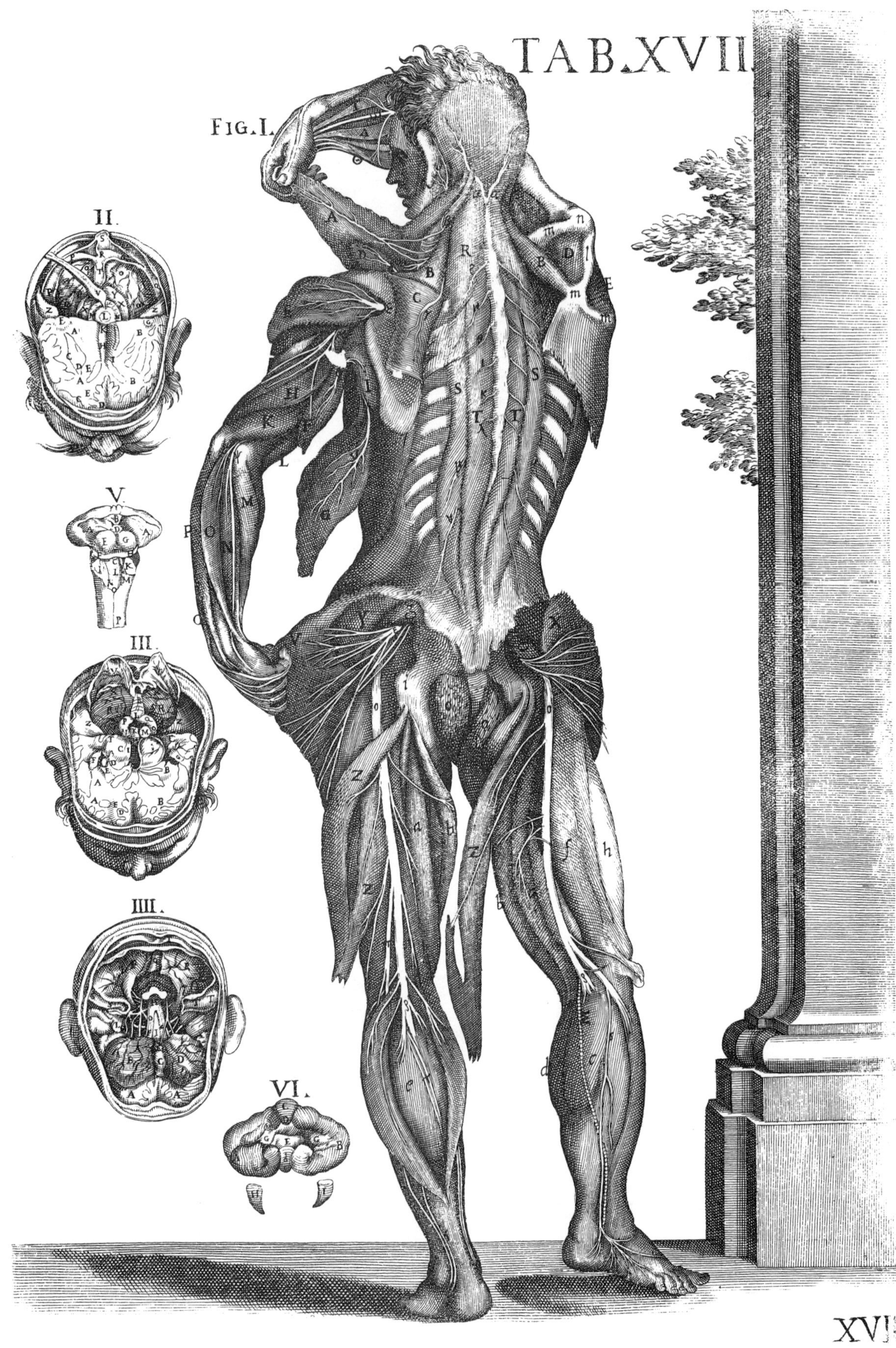

Nerves, back view

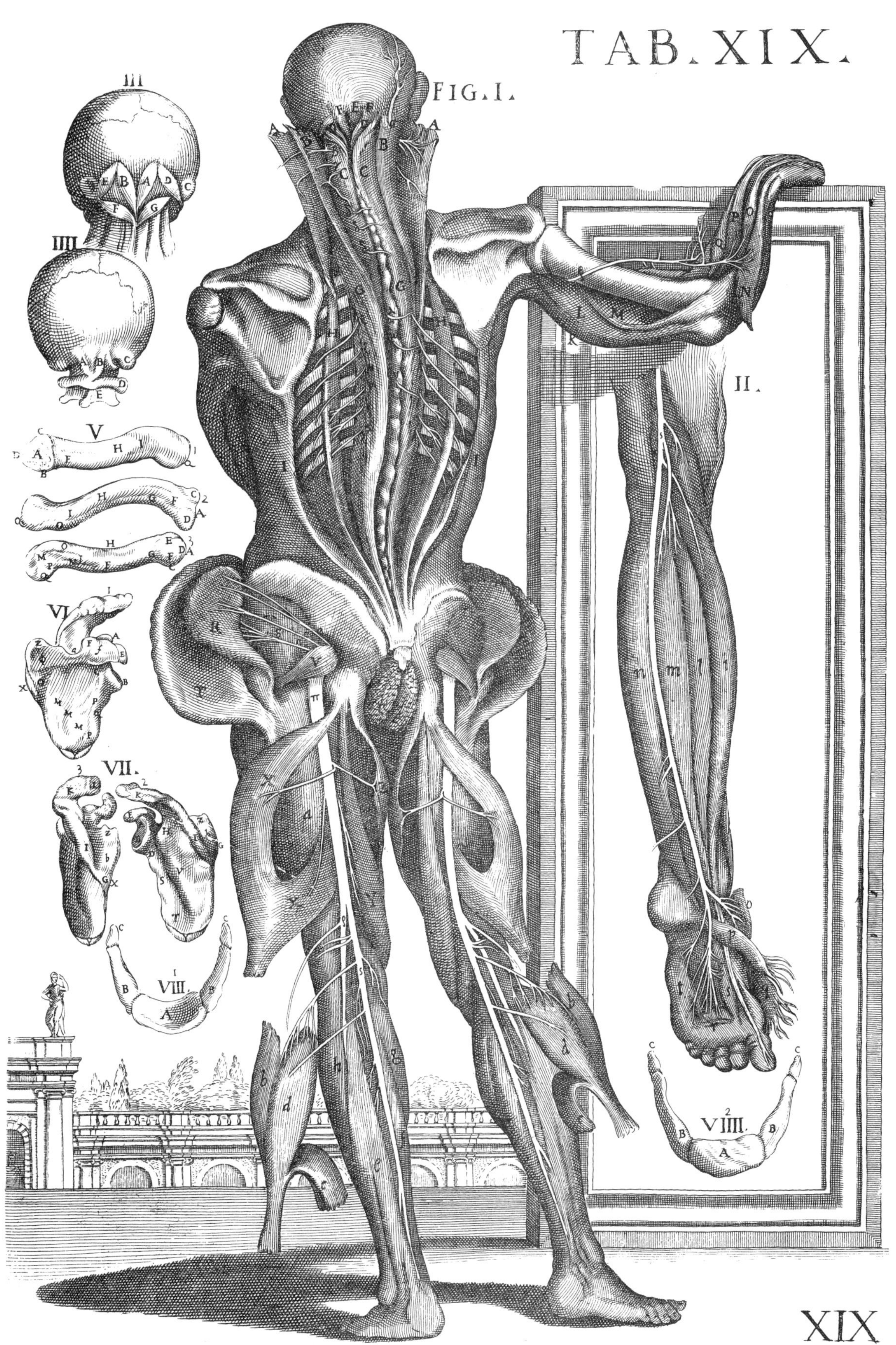

Muscle/Nerve Connections, back view

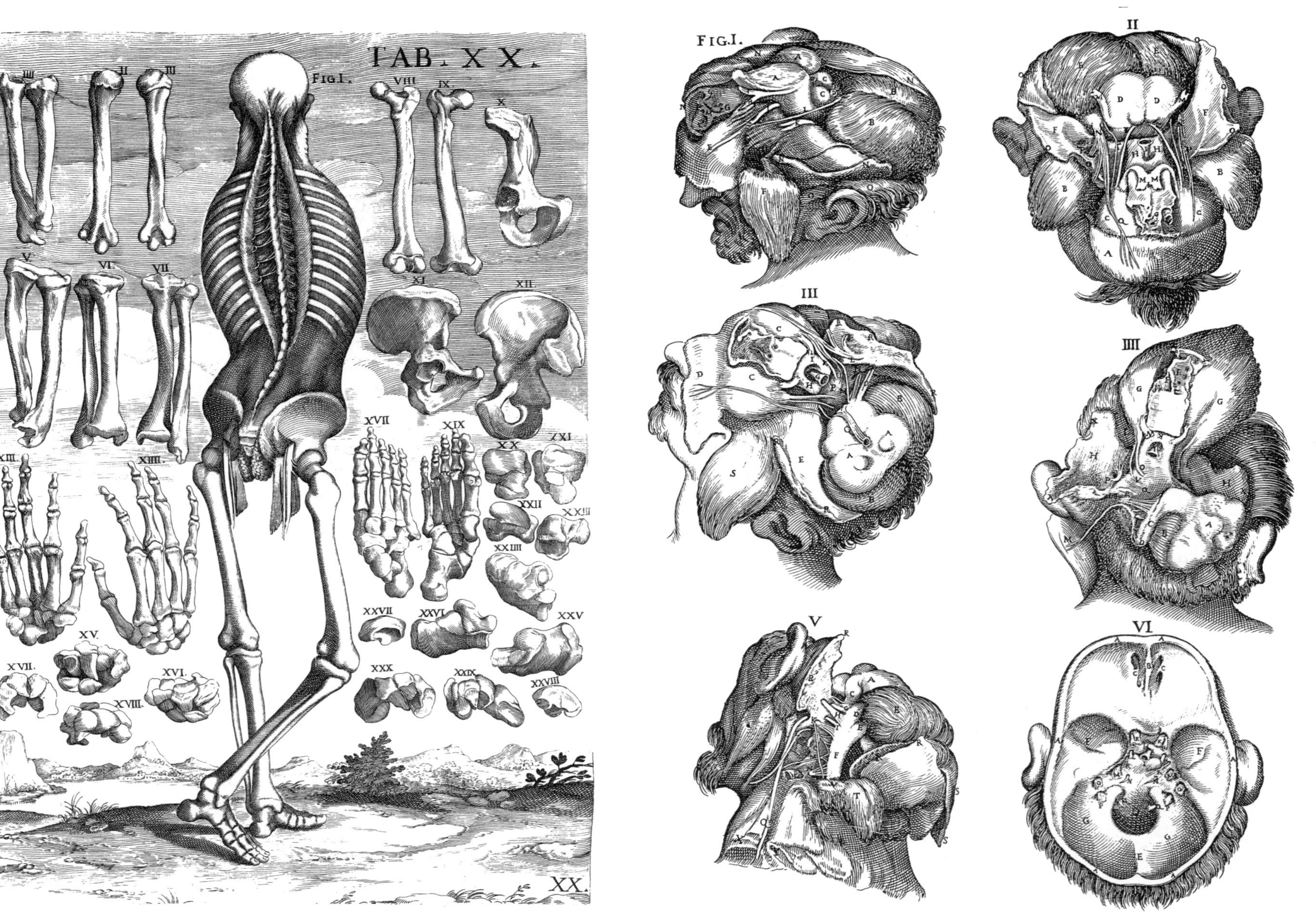

Left: Spinal Column and Bones. *Right:* Cranial Nerves.

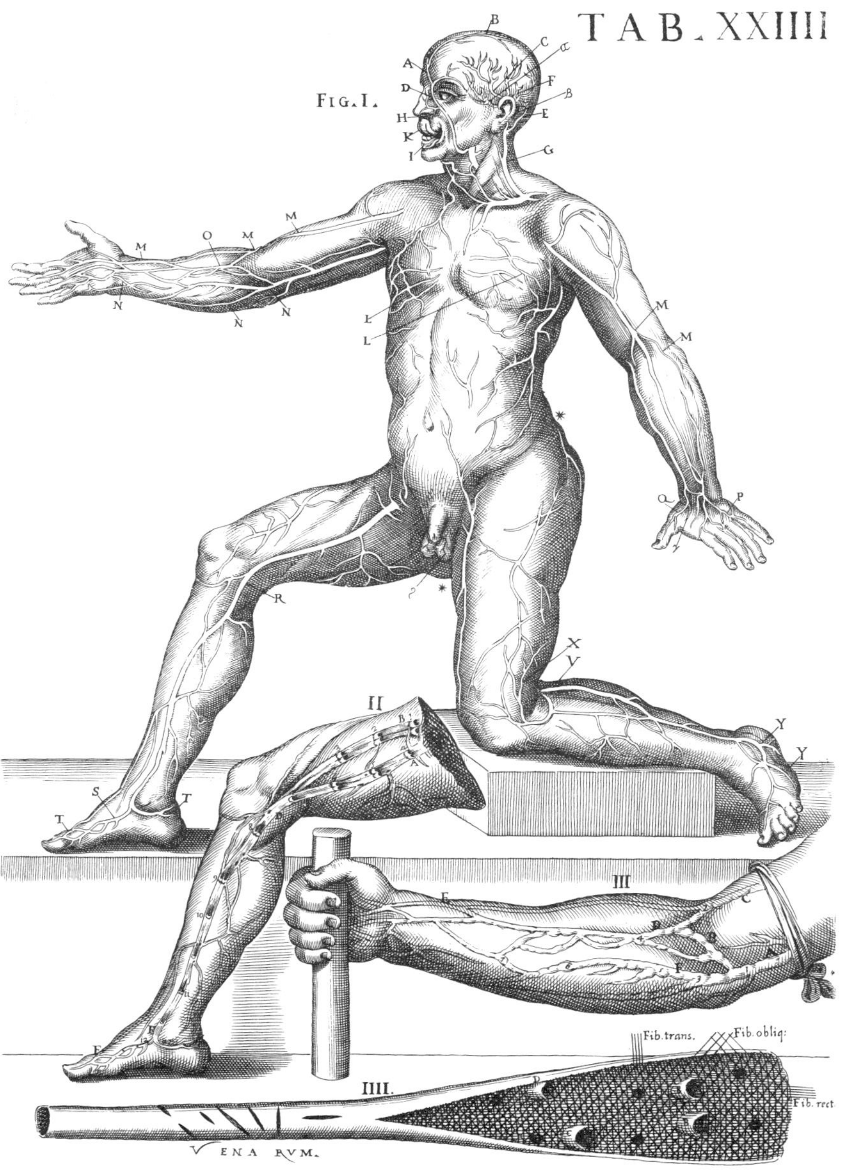

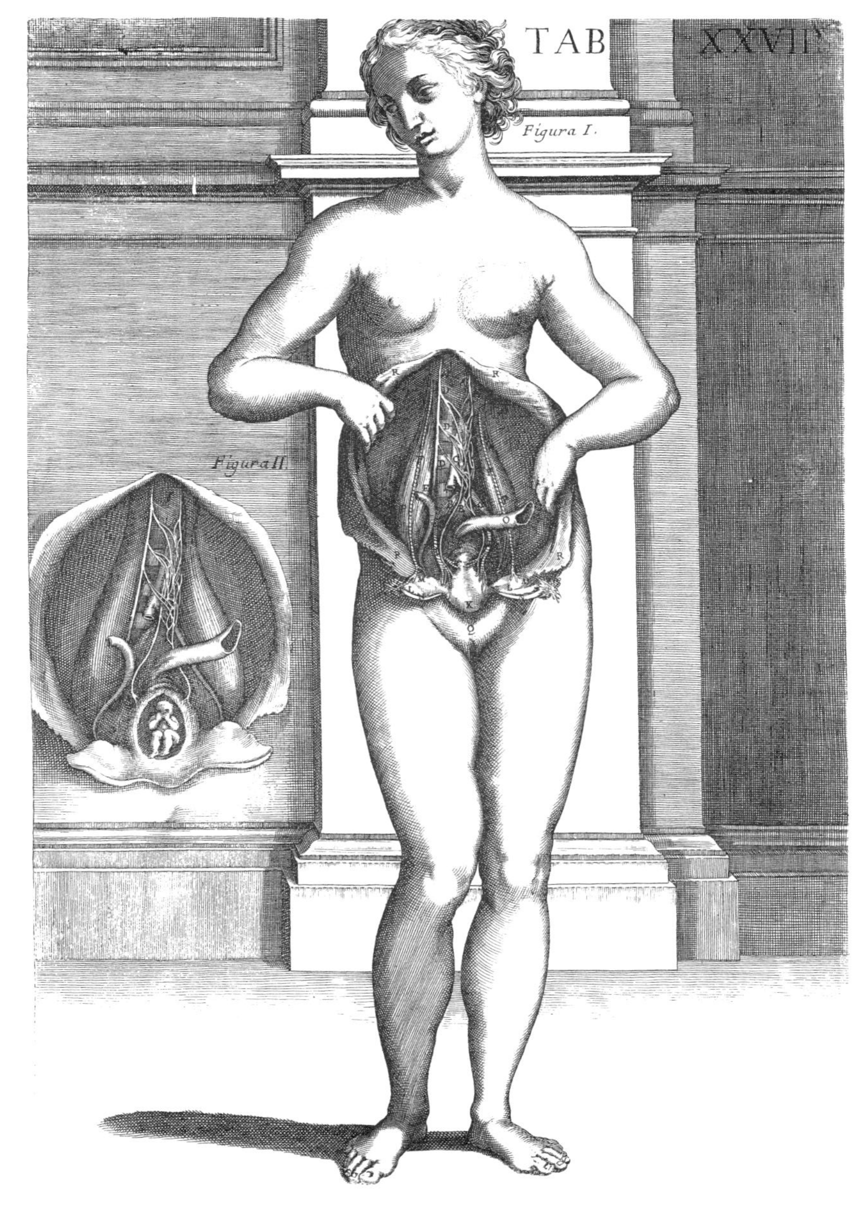

Left: Veins of the Body. *Right:* Female Urogenital System.

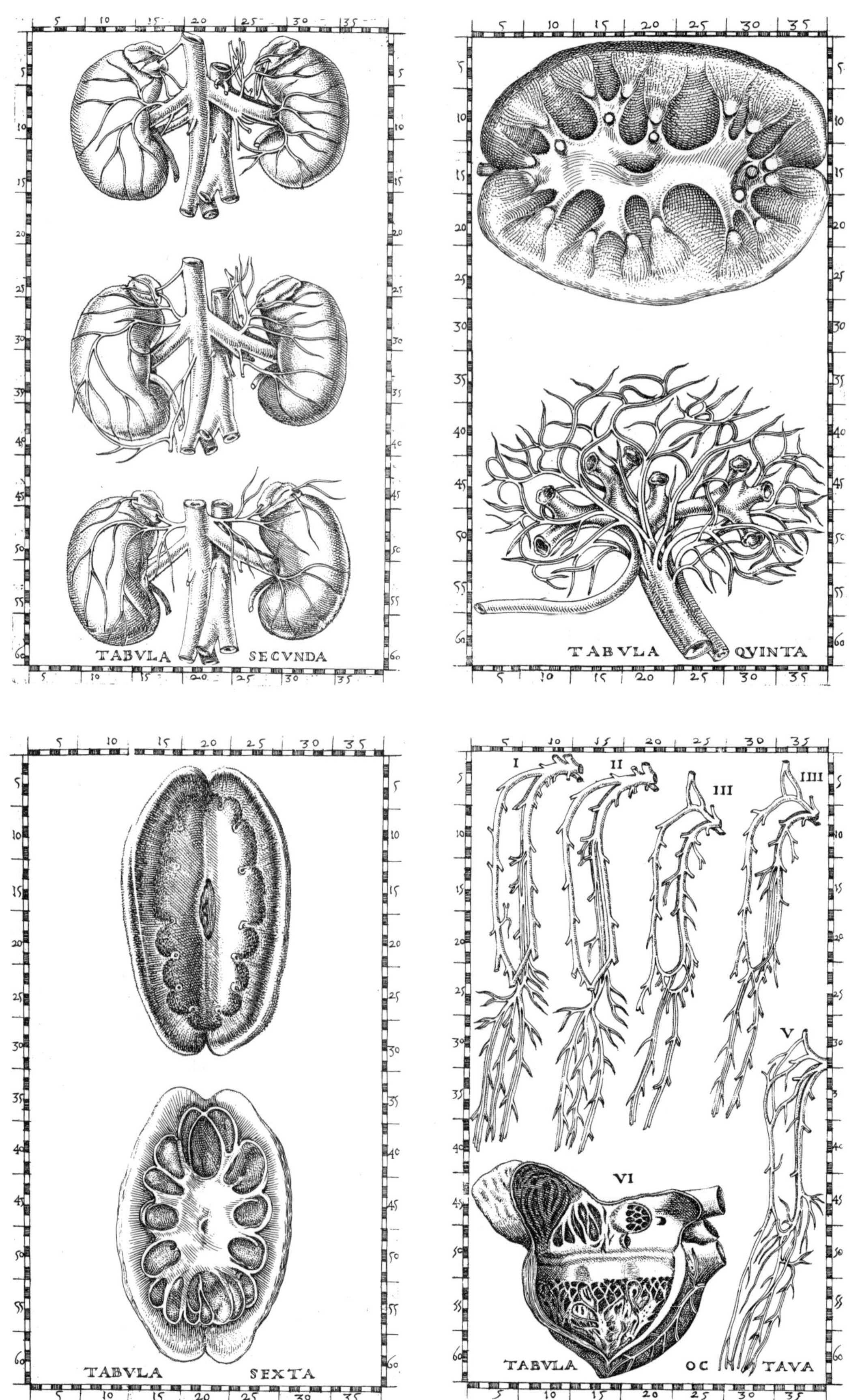

Top, left and right; and bottom, left: The Kidneys. *Bottom, right:* The Heart and Circulation of the Arm.

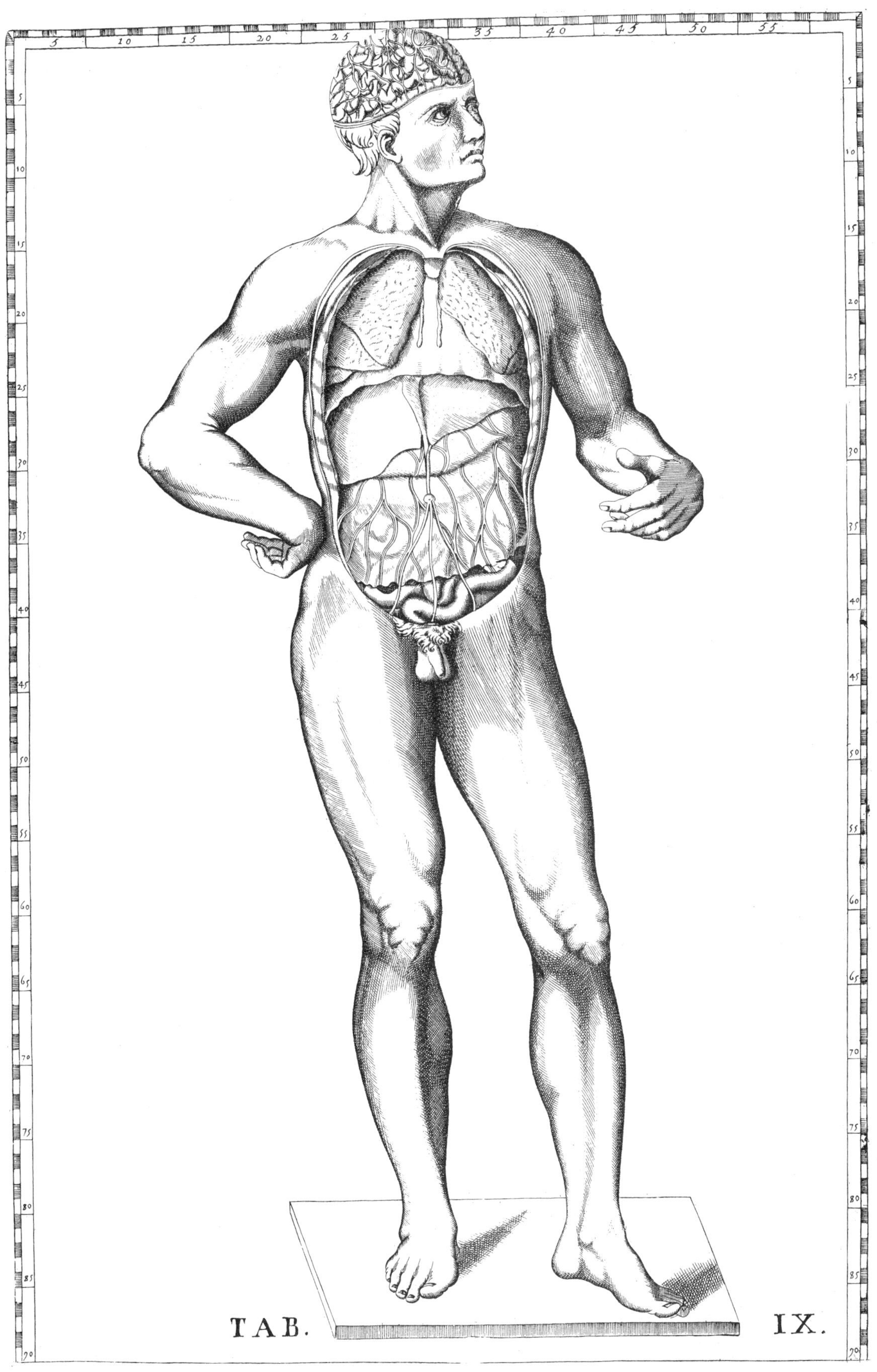

Internal Organs of the Trunk

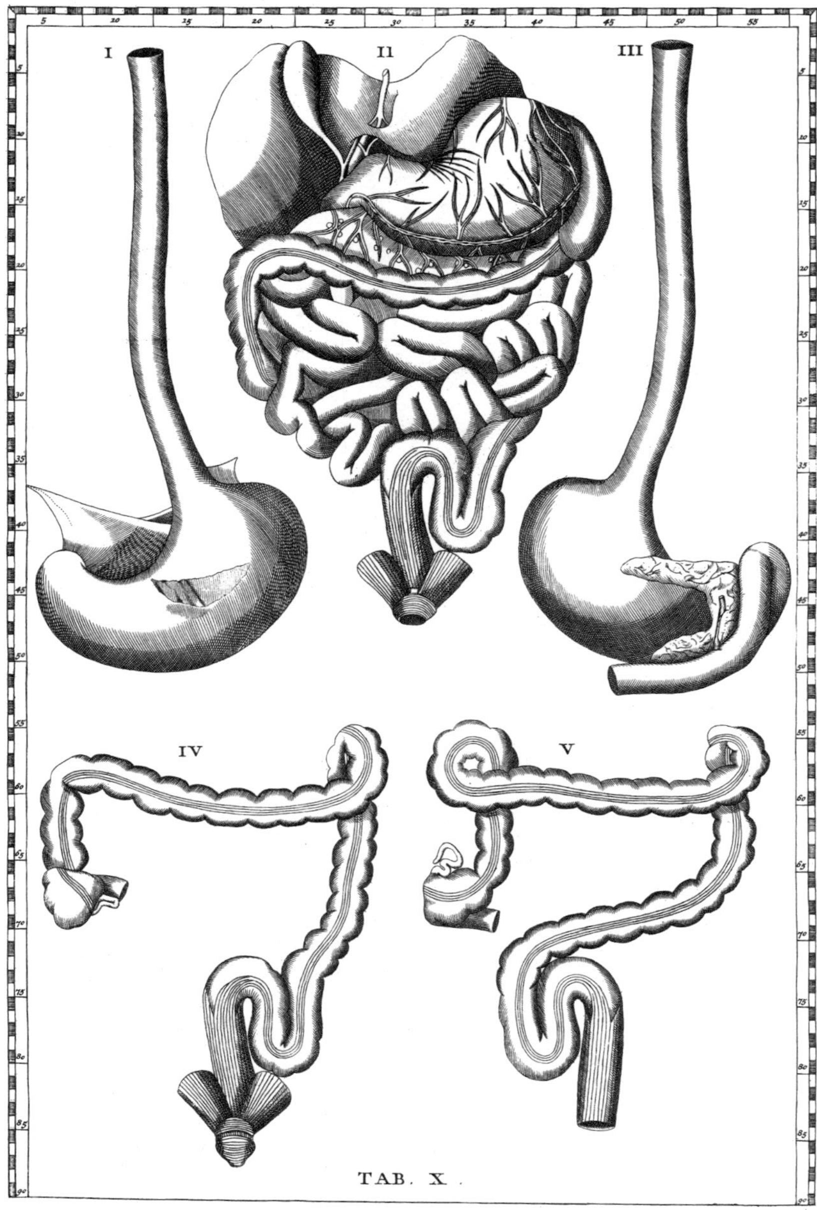

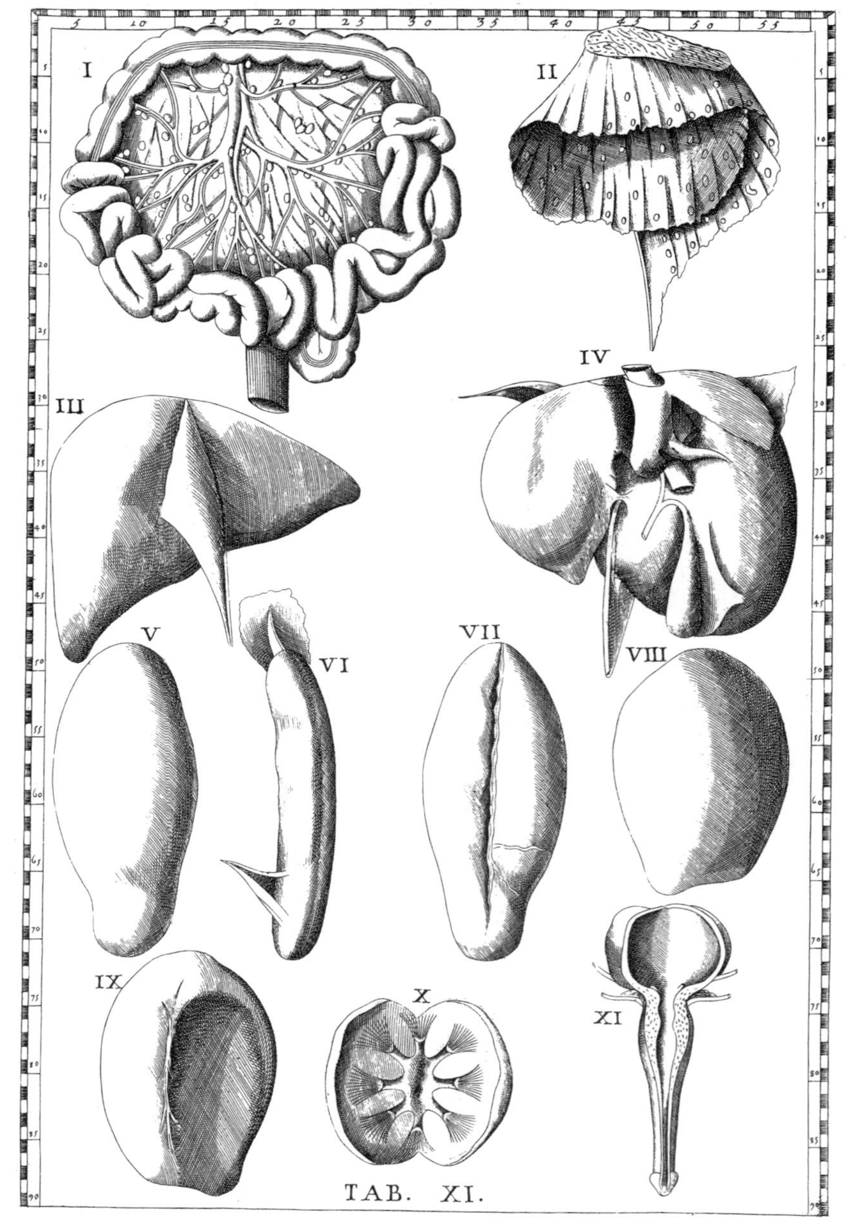

Left: The Digestive Tract. *Right:* The Digestive and Urinary Tracts.

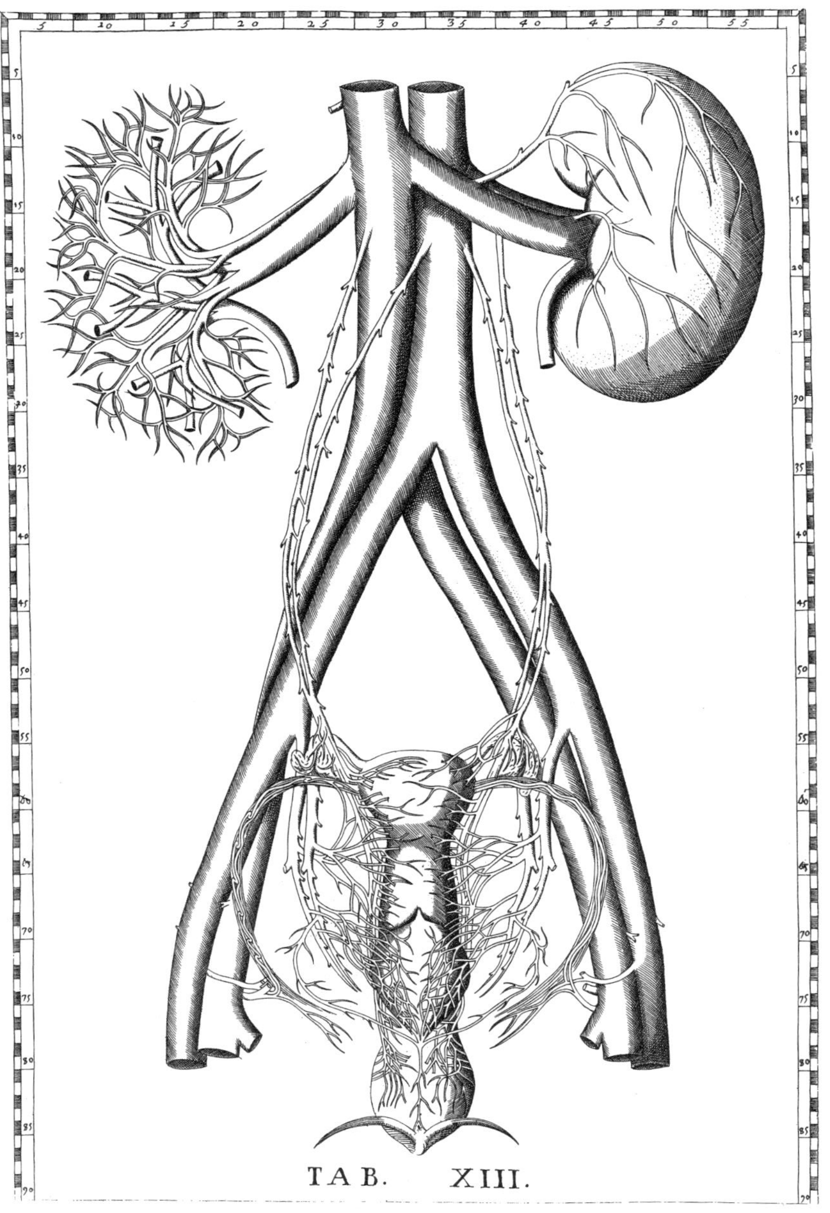

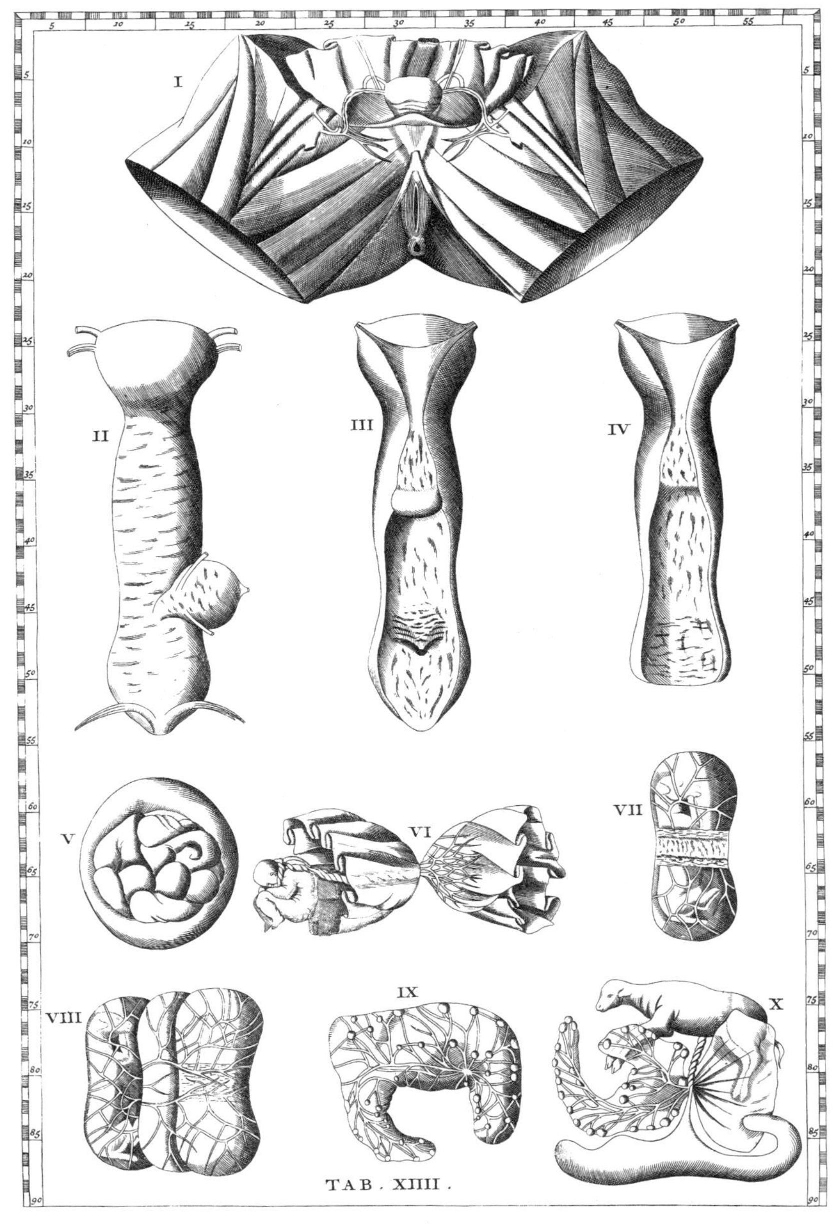

Left: The Kidneys and Urinary Tract. *Right:* Female Reproductive Organs, Placenta, and Human and Non-Human Fetal Development.

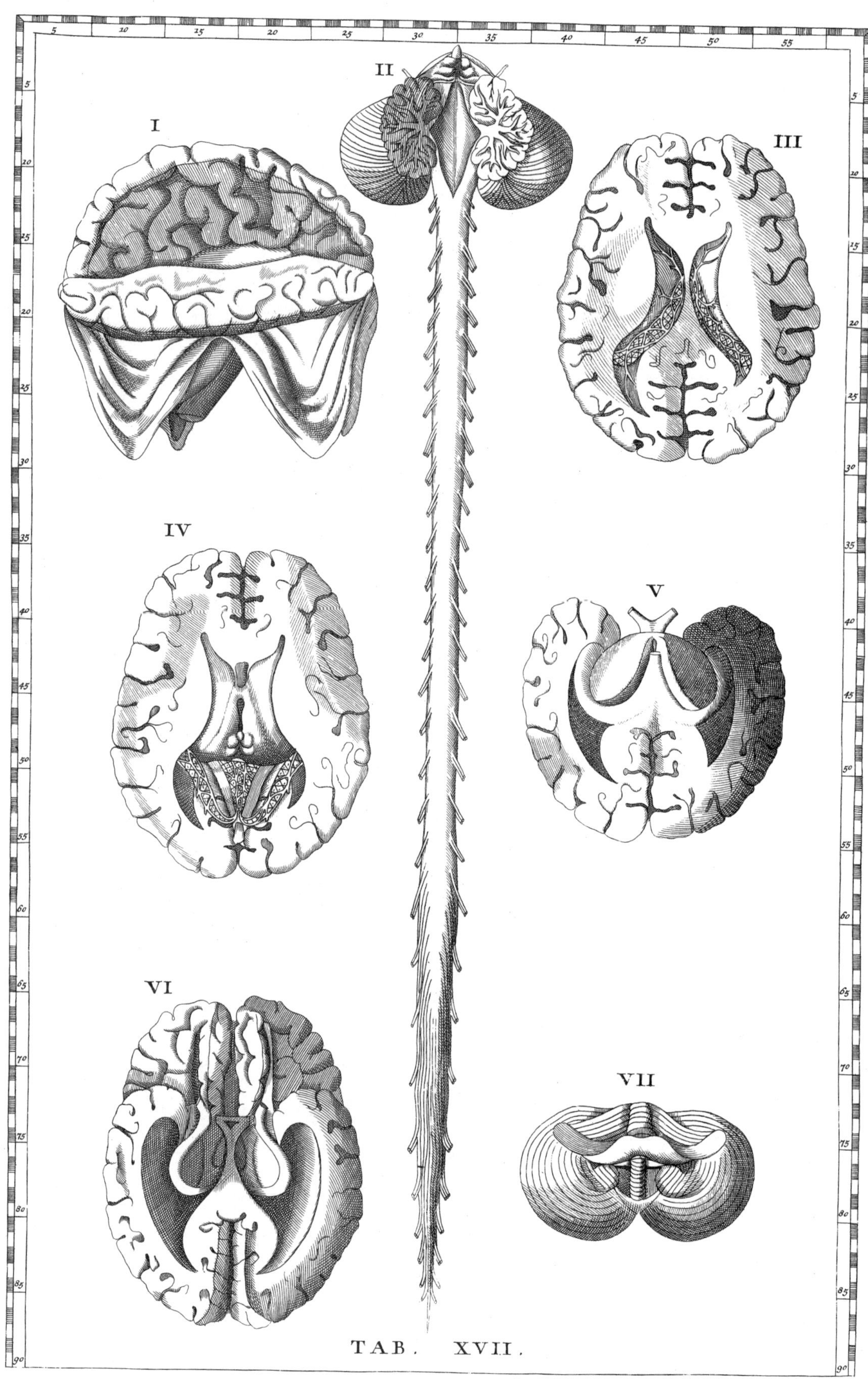

Nerves of the Brain and Spinal Column

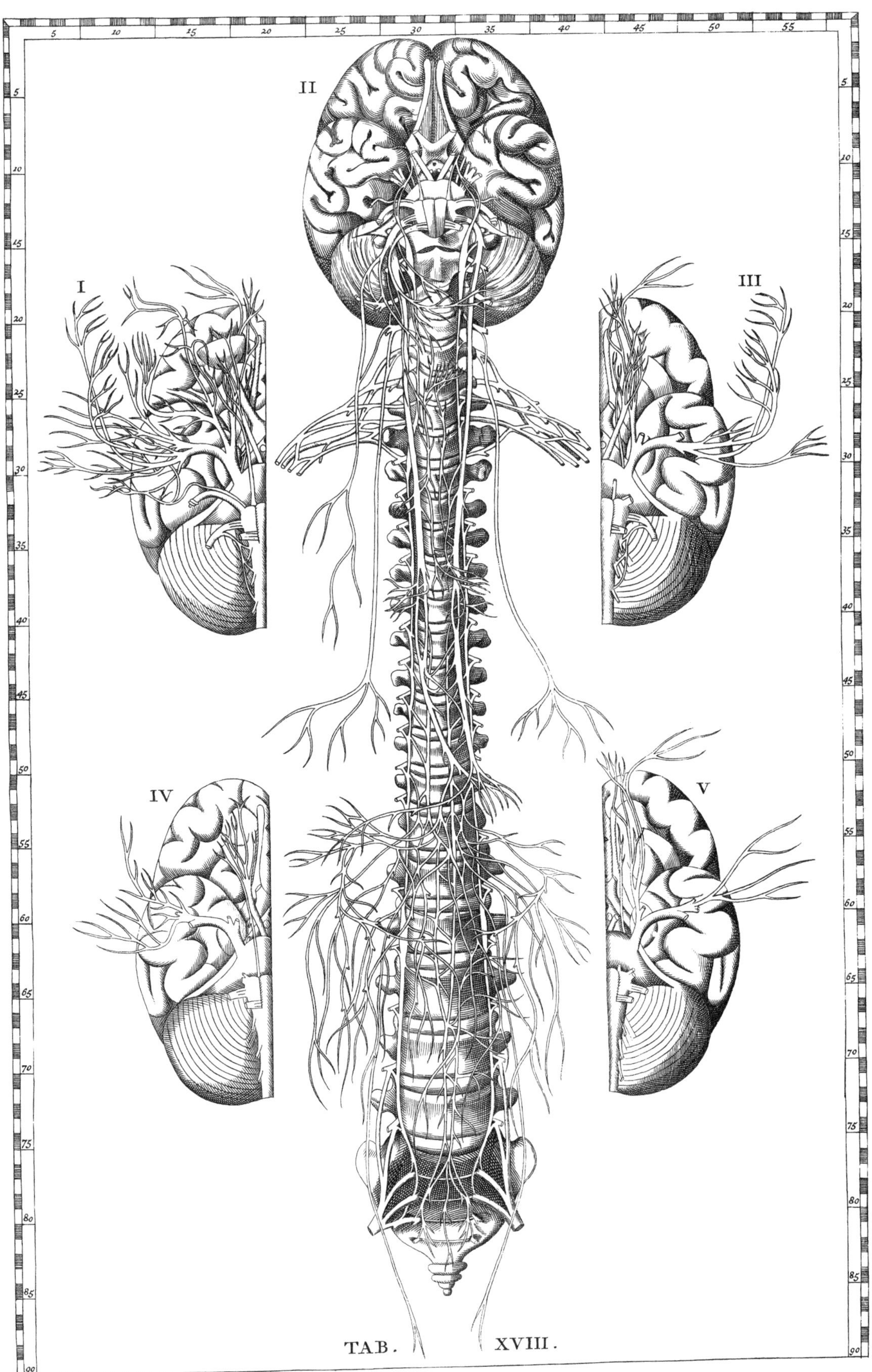

Nerves of the Brain and Spinal Column

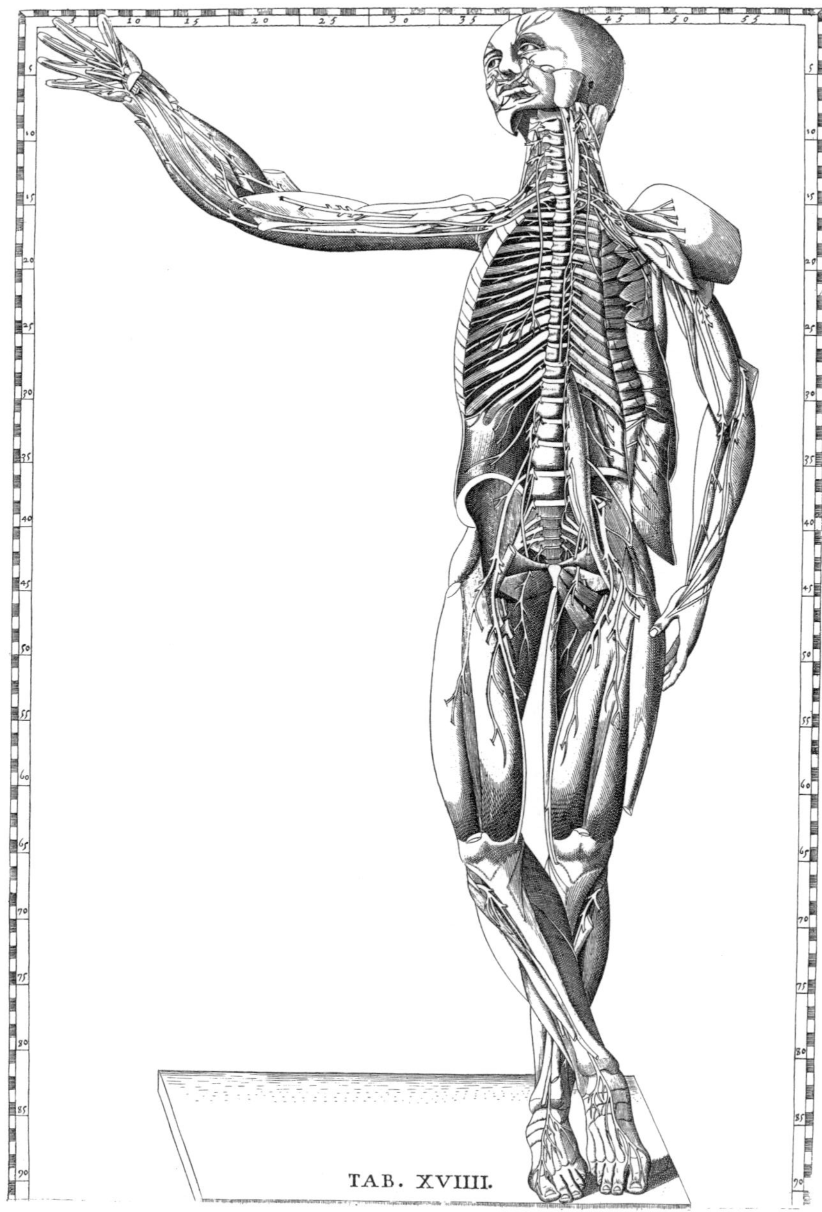

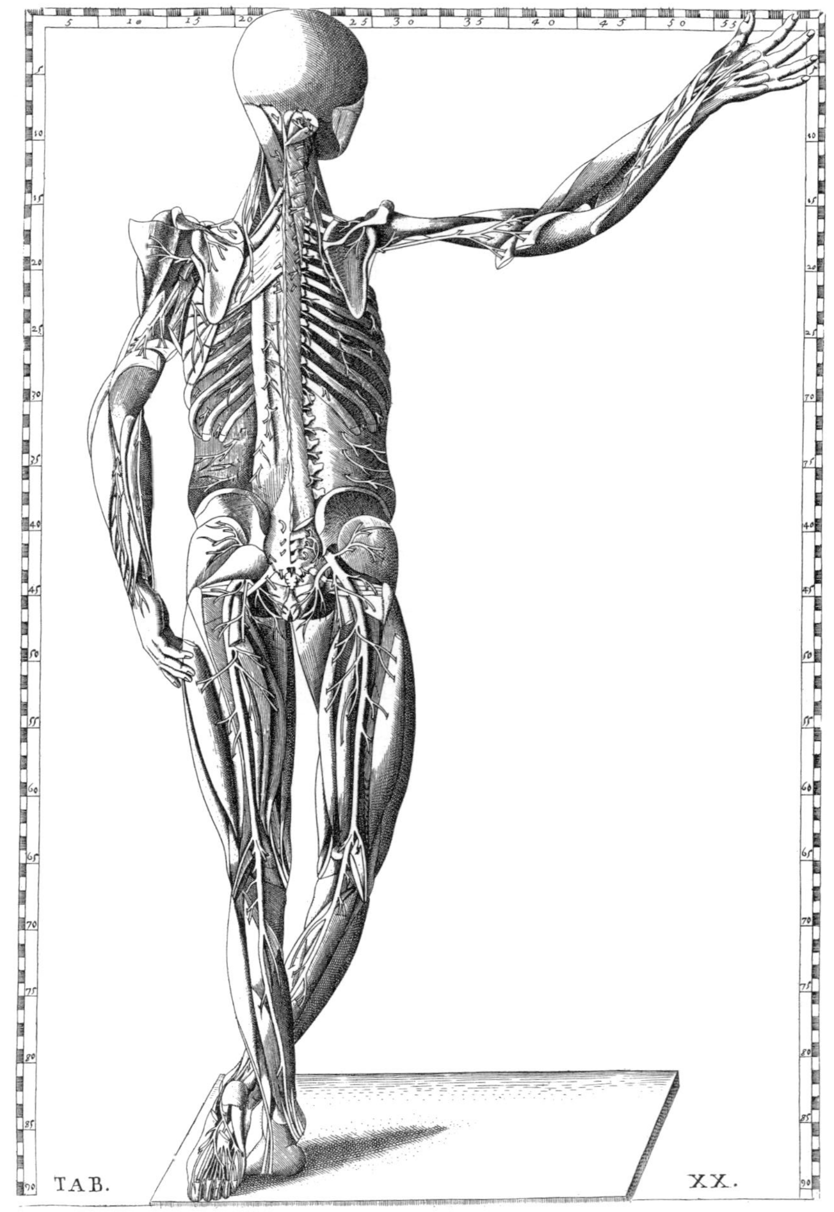

Left: Nerves and Muscles, front view. *Right:* Nerves and Muscles, back view.

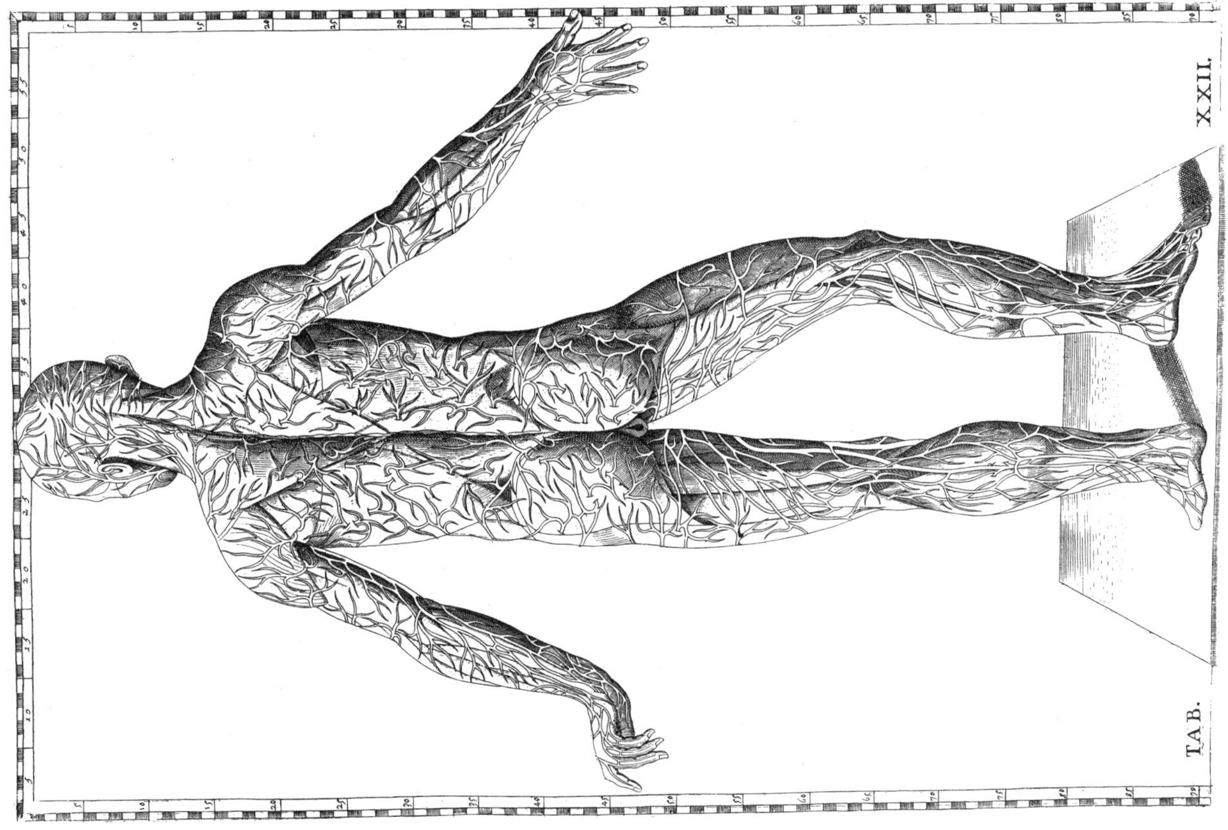

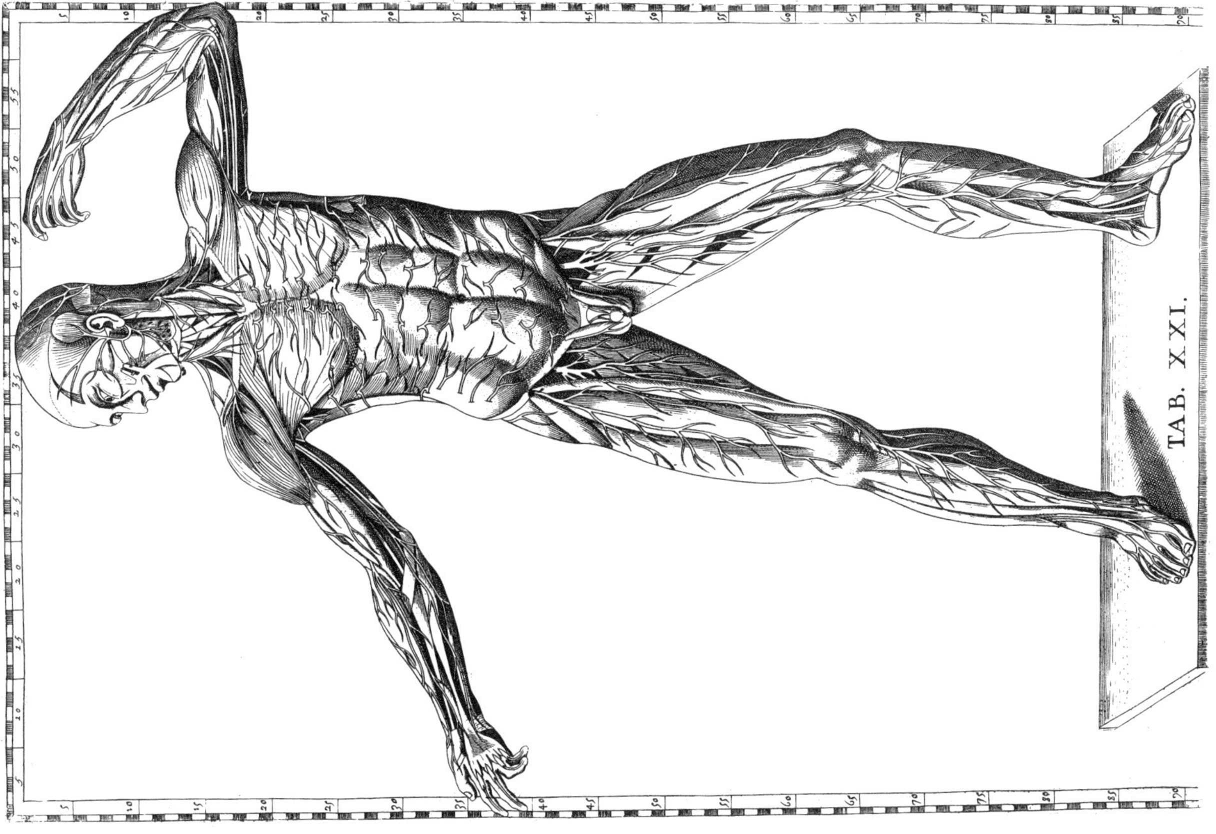

The Circulatory System, front and back views

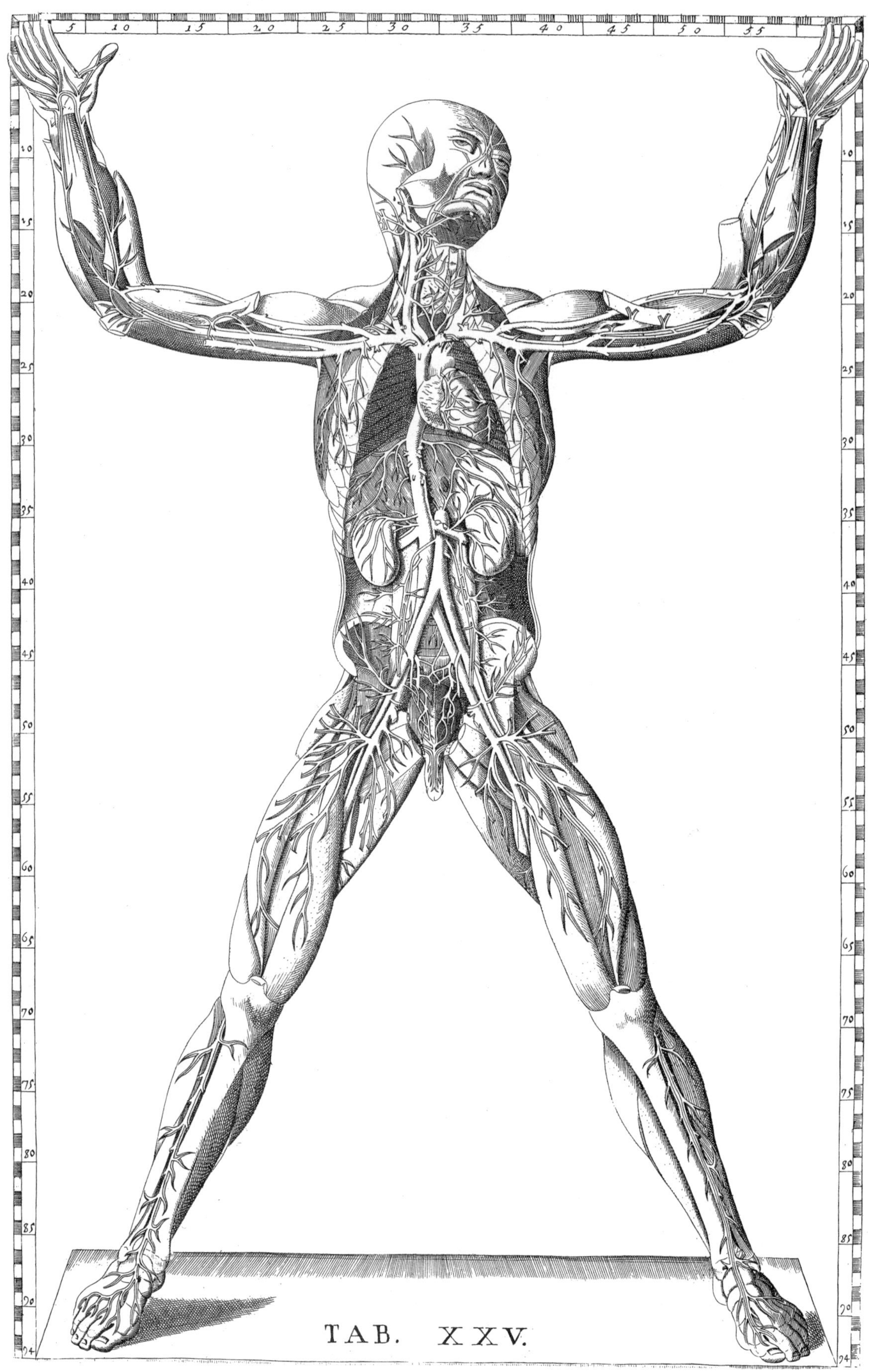

Blood Vessels and Nerves

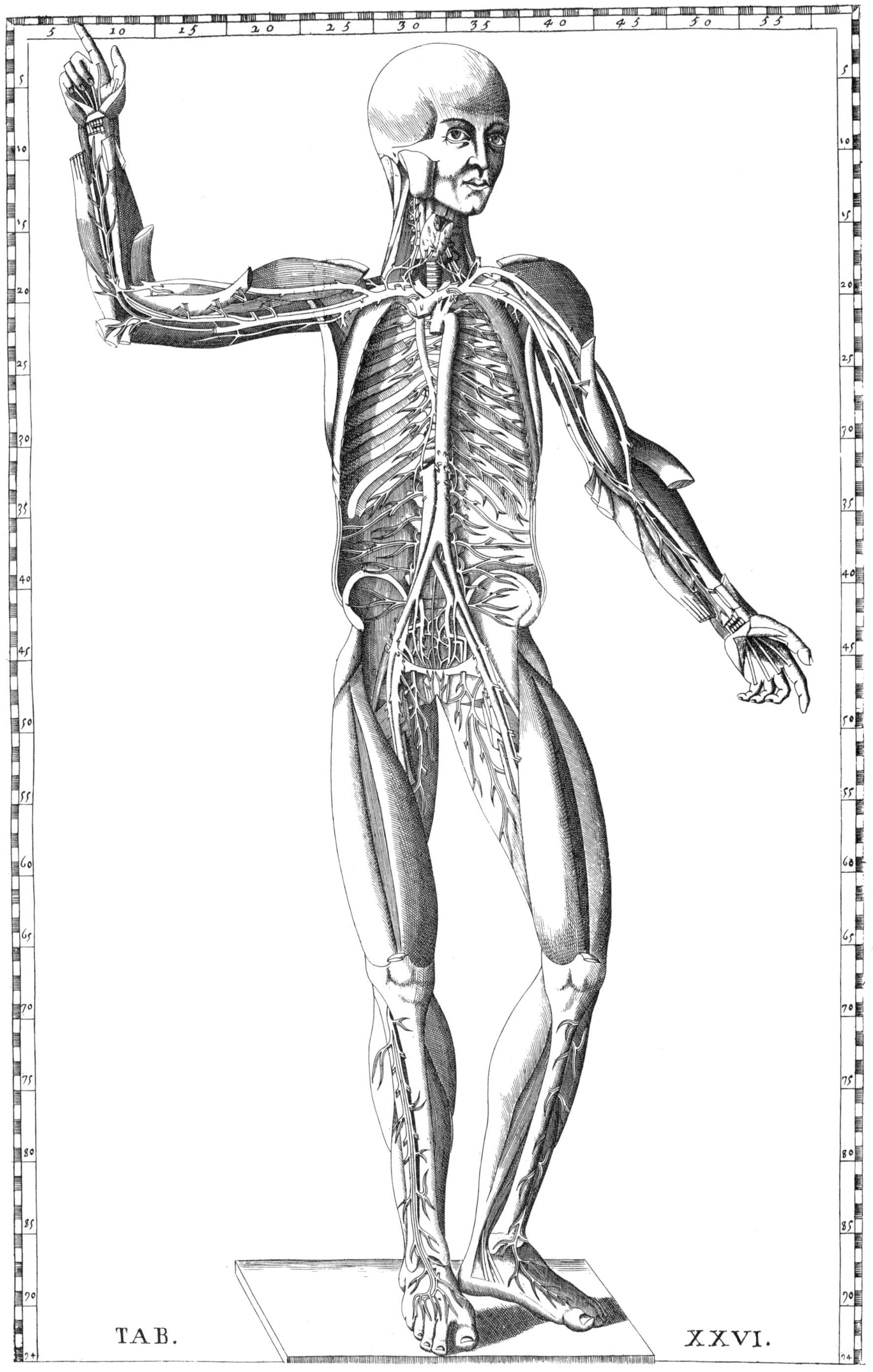

Blood Vessels and Muscles

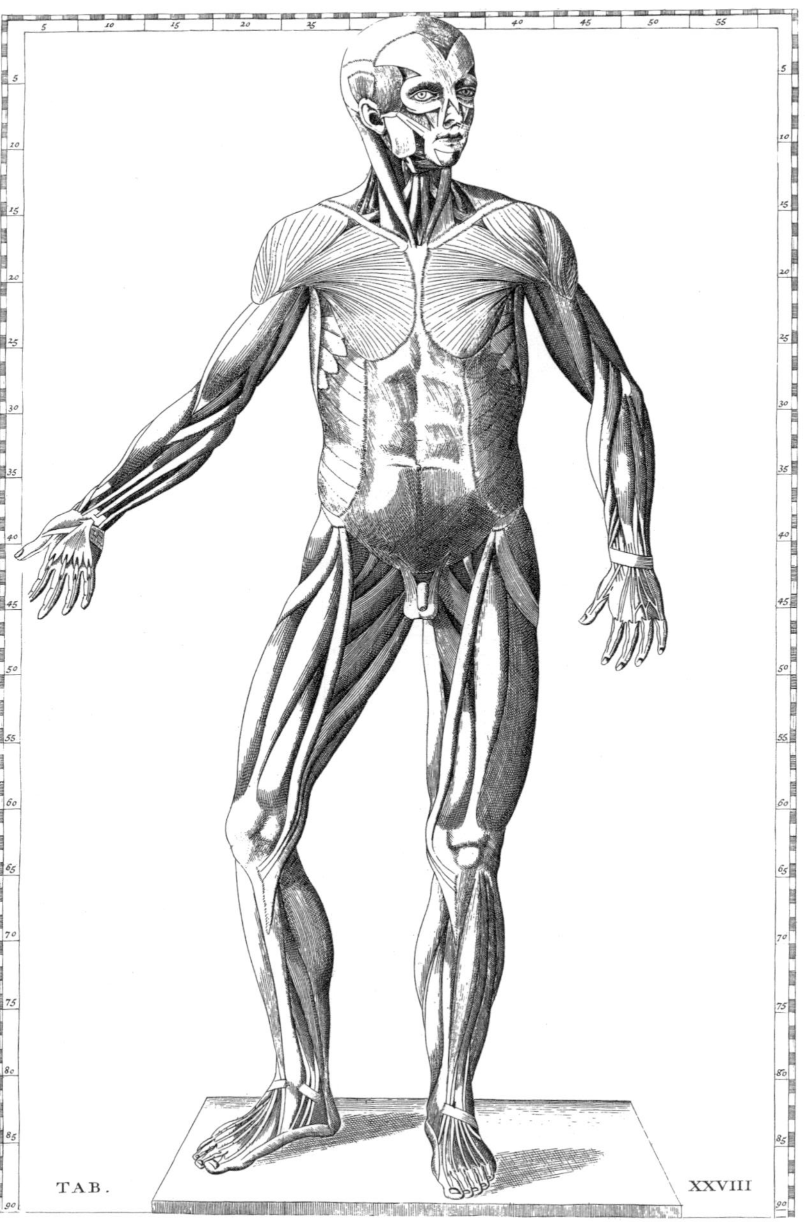

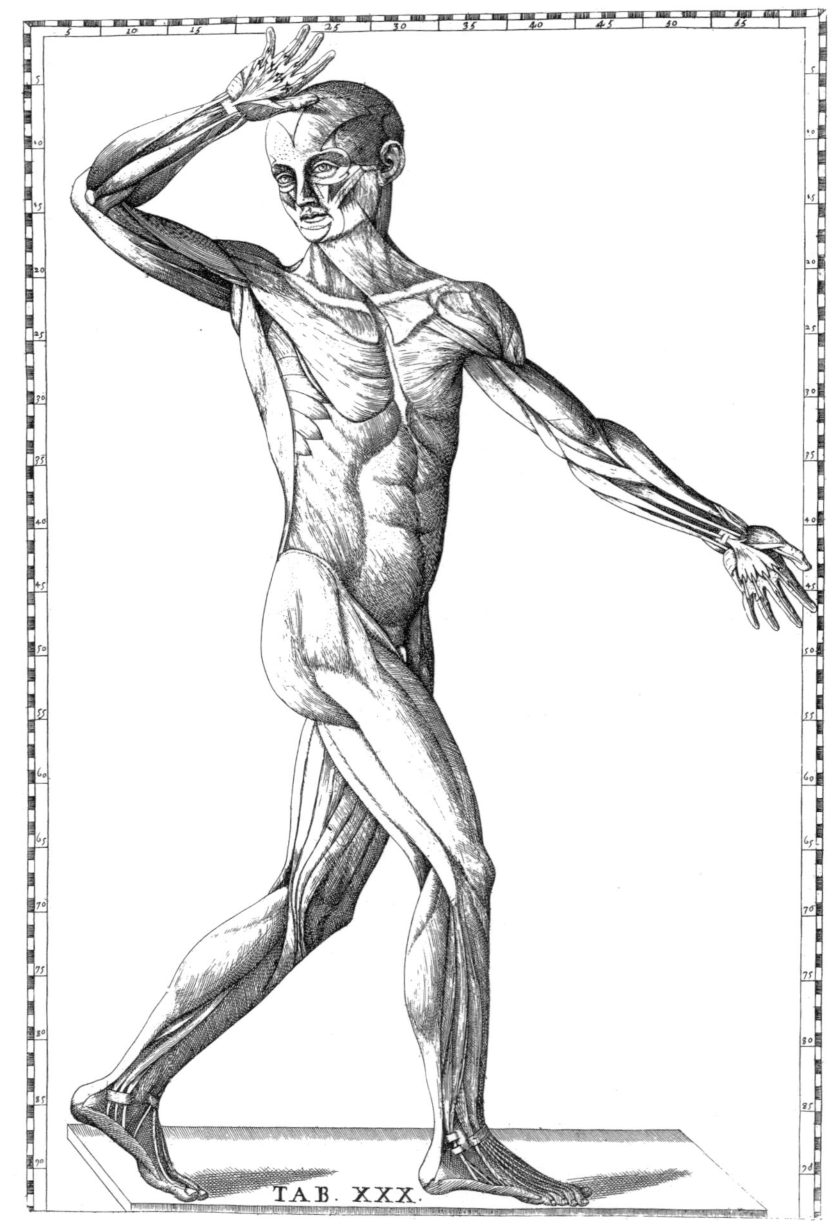

Left: The Muscles, front view. *Right:* The Muscles, side view.

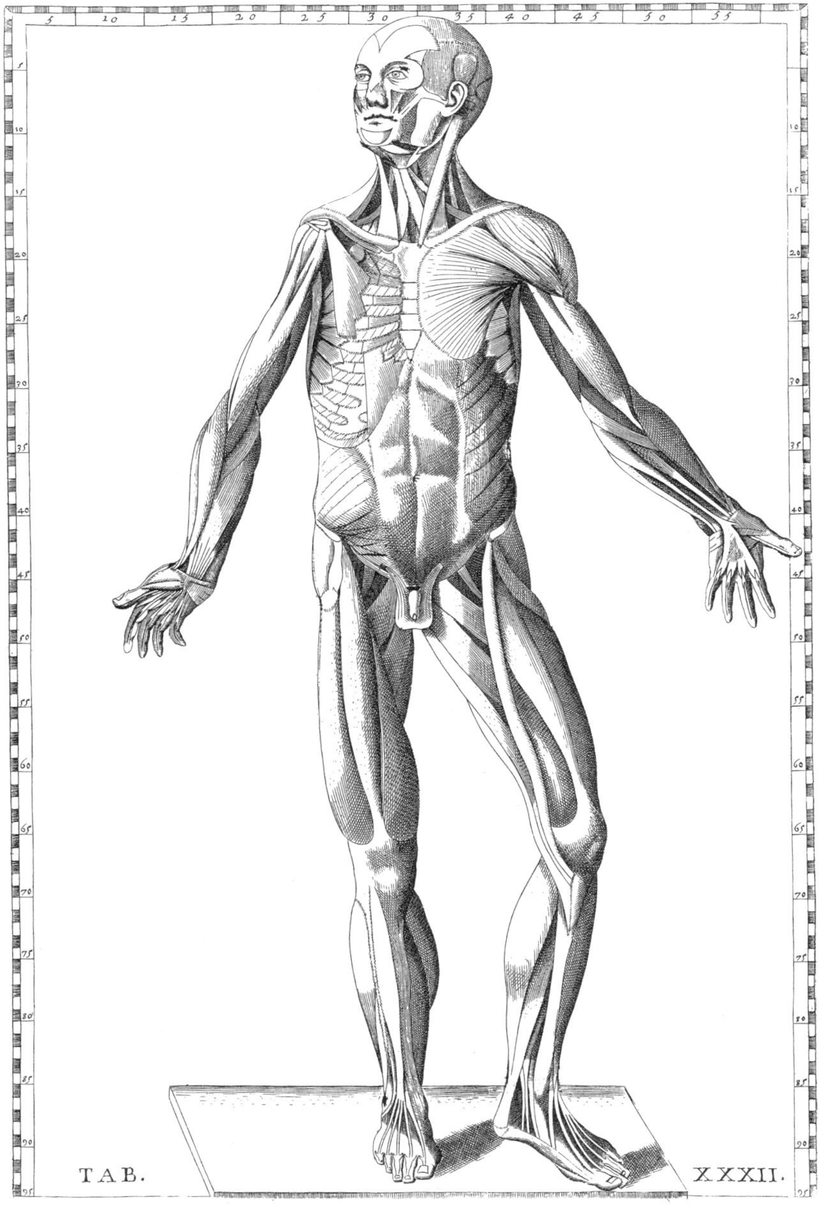

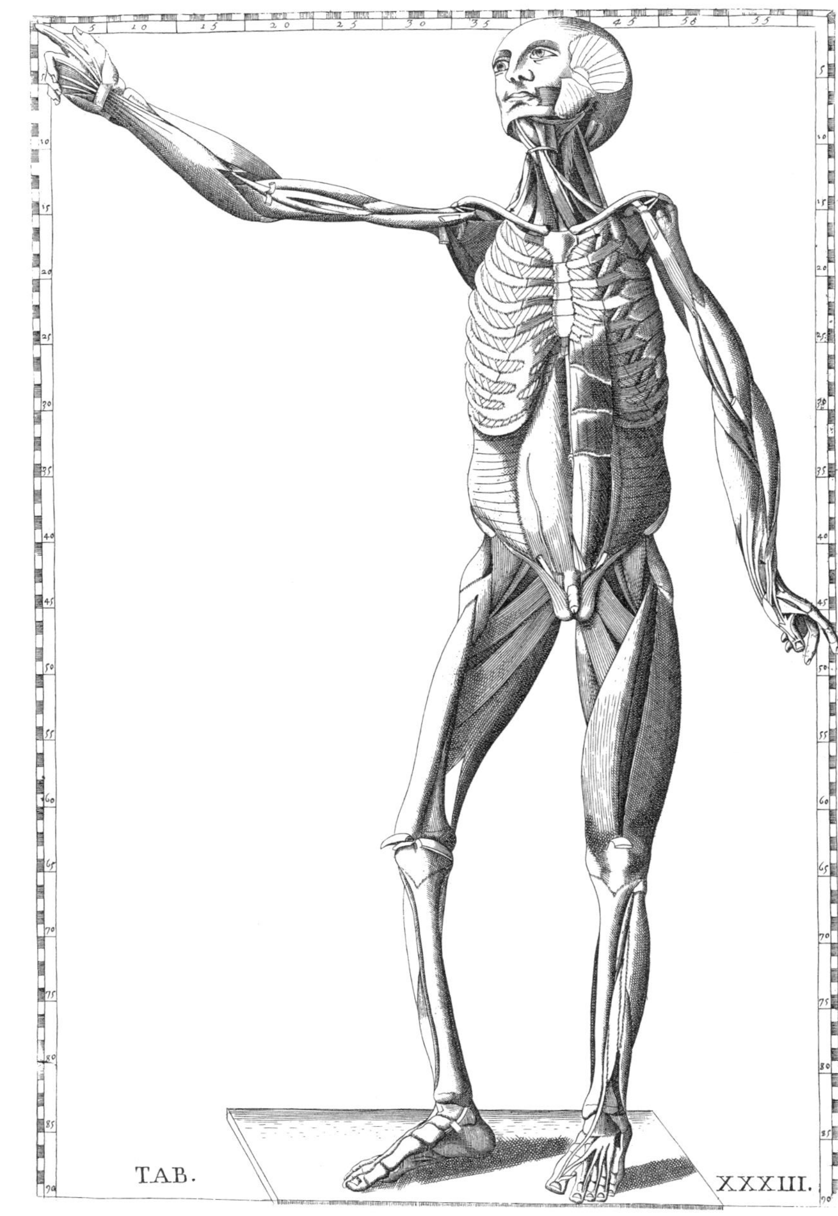

Left: The Muscles of the Body. *Right:* The Muscles of the Thorax and Abdomen.

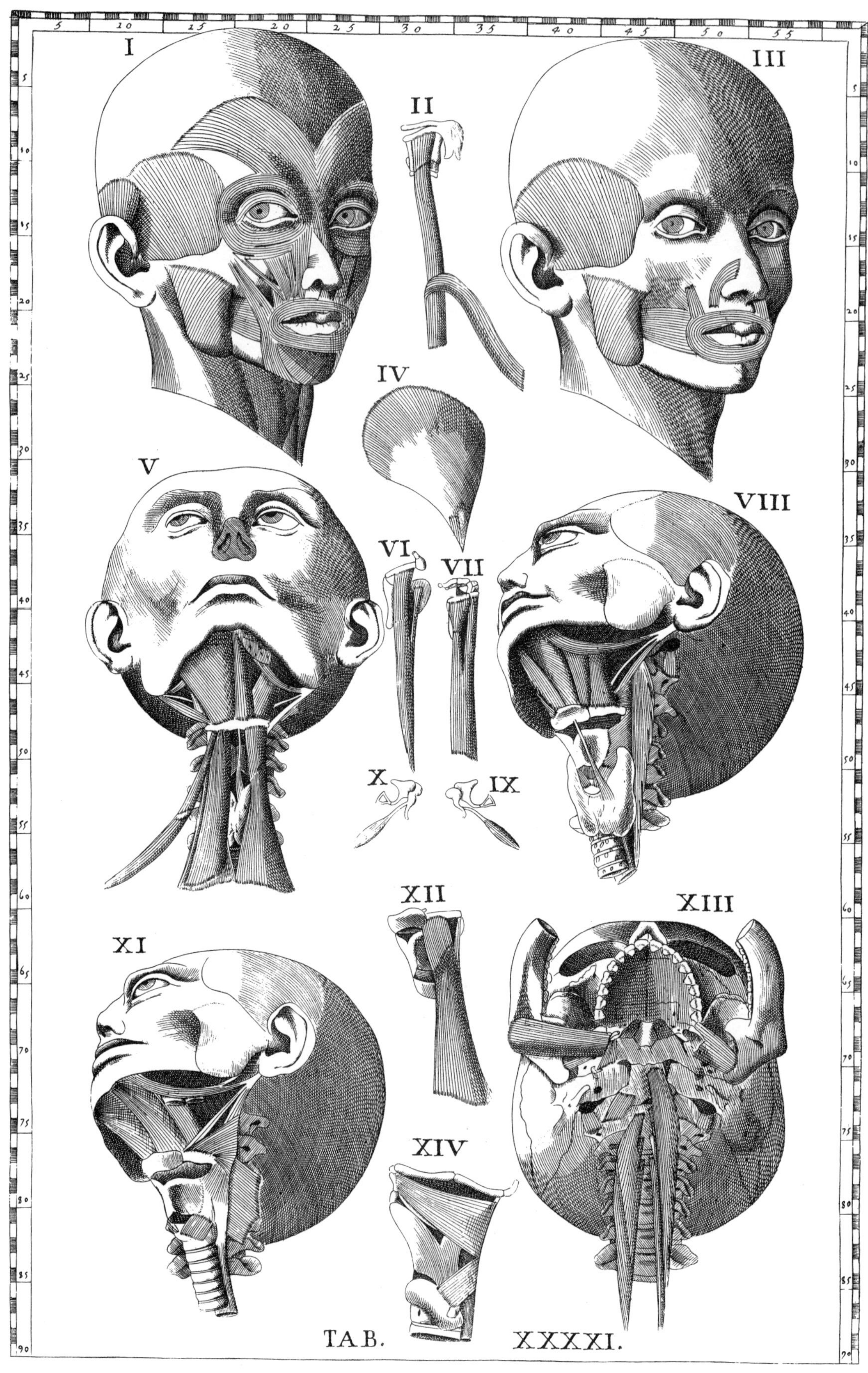

The Muscles of the Head and Neck

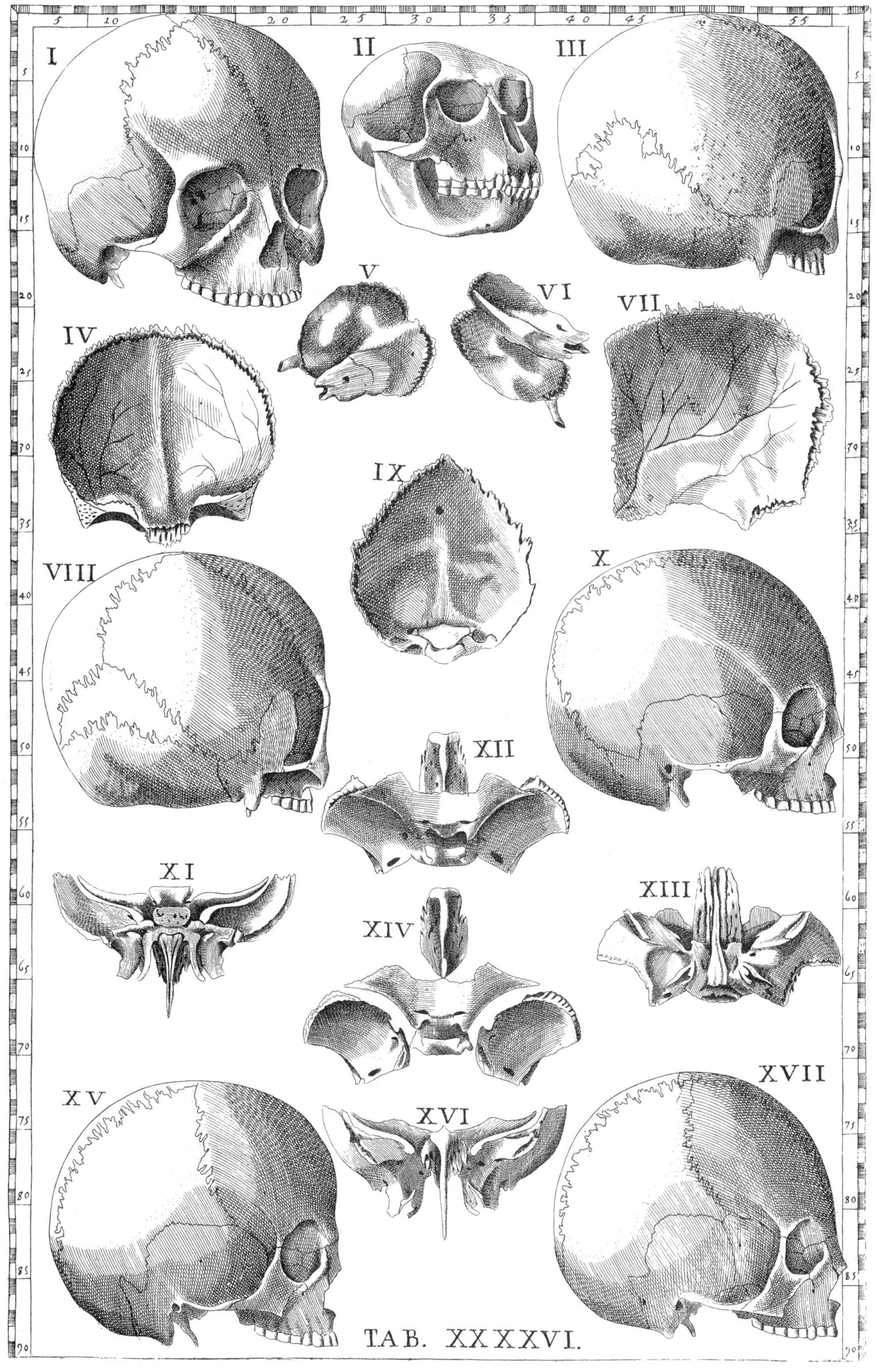
I
II
III
IV
V
VI
VII
VIII
IX
X
XI
XII
XIII
XIV
XV
XVI
XVII
TAB. XXXXVI.

The Skull

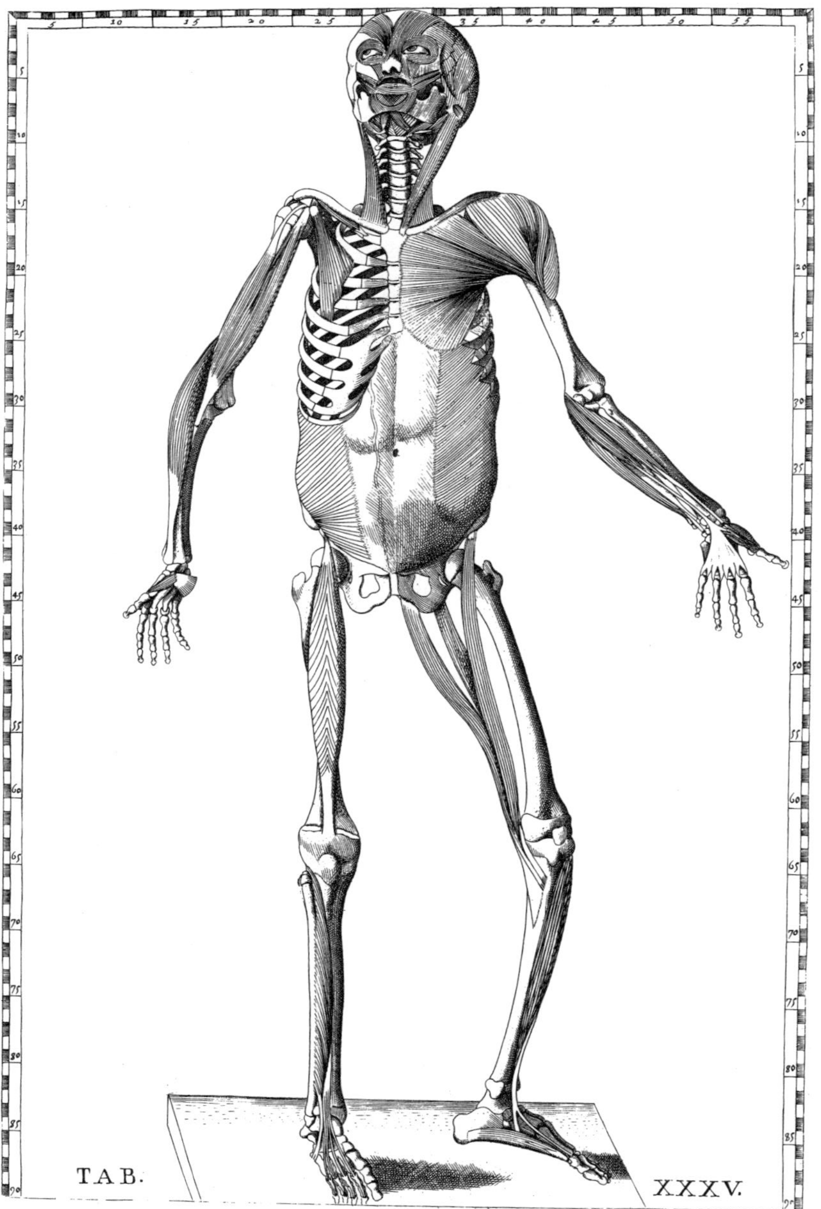

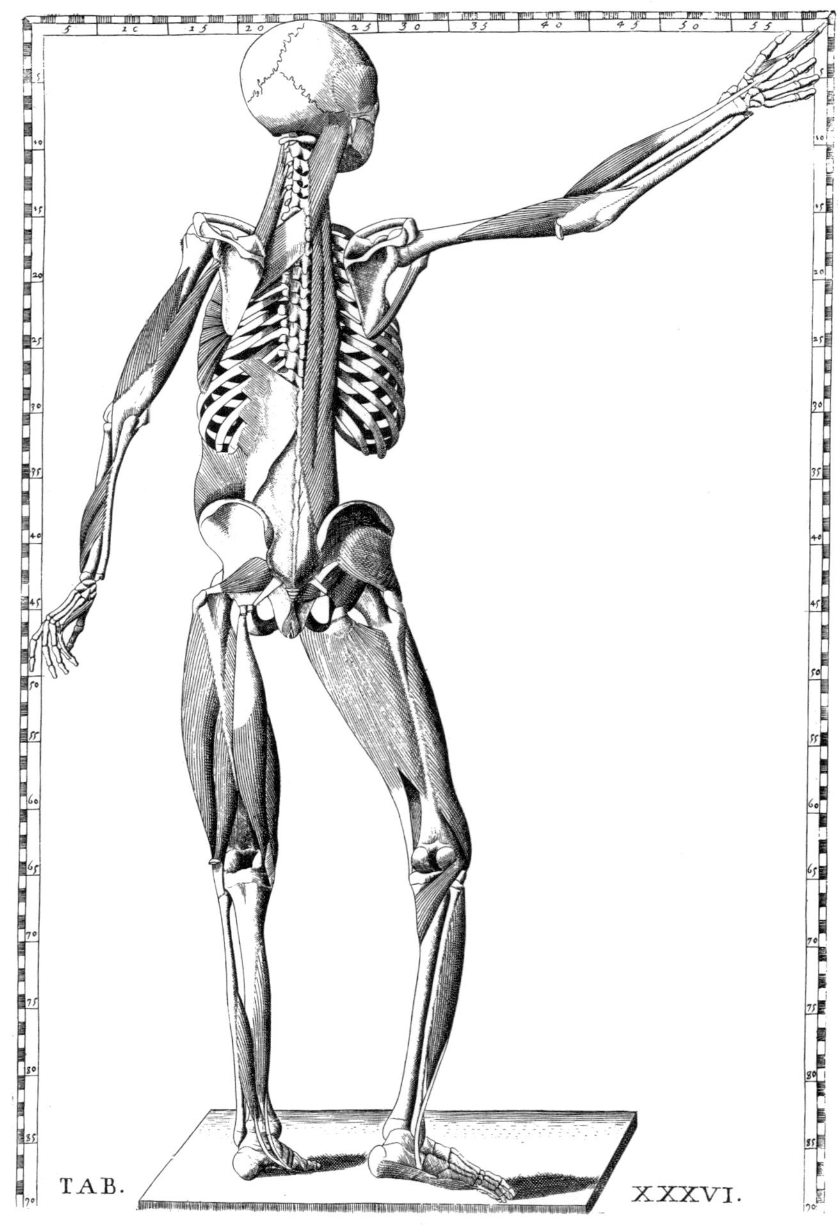

Left: The Muscles, front view. *Right:* The Muscles, back view.

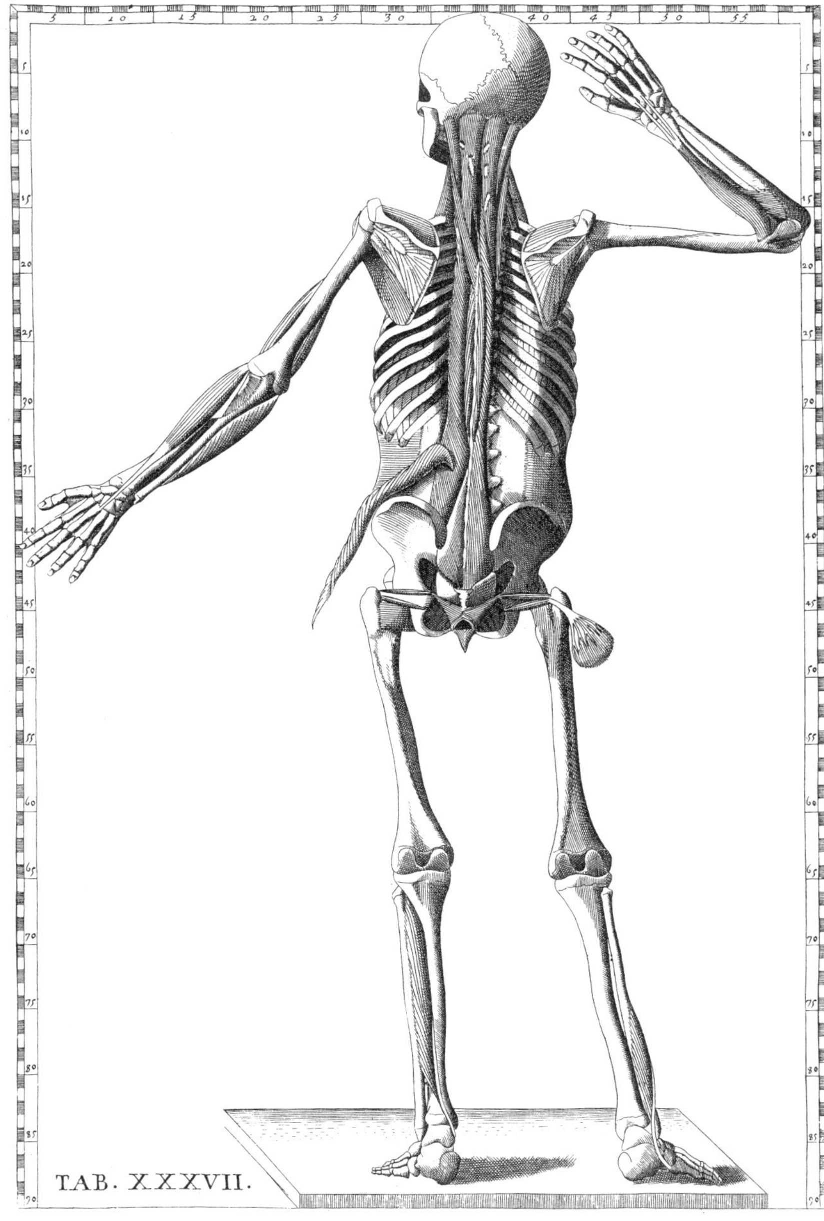

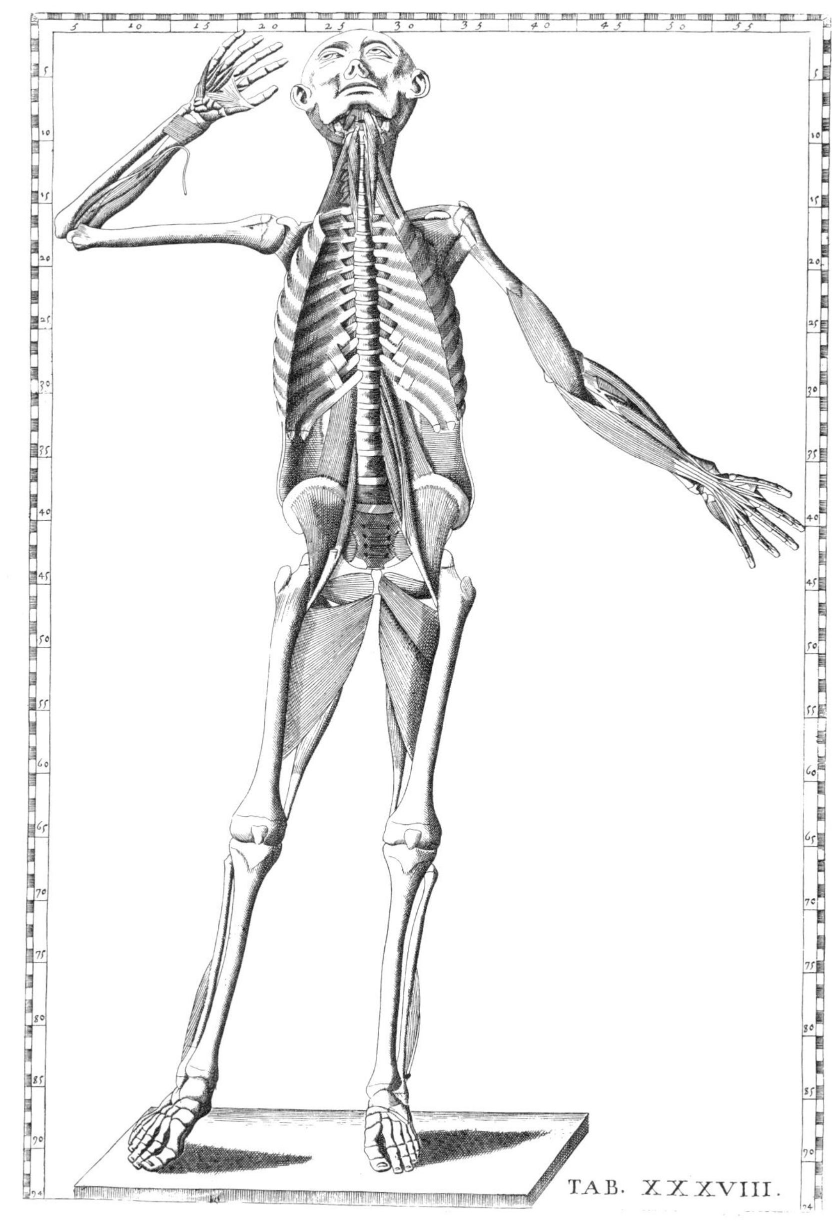

The Muscles, back and front views

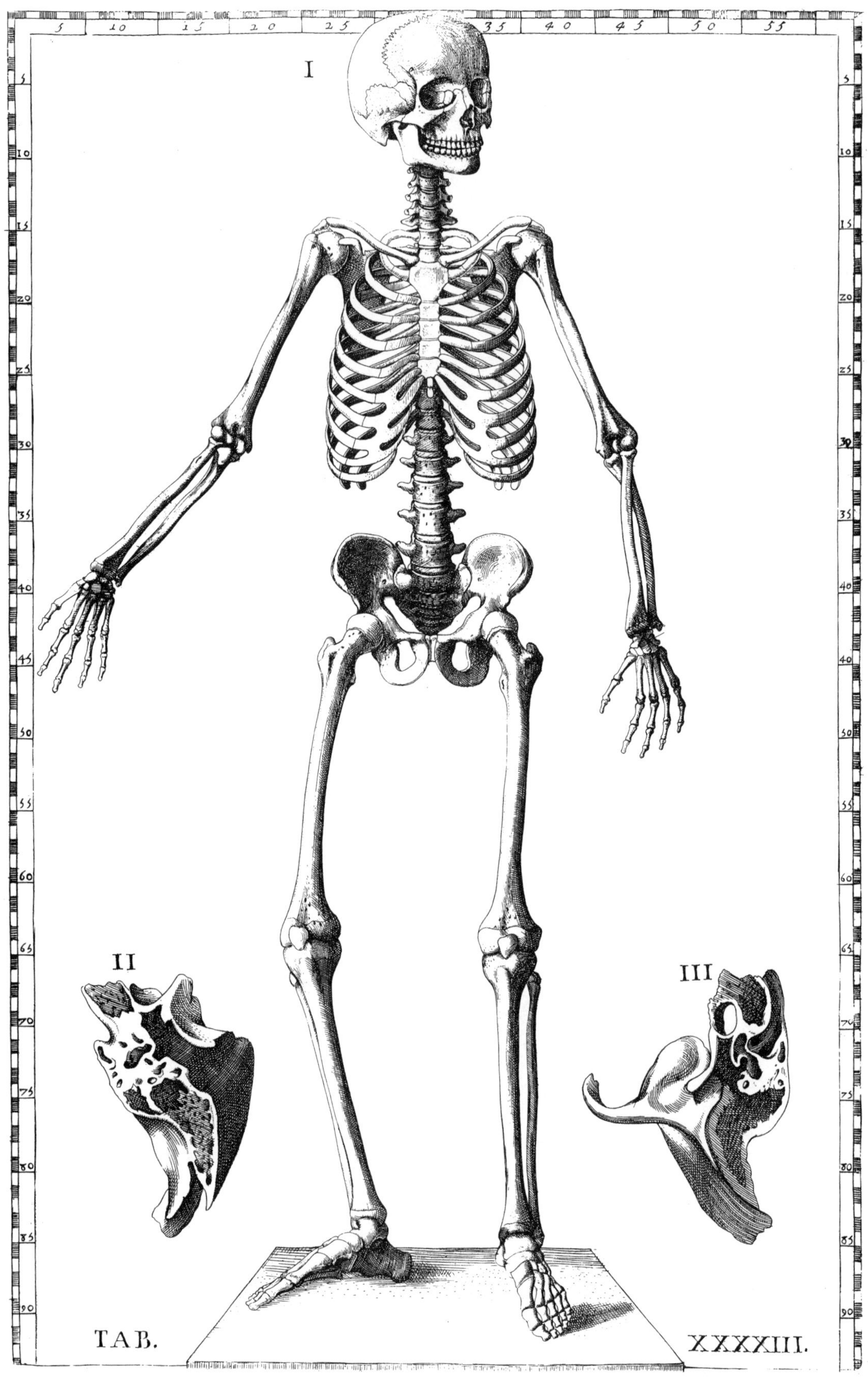

The Skeleton, front view

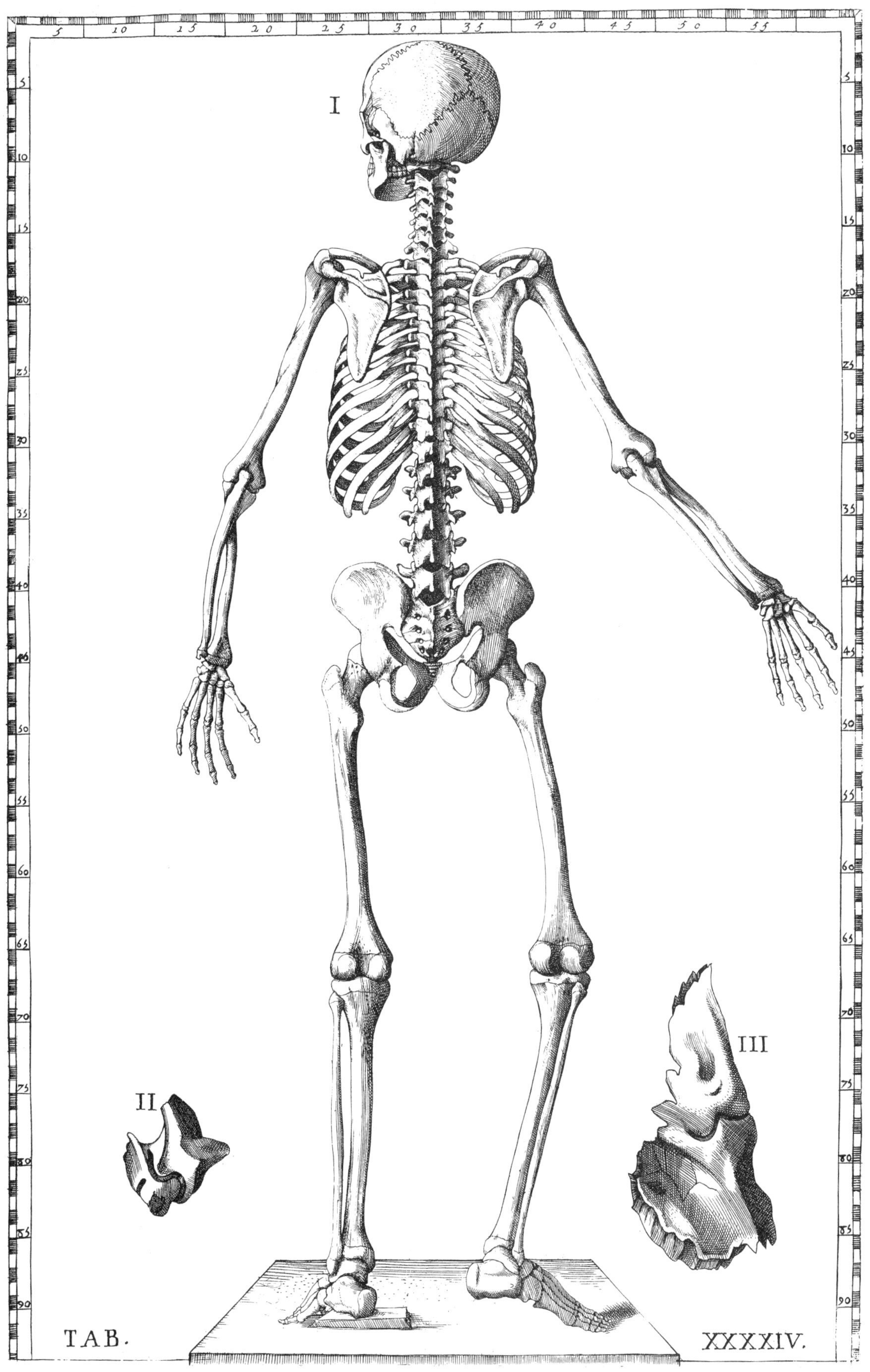

The Skeleton, back view